P9-CCR-997

THE HAPPY CHILD

THE HAPPY CHILD

A *psychoanalytic guide to emotional and social growth*

IRENE MILLIKEN JOSSELYN, M.D.

RANDOM HOUSE : *New York*

Eighth Printing

© Copyright, 1955, by Irene Milliken Josselyn
All rights reserved under International and Pan-American Copyright
Conventions. Published in New York by Random House, Inc., and
simultaneously in Toronto, Canada, by Random House of Canada,
Limited. Library of Congress Catalog Card Number: 55–8161
Manufactured in the United States of America
by The Book Press

Much of the material in Chapter 8, Adolescence,
appeared in the author's previous book, *The Adolescent
and His World,* Copyright, 1952, by Family Service
Association of America, and is here used with
grateful acknowledgment.

CONTENTS

PART I

PERSPECTIVES

1 : Goals in child care

MOST PARENTS HAVE TWO CLEAR GOALS FOR THEIR CHILD. FIRST, they want him to be a happy child. Second, they want him to grow into a happy adult who will play a significant, constructive role in society.

These are not unreasonable goals. Childhood can indeed be a delightful time of life and adulthood, equally, can be filled with rich personal satisfaction rather than with arid submission to the grimness of living. But such goals are easier set than reached, for a boundless complex of difficulties and problems surrounds the earnest parent in his efforts to help his child to happiness.

The cornerstone of child care is necessarily the fact that a child is born into a specific culture and will normally continue, both as child and as adult, to live in that culture. He may daydream about living peacefully where women do all the work or where women are goddesses, or he may have notions of how idyllic life in a faraway primitive society might be, but fundamentally he realizes that he is born into a specific pattern of society and must learn to live within that pattern. Especially in Western society, the child learns quite early that he has a right to the full pursuit of happiness, but he learns at the same time that he must not achieve it at the cost of anyone else's rights. As time goes by, the child recognizes that society, though it often frustrates him, is not inevitably his enemy. He learns, in fact, that it is an expression of one of his strongest needs: the need to live with other people harmoniously in the fulfilment of their common purposes and needs. Society, after all, is simply an aggregation of individuals; it is not a juggernaut. The task, consequently, that every parent faces is to help his child meet his psychological needs within our social structure. To the child the world about him is an ever-widening vista of experience and only the wisdom and patience of the adults around him can teach him how to understand this vista correctly and how to relate himself to it healthily.

The time was when a child just grew. What he was to become, whether aided or not by the heavy hand of his parents, was essentially a matter of chance—and even that chance was usually explained by heredity in the guise of some wayward relative, by the inherent evil of mankind or by the presence of a demon in the child. The theory of child care under such circumstances was that a good sound beating would either drive out the evil influences or provide some means by which the evil nature of the child could be controlled until adulthood when presumably he would have "sense."

Nowadays, parents are much more concerned about understanding their child more fully and, as a whole, parents probably have better insight now than ever into the wishes and hopes, the fears and agonies of their children. As parents have grown aware of the extent to which they mold the personality of their child, however, they have developed strong feelings of inadequacy and guilt. Thus beset, many parents look too readily for glib answers and easy formulas. There are no such things—fortunately—for in the end every child is an individual and every situation in which that child has a problem is an individual situation. Parents must help their children, not by relying upon simplified rules and pat advice, but by relying upon their intuitive capacity as normal parents. If the parent knows, whether as a result of reading a book or as a result of intuition, what development his child is going through, if the parent sees things from the viewpoint of the child, not taking the child as an adult in miniature—such a parent is well equipped to help his child through happy childhood into fully mature adulthood. The wise parent, fundamentally, believes in the virtues of family living, believes in the satisfaction of parenthood and believes in his own capacity to be a good parent. Above all he loves his child.

Parental love is hard to define. Many parents love their children intensely without being parents to them emotionally. Sometimes the love that parents seem to bear toward their child is in actuality only self-love. The child is not an individual to the parents in such a case but is perpetually an extension of the parents or an embodiment of all that the parents wish that they themselves might be. The child may perhaps be a symbol of a loved (or, unfortunately sometimes, hated) person of the past and the love he receives is a displaced love and available only so long as he fulfils his symbolic role. Some parents can love only an independent human being; then their child is forced prematurely to give up his infancy. Other parents love their children primarily as toys, not accepting the person inherent in the child. In still other cases, parents are so objective about their relationship to their children that they might just as well be raising amoebas under a microscope.

Paradoxically, all of these components are present in parental love. Parents are better parents if they do gain some gratification from their child as though he were an extension of themselves, for this preserves a special unity between parent and child. Similarly, if the child is loved as someone of the past was loved, the fulness of parental love is more readily available because it is in part a familiar experience. And true parental love involves gratification of the needs of a helpless child, not only when he is an infant, but when he is in temporary need of regression. It is equally important that parents respect the child's growing independence and that they love him because of it. Parents should at times enjoy their child as a plaything if they expect to enjoy playing with the child at all. Few adults, for example, can play blocks with a two-year-old for the sheer joy of putting one block on top of another; actually the child is the plaything which makes the block manipulation fun. Finally, there are times when parents do need to be objective about their child, to stand off and take a cold look at him.

If all of these attitudes occur in parental love, it should be clear that each one alone is inadequate and harmful. Parental love is more than the sum of these reactions. It is one of the supreme aspects of mature emotional growth. Emotionally well balanced parents give bountifully without knowing how much they give and without being martyred by giving. In return, they receive richly from their child's responses to them, responses which have a meaning in quality that they alone can fully sense.

2 : *The family*

FAMILY LIFE, IN THE DREAM WORLD OF THOSE WHO ARE NOT YET parents, is one of love, peace and complete freedom from anger. The dream family gathers around the organ for morning hymns, then proceeds to make breakfast together. The family gathers at the table, sharing opinions and experiences with no discordant note. Then they go off to their daily tasks, returning to a cooperatively created dinner, eaten in utter harmony. The evening tasks having been performed in an atmosphere of saintlike beatitude, the day ends with popcorn before the fireplace and reading aloud of Louisa May Alcott or perhaps even sharing the bitter realities of the past by reading Dickens. Finally, the family is off to bed in an aura of delicately perfumed love.

That dream is rarely possible. Brothers and sisters will quarrel. Fathers and mothers will too. Sons and daughters will fuss when they have to dry dishes; so will mothers or fathers. Boys and girls may prefer to play with the neighborhood children rather than listen to a family story hour. Parents may prefer at times to dine with friends rather than with their own children, or to play bridge rather than Sorry or Old Maid. TV, radio and comic books will at times be more satisfying to the child (and to adults) than a family conversation.

Other interests do not destroy the family or place it in a state of suspended animation. During those times of diversity of interests the family is not as tangible but it remains a part of the essential atmosphere in which activities are carried out. The family never disappears, although it is at times in an all-pervasive but invisible gaseous form. At other times it crystallizes into the solidity of actual family-shared experiences. The child is often more aware of the all-pervasiveness of its gaseous form than are many adults. The child cannot understand why he has to sit and talk to his parents in order for them to feel he is "part of the family" when he wants to listen to "Superman." After all neither can the average husband, engrossed in a mystery story, understand why his wife thinks he doesn't care for her because he doesn't prefer to listen breathlessly to gossip she's heard that afternoon! He enjoys just having her around while he reads.

Were it possible to live out the dream of the ideal family, its members could hardly conceive of themselves as individuals. They would of necessity have to give up their individuality to function in such a family. An individual's personality is enriched when parts of such an ideal day are in his experience. Mutual and peaceful family living is important for everyone. It cannot be the total living except as the gaseous phase diffuses through the atmosphere in which tangible, non-family events are experienced. The wisely structured family does not swallow up the individuals composing it but rather gives the individual an opportunity to be part of the concrete family structure and also to be free to leave the tangible form carrying with him a special atmospheric component emanating from the structure. Family living is not defined by what its members *do* together but rather by what is emotionally *experienced* together, not only when corporally together but also when corporally apart.

The important emotional interchanges in the family are not solely of gratifyingly positive feelings. Anger, jealousy and resentment can be a part also, and these often enrich the total experience if the more mutually gratifying feelings are predominant. Children are frequently facile in verbalizing their hostile responses while they are inarticulate in expressing the more deeply felt feelings of affection. Some adults are like that too!

The word *family* has implications over and above a description of its numerical composition. It is a living form rather than a filing cabinet. As such, because of the emotional gratification that lies in the individual's relationship to it, its characteristics are a composite of all those of its contributing members, but with a unique pattern resulting from a fusion of all. When it or any member of it is threatened from without, the threat arouses loyalty and protectiveness that erases negative feelings within the group. The family is defended against an outside enemy, irrespective of the internal turmoil that exists. Members of a family respond as parts of a total body. An individual may consider his physical form undesirable, or one essential part of it particularly unattractive, yet he will protect every part of his body from attack by others regardless of his own dislike for a part of it and his own attempts to modify or hide it. Pain or pleasure are experienced by the total physical body even though the pain or pleasure is localized in only a part of the body. Equally so, the family responds totally to the experiences of one part.

Even when, with justification, the individual rejects his family, if his earlier experiences have had some meaningfulness to him, this rejection is not without emotional repercussions. These repercussions are often either in the area of shame or guilt. Shame is experienced when a member of the family behaves contrary to the individual's concept of propriety or good taste. Guilt is experienced if an individual behaves contrary to family standards, attacks members of the family or violates social mores. He wonders what "the family will say." The individual feels guilty as a result of the meaning his behavior will have to the family. He fears he will lose the love of the family group. Behavior of another member will also arouse his guilt. He will strive to make up for the act of the one who violated some family standard, as if the entire family shared the crime and would be punished for it.

It is difficult to know when the full meaning of the family develops. Its development is probably insidious and would be expected to be rather nebulous in outline until the more primary relationships with the individual members composing the family have reached a point of some stability and predictableness. As indication of this a child whose primary relationship with his mother has never been adequately stabilized will tend to continue to struggle with that relationship rather than find value in the give-and-take of a family group. The significance of the family can be traced throughout the psychological development of the individual.*

As the small child becomes aware of the interest and protectiveness of other members of the family in addition to the mother, he finds those other members offer him security as well. The family becomes a depersonalized mother. This meaning of the family usually continues through life. A common phrase gives expression to the emotional significance of this concept: "He returned to the bosom of his family."

The family plays a very important role for the child as he struggles to achieve some equilibrium between (and some safety in spite of) his need both to love and to express his hostilely motivated, aggressive impulses.† It is important to recognize the validity and the strengthening effect of the hostile responses occurring in the emotional interchanges of the family. Such interchanges give the individual an opportunity to be a total person and in so being to learn to be so constructively. It is inevitable that an individual who has not repressed a fairly extensive part of himself will feel resentment, jealousy, anger and destructive impulses as long as he is a part of the world. Those emotions expressed in unmodi-

---

* The following paragraphs refer to stages in development that are more fully covered in later chapters. It is important that those chapters be read against the backdrop of the family as a unit.
† See Chapter 4, The Oral or Dependent Period.

fied form would militate against any really successful adaptation, not only to the world outside himself, but to his own internal being. These emotions, which in their unmitigated form would have eventually to be repressed, can be gradually redirected as a result of childhood learning experiences into acceptable and often more dynamically productive outlets. This is most facilely achieved in an emotional atmosphere in which the individual has acceptance as a person even though his act may not be acceptable.

It is in the family that the child can most readily learn to tolerate and balance these ambivalent feelings.* In no other interpersonal relationship is hostility so sharply weighted against the heavier element of love. In no other interpersonal relationship is the ambivalent response of the other person so weighted in favor of affection. In few other situations, further, are the ambivalent feelings towards another so tangibly colored by the value of the total of which each individual is a part. Not only does the child seek to reestablish and solidify his relationship with the individual toward whom his ambivalent feelings are directed but he wishes to preserve his place in the intimate group. This is clearly indicated in certain common domestic crises. A child is angry at his mother and directs the anger toward everyone near. His mother, recognizing herself as the real target, withdraws him from the family circle to attempt to reestablish peace between the child and herself. Once her mission is completed the child frequently wants, not to remain alone with her, but to return to the family group. The mother unconsciously recognizes this when she suggests that maybe he would like to go downstairs again. This readiness to return to the group is not only to share activities. Often the other members may be quietly pursuing different and solo activities. The child appears to wish to spread the newly achieved equilibrium to his relationship to the group, not only to the meaningful person who disrupted it.

* See Chapter 5.

The family as a whole may play a role also in effecting a solution to the Oedipal conflict.* It appears that part of the conflictual tension of the Oedipal period may be lessened as the father and mother become fused as "parents." The word "parent" becomes not a plural but a collective noun. The child responds to them as "parents" rather than as sexually different individuals. As parents rather than singly as a mother and a father, the relationship with them becomes re-personalized.

It is in the family above all that the child feels the satisfaction that comes from mutual living with others. At first this mutual living is a one-to-one relationship. As the child matures emotionally to the point at which the family becomes meaningful over and above the value of its individual members, he takes the first step towards ultimate acceptance of a social group as an abstraction with significance different from that of the constituent members. In this development both the positive and negative feelings are significant. The child learns that, even though his brother is a totally unacceptable child because he broke a favorite toy, he is a part of an important abstraction, the family. Loss of him would be a loss of an essential part of the family: the brother has a positive emotional meaning beyond his undesirability as an individual. Family living is the first step in adaptation to group living, achieved in a more protective environment than a less personal group would offer. The family provides a situation in which to learn gradually that a person can be an essential part of a group without losing, but instead actually in a new way enhancing, his own individuality.†

As the total psychological growth patterns are recapitulated during adolescence, family life plays the same role, though it may be reacted to differently, as it did during the earlier periods. Since the family so often has the meaning of a mother figure, an individual may have to reject it in adult-

* See Chapter 6.
† The significance of this will become clear in Chapter 7, Latency.

hood. To that person, validly or not, the family represents a mother who accepts only a small dependent child. He, so conceiving of his family, must disown it to feel he is an adult. The adolescent revolt against parents was never resolved but only transferred or extended to the family.*

The family probably is the smallest unit as an instrument for the effective continuity of the cultural heritage. The cultural patterns of behavior and ideals expressed verbally are rarely as meaningful as they are when they are a part of a living experience. The child learns his heritage both as it is given by the spoken word and as he sees it in action. It has the most significant meaning to him as he experiences it in his day-by-day living in a family unit in which those cultural patterns and ideals are the laws by which the family group lives. This is demonstrated most clearly in those closely knit family groups in which the cultural mores are at variance with the society in which the family lives. The child whose parents maintain the mores of a different national group, mores that are alien to the country into which they are transplanted, eventually recognizes that his parents and his own social peer group have different cultures and attitudes. It is a painful period for him until he can reconcile himself to the differences or divorce himself from the parents' patterns to adopt those of his social environment beyond his family.

It is in the family also that the bisexual nature of the human race is most effectively defined for the child. Through observation of the relationship of the mother and father— and their relationship to the world beyond the family—a concept of the role of each is formed. By identification with the parent of the same sex the child defines his own present and future role. By observing the function of the parent of the opposite sex, he formulates the role that he will anticipate in the opposite sex.

The importance of the family picture in the formulation of the roles the man and woman play brings to the fore a

* See Chapter 8, Adolescence.

question for which there is no sharp answer. How can a family most constructively define these roles for a child? The more subtle differences are, interestingly enough, easier to define than the more obvious ones. The feminine role is that of nourishing the young, keeping him warm and comfortable. The masculine role is more aggressively to provide and protect. Such broad yet subtle differences are difficult to translate into the actual daily living experience of the present culture. In ancient cultures, in which men devoted their lives to hunting and warring, women to that of cooking, nursing and maintaining the home, sexually determined roles were clearcut. Now a man does not hunt, except for sport; at least for short periods, he does not go to war. He may be a tailor, a baker, or president of a canning factory. On the other hand, the feminine role may be equally contradictory to the basic theoretical delineation. Women go to work to make money; they can even join the armed forces. Their role of feeding the family has narrowed to warming what has been precooked elsewhere and placed in cans or frozen, so that preparing a meal can easily be simplified to the gesture of putting something in a pan, lighting the stove and removing the pan once the contents have been adequately heated. Bread, cookies, cakes, pies are made by others, and frequently by men! Dishes have to be washed, beds made, furniture dusted—tasks which seem to require less special talent than the sexual differences would suggest are available. A simple differentiation of the role of male and female in our society is not possible.

It has been suggested by some that the answer to this confusion lies, at least for women, in a return to an earlier culture, destroying the progress-inventions of frozen foods, cake mixes and factory-baked bread. No adequate solution for the male has yet been suggested, since wild animals are too scarce and war, for the sake of war, is a violation of everyone's sensibilities. Perhaps our culture should learn more than reproduction from the bees. If women return to their role of making bread and shelling peas, men should then become drones. They can earn the money to buy the food (that they are too demasculinated to kill) from the grocer, play their role in the reproductive function and be, beyond that point, completely expendable. In some situations nowadays the female actually does behave as a queen bee; the male as far as the family is concerned, and often in contrast to his other experiences, is the drone bee in the hive. This solution may work for the bees; it has questionable merit for the human race.

In the past the man of the family had an established place —if for no other reason than that he was to be feared. Mothers implying their own helplessness threatened their children with dire consequences when father came home. The threat to tell father of a misdeed was often sufficient to bring a repentant response from the child. Children feared the powerful father. Because undesirable repercussions occurred from this method of discipline, it was—thank heaven!—deleted from the disciplinary methods of most families. A father should be more to a child than just an ogre whose homecoming is feared. In many families a complete reversal has occurred. Because the father is home for such a brief time, some parents believe he should never take a disciplinary role. The child's experience with him becomes, though brief, always pleasant. This attitude has led in some cases to the father being a charming playmate or, if he is not a playmate, an unimportant boarder in the house.

There has also been a tendency to describe the essential role of the mother and then suggest that the father imitate that role as a "mother's helper." The American child has too little contact with masculine figures. He spends a good part of his school days, at least until high school, being taught by women. His mother is the pivotal person in the home. It is important, therefore, that his father function in the patterns of masculinity, not as a mother substitute or solely as a mother's helper. To translate this into every day life is difficult to describe. A man does not lose his masculinity by occasionally giving the baby his 2:00 A.M. feeding. Nor to prove his masculinity does the man need to assume the role of a fire-spitting dragon. A man can be a man without that. The answer probably lies in a little spontaneity.

A man is born to be a man. Masculinity is not a part to be played in a stage play. Men should fuse their knowledge of child development with an intuitive response that has its roots in their inherent masculinity. If they can do this, instead of trying to respond like mothers, the father of the family will be preserved for posterity. He can still help his tired wife with the dishes and with putting the children to bed without being "mother's little helper."

Another cultural phenomenon in urban areas threatens to create fatherless families. Suburban living is offering society the creation of a social group of suburban widows and half-orphaned children. Parents move out to the suburbs to give the child a richer life. Regardless of the freer play, the possibly better schools, the opportunity to have pets, to play off the street and enjoy living in a house rather than an apartment, too often suburban living deprives the child of a father. The trip home is long. The father stays in town because of pressing business. Recreational interests may be primarily in town, so again it isn't possible to be home for dinner. To reach the office sufficiently early in the morning, the father leaves before the rest of the family are up for breakfast. A long week of work at the office combined with the hours commuting results in a fatigue that necessitates release in golf. Suburban living is ideal if it can be achieved without depriving the family of a father. But fathers are more important than play space!

3 : *Who is the child at birth*

INHERENT IN A CHILD AT BIRTH ARE CERTAIN INSTINCTUAL drives which, though they change in form, continue to determine personality throughout life. The human being has an inherent urge to be loved and to love; he has also an urge to strike out aggressively against unpleasant situations. The way from infancy to adulthood can be traced in the changing expression of these two urges. In the process of maturation, both impulses are modified. The urge to be loved—expressed first in the dependent relationship of infancy—becomes a capacity to love and be loved sexually and, more diffusely, through friendships, and to value as an expression of love the fulfillment of a role in the social world. The aggressive drive is expressed first in a desire to obtain relief from physiological distress; it gradually becomes an attack on more abstract discomforts in the immediate environment; ultimately it may be directed against abstract discomforts far beyond the immediate surroundings. The ambition of the emotionally healthy adult, for example, as well as .his enthusiasm for changing unpleasant aspects of the total social structure, is a modification of the aggressive drive.

One definition of adulthood lies within the framework of these two instinctual drives. In childhood the need to be loved may be antagonistic to the aggressive drive, since the small child inevitably seeks love from those individuals who also impose the greatest frustration on impulses. Love in early childhood is primarily self-directed; the aggressive drive most often recognizable is overt hostility. In adulthood these two originally antagonistic drives find modes of expression which fulfill each other. The adult acts out his wish to be loved and to love by aggressively attacking those situations unpleasant for his love objects, be those objects his wife, his children or humanity. His aggressiveness wins him love. His capacity to love gives him a goal for his aggressive impulses; they no longer find their outlet solely in explosive release. Ambition, expressing the aggressive impulse of the individual, is stimulated by and serves his love objects, allowing him a way to show his love and win it from others.

This direction of the instinctual drives must be achieved gradually. That is why the span of childhood is required to reach adulthood. These two drives are the tools through which other characteristics of the human species ultimately find relatively successful expression. The synthesis is so complex that time is essential; so is help from parents and other adults. Children are not miniature adults—they are the raw material of adulthood.

In addition to these general drives, the child is born with certain endowments unique to himself. They may be hereditary; they may be the result of biological experiences before birth; they may result from injury at birth or later in life. Only within a narrow range may these individual characteristics be modified.

The size that a child will ultimately attain, both in height and general body structure, is based on hereditary factors. Body growth not only varies according to the sex of the child, but also according to the size and shape of his ancestors. While nutrition has some effect upon the growth pattern, it is only within the limits determined by hereditary factors.

There is some indication that a tendency to get certain diseases may be inherited, but this is still controversial. There seems to be some evidence that cancer, for example, is more frequent in individuals whose ancestors had cancers. Children of parents who have had rheumatic fever are more prone to develop rheumatic fever—if other conditions exist that are favorable to the occurrence of the disease. It is obvious that the color of the hair, eyes, and skin are inherited characteristics.

A very significant aspect of the original endowment of the child is his mental ability. Inheritance plays a part in this. It may also be affected by intra-uterine conditions and certainly by injuries at birth or by subsequent trauma or disease. Deficiency in mental ability that was not inherent in the original germ plasm but produced by disease does not become hereditary in subsequent generations. For example, a child mentally handicapped by a birth injury will not pass on his handicap to his offspring.*

Recent studies have seemed to imply that mental retardation is not an irreversible condition, that environment plays a certain part in determining mental ability. A child in an intellectually limited, unstimulating environment may show every evidence of being mentally retarded. When placed in a different environment, he may manifest normal or superior ability. It would seem that in those cases the happier environment stimulates the growth of already existing but untapped resources. It is unfortunate if these studies have resulted on occasion in the assumption that a child *excessively* stimulated may develop beyond his basic capacity. The child of inherently limited intellectual ability then lives under a most difficult strain without actual hope of success. It has also been found that, in some cases, a small child exposed to a very stimulating environment will show an early intellectual capacity that is not borne out by his ultimate productiveness. Thus his later behavior may suggest deterioration. Actually the child, in the process of grow-

---

*This is to be borne in mind in cases of adoption. One parent of the child may be a mental defective. If this deficiency was the result of a birth injury, the child will not inherit that parent's intellectual limitations.

ing up, may only have leveled off to his inherent ability. Certain children may be mentally retarded because of the absence of some essential glandular secretion. Early recognition of this condition and correction through medication may result in increased mental capacity. Again however, the potential existed in the child at birth but was not fully tapped. Correcting this made possible the utilization of the basic ability.* When the natural secretions are adequate, artificial supplements usually will not modify the intellectual development of the child.

In summary, environment may affect the *manifestation* of mental capacity although the intellectual potential of the individual is inherent. The potential may be fully developed by the resources available in the environment; or it may be subject to functional atrophy, if the environment does not offer an opportunity for its use; and may be subject to organic atrophy as the result of certain diseases involving the brain.

A child whose ultimate mental growth is limited is not inevitably doomed to be an unhappy, asocial or unproductive individual. He is still a human being subject to the same gratifications, the same needs and the same frustrations as everyone else. The converse is equally true. A child with marked mental ability whose intellectual growth could achieve the heights of genius will not necessarily make a good general adjustment. While his intellectual capacity may make possible a very productive life both for himself and society, it may also make him more susceptible to negative as well as positive stimuli. The fundamental emotional needs are common to all children. How they can be wisely gratified is determined by the specific characteristics of each individual child. The intellectual potential of the child determines in part the manner in which his needs can and

---

* Unfortunately, the effect of defective glands of internal secretion is not always reversible. As an example, deficiency of the thyroid gland present during intra-uterine life may cause a failure in development of brain function that will prove relatively irreversible. *Each case* has to be evaluated individually to determine the permanence of the effect.

should be met, but it is only one factor to be taken into consideration in planning for his childhood.

There are perhaps other inherent individual differences somewhat more difficult to define. Some infant nurses believe that in the first few hours after birth certain characteristics become apparent. Some infants appear more aggressively eager to nurse, while others seem relaxed; still others are more responsive to stimuli. As human beings grow up, they manifest patterns of adjustment peculiar to them. Some will tend to submit; others to attack. Some appear able to stand considerable strain before becoming disorganized in their behavior; others seem unable to tolerate even slight degrees of strain. It is difficult to determine how much of this variation is the result of very early childhood experiences and how much is due to constitutional structure. Certainly the former is of tremendous importance, but it may also be fortified by certain broad, nonspecific aspects of the inherent psychological make-up of the individual.

The inherent, constitutional characteristics of the individual are the foundation of his ultimate personality, character and achievement in his adult world. To a certain extent, the foundation determines what kind of structure can be built upon it. Within the limits of any given foundation, on the other hand, superstructures of very varied architecture may arise. Upon the excavation of a house, for example, can be built an unimaginative box-like dwelling or an attractive home. This is equally true of people. A child is born with certain inherent capacities and limitations that can develop into a well-integrated personality or can form the basis for a disturbed one. It is not the foundation that determines essentially whether a house, or a personality, is desirable or not. It is what is built upon that foundation that determines whether it is wisely or unwisely developed.

In addition to these individual capacities, the newborn infant is a member of the human race; he therefore shares with all infants those characteristics which set humans apart from other animals. Since he is not reared in isolation but as a member of a distinctively human society, these characteristics obviously have a great deal to do with the way he is brought up.

This differentiation between human and other animal groups can be demonstrated in connection with their training. Methods used in breaking in a colt, a pet dog or cat, are not usually transferred effectively to the human young. The colt, dog, or cat is being trained to adjust to demands that are alien to its normal existence. A dog learns a pattern of behavior that will provide it food and care. It learns to offer that which, if you are a dog lover, can be described as love, loyalty and protectiveness. The dog becomes "almost human"—the phrase implying that he has taken on characteristics of a different species. It is questionable whether, had man not domesticated the dog, the dog would have trained man to provide warm fireplaces and government-inspected horse meat for his trainer! One difference between human beings and other animals is thus suggested. The human race is striving to adapt itself to a complex social structure which, while difficult to achieve, is not alien. The social structure as we see it today is a product, not the cause, of human nature and behavior.

It is rather difficult to enumerate the basic differences which set man apart from other animals. In part the difference is quantitative rather than qualitative. The very difference in degree in itself has an important effect on theories in child-rearing. But qualitative differences also exist and are involved in considering child development.

With a recognition of the inadequacy of the following enumeration of human characteristics, it is perhaps valid to consider certain points.

(1) The human species is a "family" species. The prolonged physically dependent period of the human infant necessitates this. Other animals also have offspring that require

a relatively long period of care, but once this period is over, the "family," whether composed of mother and child, or mother, child and father, disintegrates. Even when the parents are monogamists they do not behave as human parents. The offspring leaves to create a family of his own, without tie to those who begat him. *Homo sapiens* may find his childhood family a burden when he no longer needs its ministration, but that family remains in his reality, in his fantasy, and in his emotional patterns as long as he lives.*

(2) The human species is gregarious. Its members value and need contact with others of their kind. Inherent in man is an impulse to turn to other members of his species that has been explained as due to the long dependency period of childhood. Having found security in a relationship to the mother, man gets a similar sense of satisfaction from all human contacts. But a dog may have had the same gratifying infancy in relationship to its mother and can later survive quite happily (except for sexual satisfaction) in a world free of dogs. Given an opportunity to be with dogs, it may play or it may attack. The pleasure of dog-contact is determined as of the moment. Human beings have a persistent longing for other human beings. Thus it would appear that in our efforts to "socialize" a child we are not imposing a foreign pattern of behavior upon him. We are only expediting the expression of an inherent characteristic.

(3) Many animal species have a capacity to learn and to remember. The human species is unique in the capacity to utilize learning and memory for planning the future and for abstract thinking. Man can learn that two and two make four. Out of this and other knowledge he can blueprint a bridge or a philosophy of life. A dog can learn cause and effect. There is little evidence, however, that his inactive moments are spent in Kantian speculation upon life in general as he idly scratches a flea. In a dog world it would be surprising to dream of constructing crossing bells to warn of

* See Chapter on The Family.

an approaching train! When we educate children we do not teach them alien tricks—we only give them the tools, the stimulation and the opportunity to exercise their innate powers.

(4) The human species uses symbols. Without them it would be impossible to think abstractly or to communicate through the use of words. One suspects that animals have some way of mutual communication, but it is limited. Language permits more complete communication. It is essential for fulfilling the group urge and also makes the group experience richer. The capacity of symbolic representation of ideas and feelings is observable in many other ways. The symbolism of many religions is an indication of the capacity and the urge to express deeper emotional experiences through symbols. It is doubtful whether most dogs worship the pan from which they are fed. They may protect it because it periodically contains food, but it is probably never a symbol of gratification from a mother to be worshipped even when empty. When we fly a flag on the 4th of July, we do not teach a child merely to accept a symbol. We give him a tangible expression of some inner emotion. If the flag is not symbolically related to a love of his country (his group), he will not come to value it. If the emotion is felt, the flag becomes the external token of the inner experience.

A more significant universal human symbol is expressed in the word "home." The house in which one lives becomes a "home" when it symbolizes an emotionally gratifying experience. A child does not have to be taught to value his house as a home. He will use it as a symbol of "home" as he lives emotionally within its four walls. As the child matures he seeks a "house of his own." He who has found this a symbol for the gratifying emotional experiences of his childhood, will recreate those gratifications in a new environment and call it "home," the "home" of a new family.

(5) Man, in contrast to others of the animal world, is never independent of others. Again this is related to group

or tribe patterns but qualitatively and quantitatively differs from "pack" behavior in other animals. Dependency is self-evident in our complicated material world. The whole process of learning from books and conversation, of depending on the car manufacturer to provide a car and the mechanic to keep it running, the doctor to keep us well or cure us if we are ill, and the minister to christen, marry, guide and bury us is evidence of our perpetual dependency on others. At first glance it appears that such a characteristic is the result of a complex social structure. A little thought, however, will reveal that the social structure could not exist were this mutual dependency not inherent in the species. Again, children do not need to be *trained* to accept mutual dependence —they need only guidance toward constructively utilizing it.

Undoubtedly many other points could be added to a descriptive definition of the human species. The itemized ones are perhaps sufficient to indicate that the child is born a human being, not an unspecified animal to be "trained" to be human. To be human is not alien to him. He does need help in the course of his childhood to channel his inherent capacities into an expression that will permit their fullest gratification. He is of the human species and thus a social animal with unique tools for fulfilling his destiny.

PART II

THE

PSYCHOLOGICAL DEVELOPMENT

OF THE CHILD

PART II

THE

PSYCHOLOGICAL DEVELOPMENT

OF THE CHILD

THE FOLLOWING CHAPTERS TRACE THE DEVELOPMENT OF THE child through the stages that have been recognized and defined by modern psychology. Any such attempt to describe growth creates an inevitably false impression, as if one phase were left abruptly when the next is entered. This is not true. The child gradually passes from stage to stage without sharp lines of demarcation. It is impossible to distinguish the passage of night into day unless it is arbitrarily stated that day begins at the moment when the first tip of the sun appears above the horizon. But even then the darkness of night has already been dispelled by the approaching light. Similarly, though it is possible to recognize the developmental level of a child once it has been attained, each period is a blend of the earlier and the evolving patterns.

Psychological growth, while proceeding in an orderly fashion if permitted to do so, does not follow too closely the chronological age of a child. While statistically the majority of children will, at the age of two, manifest certain characteristic behavior and will, at six, give promise of an evolving "latency," this age chart is not applicable to every particular child. In appraising a child psychologically, a comparison of his current behavior with that recalled from a few months before is more valid than the comparison of his development with that of other children.

A further drawback in describing emotional growth in stages is that it is difficult to avoid the implication that as one stage blends into the next, the first gradually disappears. Actually each stage of development becomes a part of the next. and its characteristics are modified by maturation, not erased by it. As an example, the early dependent relationship of the infant matures until, in the psychologically healthy adult, it is expressed in the mutual interdependency with others that creates a society instead of a mass of individuals living in isolation. When the maturation process fails, the adult personality may show components of all the periods of development in immature form.

According to the psychoanalytic theory of personality development, character distortions—the neuroses and psychoses seen in children and adults—can be traced to ineffectually solved conflicts during one or several of the stages of growth. It is not, however, the conflicts themselves that cause the later illness, for most of them are inevitable in the normal process of maturation. The significant factor is the method and adequacy with which the individual resolves or fails to resolve them.

The stress in this section is on the conflicts, the difficulties the child faces in attempting to resolve them, and the role parents play in effecting the child's healthy and happy solution.

4 : *The Oral or Dependent Period*

THE NEWBORN BABY IS AN UNDIFFERENTIATED UNIT THAT, IN THE course of development, will gradually manifest three broad categories of response: the physical, the intellectual and the emotional. Though these categories become differentiated enough to be recognizable, they always remain as interrelated parts of the total person.

The infant's primary need is for food, warmth and sleep. Since he cannot provide all these for himself, they are provided by others. It is apparent from birth that these manifest physiological requirements are not solely mechanical. Their fulfillment is most adequate when enriched by human contact. It has been found, for example, that the respiratory and heartbeat rhythm, typically irregular at birth, becomes more readily stabilized if the baby is held and given the sensory stimulation of fondling rather than being allowed to remain continuously in his crib. An infant cared for in the first few months of life in an emotionally sterile environment—one considered more hygienic physically because few human beings are allowed to contaminate its purity—will bear the scars permanently if later an intensive corrective experience is not provided. Even so, he will be slow in his emotional growth until he has successfully satiated himself with the essential emotional component of infancy of which he had been deprived.

The effect of the first few months of life spent in a "hygienic" nursery is often tragically demonstrated. An infant kept for adoption in a hospital or other institution planned primarily to protect the newborn child from bacteria may appear more mentally limited than he actually is. He may be seriously retarded in his responsiveness to stimuli from outside his own body. He looks like and is a doll, carefully shaped as a healthy human body; he will not show the human characteristics that differentiate a baby from a doll. Fortunately the roots of those characteristics are in the child as they are not in a real doll, and they can be stimulated through human contacts. A few germs may come along, but a newborn baby can manage a few germs better than he can manage an environment that starves him in every area except that of physical nutrition.

Breast feeding has value since the mother's milk fills certain physical requirements of the infant that no formula can offer, and it continues for some time to be the best form of nourishment for an infant. However, as a result of increased medical knowledge, a formula, at least after the first few days, can provide an adequate diet. But scientific knowledge has never discovered a substitute for certain of the components of breast feeding. A formula, no matter how adequate for physical nutrition, is impersonal. It cannot offer the interpersonal significance of breast feeding. The infant, necessarily held during breast feeding, is maintaining as close a relationship to the mother and is approximating as closely the intra-uterine existence that he has just left, as is possible.

The immediate post-uterine contact between the infant and the mother is often referred to as a *symbiotic* relationship, in which there is an emotional exchange between mother and child. The child is maintained through the relationship; the mother develops an ability to fulfill her potential motherhood out of this mutual experience. Not only are the child's physical needs for food and warmth met but there is also a more subtle giving by the mother. The assurance and emotional nutrition transmitted to the child as the mother holds him, comforts him in his crib, allows him to sleep the proper length of time and provides adequate food for him lays the foundation upon which the child gradually builds his responsiveness to the outside world.

It is important to bear in mind that the early care of the infant should not be characterized by constant handling or perpetual feeding. The mother's arms are not the only cradle for the child. The ideal cradle is his total surrounding. The physical contact with the mother is a part of the overall gentle and peaceful world she creates as an extension of herself.

In determining the proper emotional environment, the mother's personality, the demands placed upon her by other considerations in her life and the confidence she has in her own role must be taken into consideration. A mother is often fearful about handling her own infant. Her tension and awkwardness in holding the child arouse similar tension in the baby. With practice, she will gradually find how unlike Dresden China he actually is. If a mother is harassed by multiple demands and the requirement that the baby be held seems one demand too many, it is preferable that the infant's contact with the world beyond himself be fostered in other ways.

Because the significance of overall contentment in an infant's development is recognized, "demand feeding" has become more and more accepted. In this program the child eats not when the clock says he should be hungry and not in quantities that the chart says he needs, but rather as his own body language expresses needs peculiar to him. Each child has different food requirements and different rates of food utilization. Since the metabolic system of the infant is not as stabilized as it will become, his needs vary at different times. Adults vary in their food intake from day to day. It is not surprising that an infant's requirements are even more variable than those of the adult whose life in general has reached a more uniform pattern. From a physical standpoint, "demand feeding" has a rational basis.

From the viewpoint of the infant's relationship to his mother, "demand feeding" has much justification. Hunger is a physically determined, unpleasant experience. The mother, in providing food, relieves discomfort. Furthermore, it is not just the food *per se* that is of significance. If the baby is held while fed, the pleasure that results from having the hunger allayed is accompanied by the overall soothing sensations. If, on the other hand, the infant is not hungry the insistence upon clock-dictated eating would not be apt to offer an optimum experience with the mother. If the mother struggles to force the infant to take unneeded food, quite the contrary result may occur. Not only will her own tension and effort make her embrace bodily unsatisfactory to the child, but there is also the unpleasant experience of having something imposed that is not desired. This certainly would tend to minimize the gratification. It might actually result in unpleasant associations with food and being held. The impression is often gained that some of those children who later seem markedly unwilling to accept or express affection through normal physical gestures may have been conditioned early against that form of expression because their physical contacts in infancy, through feeding as well as in other contacts with the mother, were unsatisfactory.

"Demand feeding" is not as simple to achieve as it appears. If the infant cried only when hungry, he would be more cooperative in the application of this ideal plan. An infant does cry for other reasons—he may be too cold, too warm, cramped in the way he is lying, or just responding to general tension in his surroundings. The environment, because of the mother's eagerness to be a good mother according to the book, may not be conducive to relaxation. The mother in such instances is trying so hard to be a good mother that she cannot relax sufficiently to achieve her goal. An infant often responds to tension in a mother as if there were a direct nerve connection between them.

"Demand feeding" may result in an attempt on the part

of the mother to solve all the infant's problems by putting a nipple in his mouth. Far from solving the problem, it only complicates it. Most babies have a period in the day in which they cry for reasons that are not too clear. It has been postulated that crying is physically essential for the infant because it expands the lungs. But contented babies who cry little seem to get on pretty well; they will, it appears justified to conclude, cry enough to provide whatever physical benefit is derived. It is certainly not necessary to foster crying by failing to give obviously indicated comfort. On the other hand, unexplained crying spells will not irreparably damage the psyche of the child whose environment is predominantly comfortable.

A mother who is unsure of herself under a regime of "demand feeding" will probably be a more effective mother on a scheduled feeding plan. Perhaps then she will feel more receptive to the idea that even on a schedule a child does not have to be wakened to eat, nor does he have to obey the chart that says how much he should eat at a given time. A woman who feels comfortable only if she is living by a predictable schedule will do better if she is allowed a schedule. Mothers and doctors need to consider the mother's emotional pattern as well as the baby's biological ones! The plan with which the mother feels most relaxed is the plan that will benefit the infant the most. A little ingenuity will make possible a schedule not too out of accord with the child's own rhythm.

The first step in psychological development is the oral* stage, during which the infant's most organized source of gratification is sucking. Sucking is the newborn's means of

---

* On the whole there has been an attempt in this work to avoid the use of psychoanalytic terms, partly because many of them are not used strictly in accordance with the meaning found in most general dictionaries. Many of the terms must be defined by the individual user since each one gives them a slightly different connotation or emphasis. However, there is verbal economy in the occasional use of certain terms when otherwise longer phrases would be required.

acquiring nourishment, and nature has thus assured survival by having it as an instinctual response. The urge to suck and the relief from the effect of sucking create the tension and relaxation that is the matrix of later pleasurable emotions, especially that identified as love.

When the significance of this relationship between pleasure and a physical response was first recognized the term "erotic zone" was applied to the mouth area. In this basic Freudian concept, the word "erotic" refers to love in its largest possible sense; it does not refer to love with the connotation of adult sexuality. From the experience of nursing, then, comes the child's first fulfillment of what will become the desire to know and give love.

In psychoanalytic literature the term "oral incorporative tendencies" is frequently used. Unfortunately it is usually used to refer to an individual who really "swallows" others symbolically. Such a person cannot let those he cares for exist except as they live through him or, so to speak, inside of him. He cannot love except by "eating up." This capacity for oral incorporation is not, however, discernible only in pathology. A person capable of mature love also feels that the loved one is a part of him. In such instances he feels a unity with the person, who is, though not eaten up, figuratively fused with him, remaining at the same time a separate entity.

The infant does "eat up" the source of his early pleasurable experience. This pre-love gratification results from taking in by way of the mouth. He does not have the sensory development or the capacity to differentiate between his self and his not-self, to conceive of a source of gratification separate from himself. But if this experience occurs in generally comforting surroundings in his mother's arms, the relief of hunger is accompanied by other pleasurable sensations. It does not seem beyond the realm of possibility that the child whose feeding is accompanied by comfort and pleasure over and above that derived from sucking and the relief of hunger distress will be better prepared to recognize, experience and express love through more subtle ways in adulthood. An infancy in which a child finds nursing satisfaction will condition his later responses in two ways. It should, as indicated earlier in this chapter, provide a feeling of comfortable security in the world about him so that he sees it as a friendly place in which to live, rather than an indifferent or attacking environment against which he must protect himself. Secondly it should enrich the erotic gratification of sucking by the added pleasure of experiencing love from others.

The intensity of the sucking urge varies from child to child. Some infants apparently suck before birth. Some infants respond quickly with sucking movement to any stimulation of the lips. Others will be relatively less responsive. The child with a strong sucking urge will often, in the first few days of life, suck a fist or move the lips in a sucking movement even though he is not hungry. In another child the sucking urge is satisfied during normal feeding experiences. If a small infant obtains his food too easily, if the milk flows into his mouth with minimum effort on his part, his sucking urge may not be gratified as his hunger is met. He may then continue to suck, often sucking his fist, not because he is hungry, but because his sucking response, which has served the function of gaining food, has need for still further activity.

Sucking is the first comforting experience the child has. It is not surprising, therefore, that a small child will often turn to sucking when unallayable discomfort occurs even after the first few months of life. Thumb-sucking is a form this solution may take, though other objects may be sought as a substitute. Many small children suck their thumbs only when tired, as if the thumb-sucking not only lessens their fatigue but also invites the return to the infantile state in which food brought not only relief from hunger, but the comfortable state of sleep. It is not extremely rare to have this pattern persist through life. Some adults induce sleep, consciously or unconsciously, by recreating the infantile state of sucking and falling asleep.

Other children suck their thumbs because they need comforting the environment does not offer. Such a child has, at least transiently, abandoned his urge to gain gratification from without and has turned to himself as the only means upon which he can depend to meet his longings. A child who has found his surroundings chronically unsatisfactory may use this solution. Sometimes the deprivation he has experienced would have been avoidable had those about him known how to fill his needs. At other times, circumstances such as the birth of another baby, a crisis in the home or an increased burden of demands upon the most meaningful adults in the child's life may have resulted in a realistic but unavoidable deprivation. The child, refusing to submit to the uncomfortable state, uses his own resources, his thumb and his ability to return to infantile gratification, to fill the void in his environment.

Thumb-sucking as an attempt to gratify legitimate needs is a poor but valued resource. Transient episodes (including those occurring only with fatigue) suggest that the immediate experience of the child is taxing his ability to deal with it except by this self-comforting. If possible the environment should be changed to gratify the child's unmet need. When this cannot be done, for whatever reason, the child should be allowed his own answer until the ingenuity of adults develops some more constructive plan.

It is obvious that there are disadvantages for optimum psychological growth if the child's most satisfying answer lies in sucking his thumb. In essential areas he is limiting his world to his own physical orbit. He is failing to have sufficiently meaningful relationships with those about him. The damage done to his teeth is minor compared to the damage done to his psychological growth as a result of the emotional starvation he feels. But to force him to give up this gratification of thumb-sucking without offering him a more meaningful environment is to threaten him with still greater starvation. The Chinese coolie who eats only rice needs a more balanced diet. Since his budget cannot provide this diet, it would not be wisdom to deprive him of his rice. Only if a wiser diet could be afforded should he be encouraged to lessen his rice intake. Of course, he might be so used to rice he would reject other foods. Similarly, children who are persistent thumb-suckers find it difficult to shift from self-offered comfort to that offered by others. The mode of gratification of a need has become a "habit." At that point, gentle pressure to abandon the habit may be indicated. Often the question as to whether that point has been reached cannot be answered by the parents but requires expert evaluation.* More frequently the child stops thumb sucking spontaneously because it is no longer required.

It should be borne in mind that, as indicated earlier, infants show differences in their sucking urge. The stronger the urge, the greater likelihood of its being unsatisfied and therefore the greater probability of thumb-sucking. This, as well as all behavior patterns, should never be used as an isolated symptom to evaluate a child's needs, his adjustment, his problems and his emotional development. It must be seen as only a part of a whole. The whole must be known before the significance of a part is judged.

As the infant becomes a little older, his teeth are ready to erupt. The gums become more or less tender and painful. At this point Nature provides a means of getting relief which also fulfills the physiological function of stimulating the growth of the teeth and maintaining healthy circulation in the gums. The infant begins to bite as well as to suck on those objects that enter his mouth—a response which signalizes the beginning of the oral aggressive phase of development. The pleasure of biting and the relief it brings has psychological as well as physical significance throughout life. Biting becomes a way

* When and where to seek help, p. 394.

of relieving the tension of pain—as when a person with a toothache bites down on the tooth for relief—a gratifying means of oral stimulation, and a means of reaction to psychological frustration. If it is excessive or if it remains at the infantile level, it becomes a part of a neurosis or character disorder. If entirely absent it is just as indicative of a distortion of normal psychological growth patterns.

The permanence of the oral aggressive phase is indicated by the common expression "get your teeth into it," used when a difficult task must be undertaken. "Oral aggression" is part of the pleasure found in chewing solid foods. An extract of steak can be made that would be just as nutritious as the steak itself. The bulk provided by the steak could be obtained by swallowing pills of cellulose. Who but a person inhibited in chewing and thus burdened by conflict would give up the pleasure of chewing steak? Similarly, gum would be less popular were it not relatively universal to enjoy chewing for chewing's sake. This enjoyment is not a carry-over of infantile pleasures into an adult neurosis nor does it imply inadequacy in development. Most infantile patterns of response do not disappear; they mature to adult patterns. The pleasure of chewing firm food is a maturation of the infantile chewing response. It is probably a legacy from our carnivorous ancestors, and although it is no longer imperative for survival, the pleasure remains.

Biting as a response to frustration is a common response of mature adults, who "grit their teeth" and face a problem or threat. Often this is not merely a figure of speech, but an actual physical response under tension. The jaw muscles are fatigued when the effort is over. "I sure chewed him up," or "he bit my head off" suggest the survival of an immature way of expressing anger that in the adult has become only symbolically expressed by verbal rather than actual attack. There is nothing strange or unfortunate about this. Feelings have to be released in some way. In the immature person certain direct channels are used, while in the mature individual symbols of those channels become effective. This symbolization alleviates the necessity of totally repressing the feeling, for total repression would only create an internal atom bomb, always threatening to explode.

When the child bites down upon the nipple, and it happens to be a rubber nipple, others have little awareness of the child's gesture. If on the other hand the sharp little teeth bite down on the mother's breast, the effect is more electric. The mother may be startled or may actually experience considerable discomfort. She may then abruptly withdraw the breast, both in self-defense and to punish the child. Such behavior on the part of the mother may give the infant a memory pattern that will have two possible outcomes. He may later rediscover biting as a channel of outlet for anger because the memory pattern of the past indicates that this is an effective way to attack. Another infant may find the memory pattern tinged with fear. Biting brings withdrawal of the loved object accompanied by a feeling of desertion and loss. Thus an aggressive act like biting is too dangerous and must be curbed at any price. Undoubtedly *some* feeding problems in adults, such as some examples of inability to eat in public, may relate to memory patterns of this period. This does not mean to say that every child who bites his mother's breast with a resultant withdrawal on her part is going to be unable to eat in public. There would be a dearth of restaurants, and we would have developed secrecy in eating customs similar to bathroom customs, were this true!

The experience of the infant in this connection is probably most significant when it occurs at the time the child is also suffering frustration from another source. If, for example, the breast milk is not adequate and the infant is therefore not satisfied, the gratification from biting may not only be related to his erupting teeth but to the relief that biting provides from the tension of his frustrated hunger.

During this period of development the child should have something to bite on. He will provide it for himself by utilizing his toys. The pediatrician offers some help by modifying the infant's diet. The child may chew on his own fists. Mothers who have become sophisticatedly familiar with the concept of masochism and self-punishment sometimes become frightened at this and wonder if it is the beginning of a masochistic self-mutilation. Perhaps the infant does enjoy the stimulation of self-controlled mild pain. There are many bodily sensations that are mildly tension producing but still pleasurable, such as those caused by rubbing the skin, tickling and other familiar ways of skin stimulation. Pain is only excessive stimulation that goes beyond the level of pleasure. The infant who bites himself during this period is not fated to become self-punishing and masochistic unless he has some reason in his total subsequent life situation to find pain and self-punishment a permanently gratifying way to relieve otherwise unbearable tension.

The intensity of the urge to find satisfaction through oral stimulation gradually decreases as other gratifications become available with the physical maturation of the body and the infant is able to channelize some of his oral desires into sublimated forms. It is at this time, were one able to recognize it clearly, that the child is ready to be weaned and will sometimes, given the opportunity, wean himself. An infant existing in an environment ideal for his maturation probably would never have to be weaned. But such an environment cannot be created—it is not a part of a real world. Some infants, in spite of drawbacks, do wean themselves.

Weaning cannot be timed by the calendar or chronological age. An infant may persist in wishing to suck a bottle at bedtime longer than other children do without its being of any more significance than that he is not yet ready to give up that particular pleasurable activity. An infant is able to give up the pleasure of attaining food by sucking if the withdrawal of the opportunity is gradual and done when the child can find other available experiences gratifying. Rapid, poorly-timed weaning places an excessive demand upon the child's adaptability. Obviously when a child is ill is not the time to institute a withdrawal of the breast or bottle unless the child shows a preference for solid food or milk from a glass.

A child who has reached a level of development commensurate with giving up the direct oral gratification of the bottle but who fights against this step in maturation may be indicating that other gratifications are missing. It is then important to explore the reasons for the absence of other gratifications before insisting that the one so important to him be abandoned. As with persistent thumb-sucking, parents often do not have sufficient perspective concerning themselves and the child to judge the wisest way to help the child over this hurdle. Professional help, not consultation with the neighbors, is indicated. It is not that the symptom itself is so serious, but rather that unwise handling of it might have a more serious aftermath.

The first year or so of life is the time of maximum passive dependency. The child is totally dependent upon his environment for the fulfilling of most of his essential needs. Out of the gratification of those needs comes physical well-being and, equally importantly, emotional well-being and fundamental security in the world about him. If the world he is introduced to provides a comfortable feeling of warmth and responsiveness, it gradually becomes increasingly inviting. As the sensory organs develop and their connections are established with the cognitive part of the brain, their stimulation is experienced as pleasurable. If, for example, as vision improves and the infant is able to see the mother and connect her image with many pleasant experiences, she comes to be recognized as a person towards whom to turn and finally to seek out as a happy contact. The first cognizant step towards gratification of the desire to turn outward for pleasure instead of depending only upon the self, is taken. It is one of the early steps towards ultimate achievement of a meaningful relationship to others.

During this period the infant, again as a result of physical development, is gradually coming to divide his world into two broad categories—the self and the not-self. This separation does not occur suddenly. It probably extends over some period of time. It is thought that the first recognition of the mother is not as of something separate from the self but rather as one with the self, that every person or thing, in this early phase, is recognized within the same boundaries. One basis for this assumption lies in the inability of some mentally-ill people to differentiate self from the not-self. Since so many of the symptoms of mental illness seem to be determined by a distorted return to childhood or infancy responses, it is suggested that a similar return causes this symptom also. In a mentally healthy individual there would also appear to be a constructive remnant of this. An emotionally mature individual feels himself a part of the world, suggesting that he never has completely separated himself from the world external to his body, but rather has come to recognize that the world is not part of him, but he is part of it.

The above paragraphs are not inserted as a philosophical digression from the main purpose of this book. They rather suggest certain conclusions in regard to the needs of the infancy period. For the infant to carry to fruition the inherent urge to turn outward for satisfactions, the groundwork should be laid by his experience before physical responses are differentiated from emotional ones. In order for him to separate himself from and yet remain a part of his environment, he needs contact with that environment in a framework of security. An infant could be secure in a room that is soundproof, thermally controlled and provided with an automatic feeding device, but this offers no preparation for responding to the real world. He could become aware, on the other hand, of the external world by too constant stimulation from without. He would then find no peace or security except by his own mechanisms of defense, which might be

limited in his early period to repressing responsiveness because to be aware would be too frightening.

These thoughts can be translated into directly significant
recommendations to the mother. The bottle-fed baby should
be held when fed. In the first few weeks of life little more
is needed since sleep takes over for the rest of the time. As
the periods of sleep decrease, contact with human as well as
material aspects of the environment should increase. Toys
with which to play become important. The infant needs also
to be alone in order to become aware of himself, to enjoy
his own body, to feel his own toys and to make his own noise
with his rattle. He needs pleasant experiences with the not-
self of his environment as well as pleasant experiences with
the self without too much outside stimulation. He is ready
to begin to learn "I am fun; you are fun."

As the infant begins to identify the mother and others as
separate from himself, a response trying to the parents and
to the infant often occurs. The infant does not want to be
left alone. Awake, he cries for attention, not because he is
hungry or physically uncomfortable, but because he is emotionally uncomfortable. He does not have the gift of philosophical verbalizing so he cannot tell what the uncomfortable sensation is. Maybe he feels anxiety over the impact of
the unknown that he is just beginning to recognize about
him. If so he wishes the support the mother, or other people
with similar roles, have provided. Perhaps these meaningful
people are not yet separate entities and their absence is as if
part of his self were mislaid. Or perhaps the gratification
these persons have offered has been so satisfying that nothing else is quite as desirable. Whatever the reason, the infant
seems "spoiled." He wants attention "all of his waking
hours."

The child is on the threshold of a new and important
learning experience. He is about to learn (and it will take
time for him to learn) that temporary absence does not
mean permanent disappearance. At first this is compre-

hended only if the separation is limited to the length of time he can tolerate. Gradually his tolerance for separation increases, accelerated probably as the older infant develops some capacity for memory and an ability to enjoy a simple fantasy—the fantasy of the mother in the physical absence of the mother.

It is interesting to speculate whether this simple fantasy about the absent mother is actually the beginning of the capacity for abstract thinking. It has been observed that many individuals who were reared in the older type of large impersonal orphanage where meaningful relationships with parent substitutes were not available, have, regardless of their intellectual endowment, a relative inability to deal with abstract concepts. As in all aspects of human personality, however, there is not only one cause for a given result. There is also probably an inherent variation in the ability for abstract thinking in different individuals and there are many other conditions that will foster or curb its development.

When the baby, previously content to be alone, suddenly shows unhappiness when no one is with him, it is not indicative necessarily that he is fundamentally an insecure child or that he is "spoiled." "Spoiling" occurs as a result of the way this period is handled. If the parents are frightened by the infant's behavior and feel that one of them must always be present, the infant not only is not helped to go beyond this stage, but whatever fear he has will seem justified by the parents' anxiety. If the child is forced to tolerate periods of separation and anxiety beyond his capacity to master them, he may become chronically fearful of desertion. On the other hand, he may deny his psychological hunger for something that is not sufficiently available by the infantile equivalent of "sour grapes."

Some children never show this concern over separation. Such cases do not necessarily mean that the infant is failing to distinguish the parts of his environment but, perhaps, he is successfully mastering the problem. Only consideration of the total picture can determine if this is true. The major criterion is the child's responsiveness to the presence of others. If he is selectively responsive, he is probably handling this maturation step healthily regardless of how he reacts to absence. His failure to respond to both presence and separation is indicative of something unsatisfactory in his developmental process. This may be due to a congenital defect. The child who is markedly retarded mentally will often show the first discernible symptoms at this point. On the other hand the child may have, for unavoidable reasons, been deprived of the necessary attention prior to the development of an awareness of his environment. If no one really loves the infant, he may be just giving evidence of the effect of that lack of love.

If parents of an infant are concerned about the absence of this pattern of responsiveness at a time that *statistically* it should occur, they should not lie awake nights worrying. This compounds the felony. A tired or worried parent complicates a child's life. They should not try to force the child's responsiveness by overstimulation. They should not ask the neighbors, no matter how statistically normal the neighbors' child is. It is again time to ask a professional person who knows.

This period of development may also be accompanied by shyness. Previously the infant, feeling comfortable in his environment, seemed to like anyone and everyone. All the effervescent friends and shoppers at the grocery store could hold him or coo at him and he would lie in his buggy peacefully or smile winningly. Now suddenly he turns away, refuses to smile or, even more disconcertingly, lets out a lusty wail. Parents then are frustrated. They can't show off their beautiful creation and the evidence of their success as parents. If more concerned about the baby than themselves, they see that the child is suddenly insecure and frightened by the world. That fear is not surprising: the infant has separated parents from non-parents, the known individuals from those who are new.

All people should be cautious in investigating the unknown until it becomes sufficiently the known to alleviate the need for caution. The infant doesn't have the equipment for rapid evaluation of the unknown, so his caution is expressed only in the crude form of fear. If, at this time in development, friends and grocery-store acquaintances would abandon their dive-bomb techniques, the child would show less fear. Since that Utopia cannot be hoped for, the parents must weather this time during which the infant, as a result of his growing awareness of a world separate and strange, is evaluating the significance of his discoveries.

There are great variations in the rapidity or success with which the children overcome this shyness. Certain children are more sensitive than others and find it more difficult to feel really secure in their expanding world. The more sensitive they are, the more they will require support and acceptance of their shyness. A world made up of outgoing, hail-fellow-well-met people might be a little boring. It is pleasant to know a few people who exercise some caution before they embrace you as a bosom friend.

A child deserves the privilege of being shy and of being many other things that the so-called "normal" child is not. In this era of microscopic evaluation of personality, and particularly of childhood, there is a tendency to establish a yardstick for normalcy so finely calibrated no child can be measured by it and be adjudged psychologically healthy. If a child is not sufficiently shy he is considered unpleasantly bold, a state indicative of problems. If he is shy, something is wrong. There is also a tendency to believe that unless parents can find a defect in their child or somebody else's child, they are not astute. In spite of what is seen under the microscope, children are macroscopically human beings and have as much right to unique personality traits as they have to their own individual fingerprints. If an infant doesn't want to smile at a gargoyle face belonging to his mother's best friend hovering over him, it would seem that he has a right not to smile. He can even go so far as to show distaste for anything so alarmingly grotesque. It is time for adults to think about how they look to the child rather than expecting the child to assume the facial expression that is pleasant to the adult.

THE DEVELOPMENT OF COMMUNICATION AND LOVE

During the first period of life the child becomes increasingly skilled in communicating with others. Purists may suggest that real communication does not develop until thought does, and until words can be used as symbols to convey thoughts to others. No one who has been awakened by a hungry infant's wail at 2:00 A.M. will deny that the baby has communicated effectively with the adult.

Communication between a child and the world beyond him begins perhaps before birth as a result of sensory stimulation and soothing experiences during intra-uterine life. Immediately after birth, it is mainly a physical phenomenon between child and mother through their bodily contact. A little indulgence in fantasy would suggest that the child's first question is expressed by sucking. The mother's first answer is given in the flow of milk. The infant's wail communicates its distress to the mother while the mother responds by alleviating the discomfort and by making soothing sounds. The presence and importance of this intercommunication is shown by the study of a condition called marasmus, rarely seen now but more commonly described in the textbooks of the past. The victims were infants who had no meaningful communication with others during their first few months of life, did not manifest any answering response, and eventually died of malnutrition. Their death is tragic proof that growth itself is checked unless the instinctual human urge to turn outside the body structure for gratification finds expression, and that communication with others is essential to human life.

Since the early communication is through the physical structure, the mother's behavior is directly reflected in that of the child. If the mother is tense, the child becomes tense; the child of the relaxed but responsive mother is calm. A mother whose relaxation is due merely to indifference, however, may have a child who is either equally indifferent or who is tense. If this is doubted, observe a day with two pediatric nurses in the infant's ward of a hospital. Both, because of training, temperament and experience, will be relaxed in handling infants. The nurse who responds positively to babies will quiet many more upset infants than will the nurse who sees them solely as objects that create employment for her.

As a child becomes more aware of his environment and as the meaning of the environment becomes part of his mental processes, his responses become more organized and broader in scope. Long before he can talk he develops movements and sounds that clearly convey his wishes to those who are familiar with his own particular nonverbal patterns of expression.

Just as sucking and the response of the flow of milk from the mother's breast is one of the basic communications between mother and child, the flow of sounds to others and of others to the child becomes an important device for later communication As the infant begins to produce sounds other than crying, he appears to enjoy the noise he makes. Some of this pleasure may be conditioned by the similarity of the sounds to those he hears his mother and other meaningful adults make. He may be recalling those delightful people to his presence by imitating them. He continues and increases these noises in the presence of others as if he found pleasure in making them for others and hearing their answer. It is probable also that pleasure accompanies the use of the tongue and those throat muscles that make sound possible.

A universal past experience of this nature is reflected in the phrases we use to describe speech: "He had to swallow his words," "He talked as if he tasted every word he said," "His words were biting," "She spoke with a sweet voice." Anyone examining his own particular vernacular will find many oral symbols used to describe his own speech or that of others. Speech is one of the more mature expressions of the infant's oral eroticism. A common parlor game at present is to label someone an "oral" person because he enjoys talking and eating. Fortunately for nutrition and communication everyone remains an "oral" person. Speech is another proof that "orality" does not disappear but matures with the passage of time.

The increased capacity of the infant is paralleled by the development of language. The child can understand the speech of others and finally learns, by imitation, to use words himself. His achievement opens a whole new world of pleasure to him, which he explores so thoroughly that the parents, who have eagerly anticipated the time when he can talk, now complain because he talks all the time!

The development of speech is affected by several conditions, such as the rate of intellectual growth and the strength of the urge to communicate. Slow speech development, however, is not necessarily indicative of either slow mental development or a weak communicative urge. It is not talking alone that is enjoyable to the child. Talking is only a skilled way of fulfilling his desire to communicate and is more quickly attempted when other methods fail. Many infants, prior to talking, seem frantically to try to transmit a concept or a wish to others and cannot find a means of doing so. This offers an incentive to achieve a mastery of speech. Other children show remarkable skill in transmitting their thought processes without verbalization. They have parents or siblings who can readily understand nonverbal communications and only later, with more complex ideas to express, does speech appear necessary to them. There is no reason to thwart these children in their successful nonverbal communication. They will learn to talk when the need arises. In the meantime they are having the intercommunication with others which is important for their further development. Delayed speech is indicative of serious voids in the infant's life that will later have psychological implications only when it is delayed because the infant has not found attempts at communication rewarding. He has abandoned any hope of satisfying his urge to relate to others because others have proved either unpleasant or unresponsive to him.

In this chapter we have been tracing the steps taken by the very young child in establishing a place in his own particular world. We have seen him, if fundamentally secure, begin to identify a world separate from himself and to turn toward that world for gratification. We have watched his growing responsiveness and desire to communicate with others in various ways, culminating in the use of language. So closely interwoven with all these steps that it can hardly be described separately is the development of the instinctual urge to love and be loved. And although this process eludes definitive description during the early oral period, it is readily recognized through its effect upon later stages of development.

It is often said that the infant's "love" is directed only to himself. Infancy has been called the period of "primary narcissism," and only in the process of maturation does the child come to love others. This concept would appear an over-simplification as well as very thwarting to parents! It is also, stated in this way, in conflict with another theory we have discussed, namely, that the very young infant does not differentiate from the self and the not-self. If the not-self does not exist, it is questionable whether the self exists either. More accurately speaking, the infant world is a whole. Within the limits of his emotional response, the infant reacts positively or negatively to any part of the world which offers stimulation. As he comes to differentiate between the self and the not-self there is no indication that he loses his emotional investment in the not-self. If he did, one would anticipate that at that time he would temporarily withdraw his responsiveness to the positive experiences from the not-self and try to encapsulate himself for protection from the unpleasant experiences. Such behavior occurs only under very abnormal circumstances when the positive experiences are minimal and the painful ones overwhelming. The infant then does retreat from anything that is the not-self and tries to wall himself in; he may become only a breathing, metabolizing vegetable, finally to abandon even this and then cease to exist.

The infant living in a relatively normal environment does not retreat. One of the indications that the infant turns towards the not-self at the time of differentiation is the criterion used to identify this step. The baby smiles or coos to the approaching mother, makes gestures that express pleasure or the desire to be taken. The mother has become someone separate from the self. It would appear that this is the beginning of a love response as well as a wish to be loved. Just because an infant cannot speak the words of love, cannot make noble sacrifices, cannot give up his own instinctual needs even if when gratified they will disturb parents, does not mean the infant does not, within the framework of his level of development, love.

This point is not stressed for the purpose of enjoying mental gymnastics. It again emphasizes the importance of the early period of infancy and the infant's relationship to his parents. A belief that the infant wants love but gives nothing suggests that the source of the love does not matter. Anyone or any number of people providing sufficient comfort to the infant will give him the resources with which to develop love in turn. It also implies that the donor gives and gives with no immediate return, the books to be balanced later. But it *does* matter who provides the love and the infant, in its own way, does make a return. He benefits if the giving is by a small number of people who will continue to be important to him. As soon as an infant differentiates between the self and the not-self, in other words after the first three or four months of life, the individual givers become important. The child will, if cared for solely by a nurse, react to the replacement of that nurse. He has not only lost a familiar part of his environment, he has lost a love object. A mother intuitively senses that the infant's response is the precursor of more definite love for her. Only non-mothers ridicule the mother's concept and say that the child has colic. Between a mother and her new-born infant there flows a two-way emotional exchange so close that they are almost fused into a single identity. As this gradually shifts to the establishment of two individual personalities, both continue to love the one who shared the earlier relationship. In early infancy the foundation is laid for that important ultimate structure, the capacity of an individual not only to accept the love of others but also to love in return.

5 : *The anal period*

WHETHER OR NOT THE INFANT ATTAINS FULL GRATIFICATION
during the period of oral dominance, his physical development will propel him toward the next level of psychological
growth, the anal stage. At this time the child's neurological
maturation is such that he has an increasing ability to control the muscles involved in walking as well as those required
in finer, more directed movements of all parts of the body.
The nerves innervating the sphincter muscles of the bladder
and rectum have matured sufficiently so that the child is
ready to control his excretory functions. The "erotic" zone
of dominant importance now becomes the anal zone. Urination and defecation are pleasurable; their control, when it is
established, becomes equally pleasant and brings with it an
increased sense of power and self-respect. The characteristic
problems of this period arise when the exercise of the child's
new-found abilities conflicts with his continuing need for security and parental love. Nowhere are the opposing forces
marshalled more directly or with more trying results than
over the issue of toilet training.

Theoretically, pleasure in the excretory processes and in
their control should create an ideal situation for toilet training. It should be begun at the precise point when the neurological development results in easy control and pleasure in
achieving it. As in most areas, however, reality does not

follow theory so simply. Nobody can pinpoint that exact time of development. Furthermore, many other past and present factors will contaminate the purity of this psycho-neuro-physiological harmony.

A child can be toilet trained before this level of physical development has been reached. Some infants, for example, have a predictable rhythm for defecation and even urination. Early success in this case does not mean that the child is trained but that the parents are. It is also true that some training can become effective, by extreme effort, before sphincter control is facilely achieved, as in the case of older children who, under parental pressure, master the art of control in spite of an inadequate neurological development.

There are those who advocate no attempt to toilet train a child until after the child learns to walk. This is a crude neuro-muscular yardstick based on evidence that the neurological development that makes walking possible just precedes the effective neural control of the sphincter muscles. In some cases this program has worked efficiently, in others it has resulted in real difficulties.

Sphincter control is not the only factor in the problem. It involves, in addition, becoming accustomed to sitting on a potty, or, more frightening for some children, sitting on a toilet seat which suspends the child over what must seem a rather large chasm from which, with a magical flick of the hand, things suddenly disappear in a swirl of water. The parent who institutes familiarity with sitting on a potty, a potty chair, or a toilet seat before the child is ready to control his excretions is probably wise. The child then has an opportunity to master one situation, his relationship with a receptacle, before he has to face the problem of giving or withholding his excretions according to the dictates of another.

In order to understand some of the more subtle aspects of toilet training, the multiple meanings it may have to a child, and their relative importance, should be considered. What these meanings are and how the child deals with them will determine to a large extent the effect upon his personality of the toilet training period. The implications of experiences at this age and later are no longer speculative as they were in the oral period. Children have told parents (though parents do not always understand) and psychiatrists (who understand more) what toilet training means to them.

As the child becomes aware of the pleasure the excretory processes offer, the resulting production becomes valuable to him. A child of 18 months doesn't have the distaste for feces that the adult has. He likes feces. He likes their odor, he likes the feel of them and he likes what he can do with them, namely, smear them. After all, the feces have come from himself, and if he likes himself, it is not surprising that he likes what he can produce. If an adult produces a work of art no one questions his pleasure in it. If he denies its merits, he is criticized for false modesty, or is considered neurotically self-depreciating. The child's feces are *his*.

But parents do not show real appreciation for this creation. They object to it being smeared over the bed and walls; they indicate a distaste for it; they throw it away. If it is hard for an adult to understand the child's evaluation of feces, consider how hard it must be for the child to understand the parents' rejection of the gift for which they have asked!

The child faces a confusing situation. During the period of toilet training parents ask for a gift, his feces or urine. They urge the child not only to be generous (so as not to become constipated), but also to be so at an appropriate time (so as to be toilet trained). If the child complies, what happens to his gift? It is thrown away. Sometimes the child's own high evaluation of his excretions is reinforced by the parental demands. Parents show that the feces are valuable; the child agrees. He then hides them from the parents' destructive impulses, depositing them behind curtains, secreting them in his own rectum, in closets or under furniture. In the child's eyes it is his responsibility to protect the valuables he creates from the predatory aspects of his parents' ambivalence.

The parental attitude may convince the child that his creation is undesirable. It becomes something then that should not be given. Controls become important but constipating. To give is to give something bad and thus an attack. The child so convinced of the significance of the feces may attempt to withhold them in order to protect the parents from his own hostility. If the feces must be discharged he hides them to hide the implication of his own anger. He may give them in the form of a diarrhea or soiling because this does offer a physiological way to express hostility. (Sometimes, however, diarrhea is due to a disease-producing bacteria that probably does not have an analyzable psyche!)

The ability to control also becomes important to the child. Previously, he had been omnipotent in his world, but his omnipotence was something passive, like that of the pre-war Japanese Emperor. He could do nothing to modify his power. While he was monarch of all he surveyed, he was so only because what he surveyed made him a monarch. With the development of control there comes an increased sense of self-power and therefore self-respect. If his control is convincing to him only if exercised according to his own whim and not that of the parent, he may become toilet trained to a rather unique pattern. It is not just coincidence if the feces are never produced when and where the parents want them, but always when and where the parents do *not* want them. The child is then toilet trained, but at his own dictation and in violation of the dictates of the parents.

Any of these attitudes towards toilet training would be solvable for the child, if not society, were it not for the child's wish for the continuation of a positive relationship with his parents. He wishes their love and the security that their love has provided. If he acts in a way of which the parents disapprove, he becomes anxious, for to him the disapproval is synonymous with the withdrawal of parental love.

Pleasure in independence and control loses its flavor. Also, no matter how confused the parents may be in their attitude towards feces, obviously they want the gift given, given in a prescribed place, and they want the privilege of throwing it away. If the child wants to feel secure in a relationship with people whose reaction is so inexplicable, it may appear wiser to him to conform without asking the reason why. The desire to perpetuate the essential security resulting from the love of the parents paves a way favorable to the acceptance of toilet training.

The child does not always yield quickly. It arouses his anger to have to pay the price. He has to give up a pleasant experience in order to preserve the parents' love. It is also anger-arousing to have to conform to the dictates of such seemingly confused parents. To accede to their wishes is, to a certain extent, humiliating and self-depreciating. The new-found ability to control is not all it would appear to be, if it must so quickly dissolve before the demands of others. The child often indicates the dilemma he is in by vacillating between compliance and anger at the parents.

The anal period in development is a time of normal, sharp ambivalence towards the same person or object. The child manifests both hostility, with denial of any need to be loved, and an acutely anxious wish to be assured of being loved. It is as if he were weighing the price he must pay to be loved against the price he must pay to be able to assert himself in the frame of his own desires.

This culture, among many other characteristics, is a toilet-training culture. Social anthropologists do not find our compulsive neurotics and "anal" characters in those cultures in which toilet training is a negligible part of social adaptation. But there are many other psychological patterns absent in primitive cultures. The social anthropologist does not find the sanitation, the freedom from plague, the productivity of research, the breadth of learning or the refinement of artistic production in the primitive cultures. The reason for these differences between the two cultural categories is related in part to how the anal period is handled by the culture as well as by the individual.

OTHER ASPECTS OF THE ANAL PERIOD

The anal period of psychological growth is one of attempted overall, dynamic mastery of the external world. Previously if the child wanted something he often had to cry for it, dependent on the chance understanding of the parents. Now he can walk to it and reach for it. One cannot observe the first steps a child takes without being impressed by the sheer joy he seems to get from this achievement. New vistas open for the child as a result of this ability to propel himself where he wishes to go. Paralleling the development of this skill is an increased capacity to understand what is seen, heard and felt, with an accompanying curiosity about those things not yet cataloged in the child's mind. He is, to quote parents, "into everything."

The child's conception of what he wants is often clear. He sees a glass ashtray on the coffee table. He wants it in order to bang it on the floor and make an enjoyable noise. He can gratify this wish by walking to the table, picking up the ashtray and throwing it down. This gives him a sense of real independence and of adequacy in meeting his own needs. But the aftereffect of this pleasurable experience is often an unpleasant one—his parents disapprove and punish him for his behavior. Even more anxiety-creating is the danger that the parents' disapproval and punishment indicate that their love has been withdrawn. The child is faced with what may appear to be an unsolvable dilemma. He wishes the satisfaction that comes from the fulfillment of a desire. He does not want to lose the new-found confidence in and respect for himself that his new talents offer him. He does not wish, on the other hand, to forfeit the security that is provided by the parents and that is equally important to him.

This is the age when negativism is so prominent in the child's pattern of behavior. Part of this response is related to the child's inability to tolerate any frustration of a desire. He cannot accept the restrictions nor does he have the ingenuity to find an acceptable way to gain the same end if the spontaneously-chosen path is blocked by disapproval.

The child also derives considerable pleasure out of being negativisitic for it creates a picture of his own individuality and mastery. He feels strong because he can say "no." He is like parents who claim to have shown the child who is boss by saying a peremptory "no" to a child's request. The author has never had the experience of having parents report that when their child asks for something they say a quick "yes" in order to show the child who is boss! (The only exception to this is when the contest is between the parents rather than parent and child, with the child simply the pawn in the battle.) Parents believe they demonstrate their strength by being negativistic. It is not surprising that the child should use the same technique for testing out his own power. During this early period of ambulation and exploration, there is probably no word the child hears or says so repetitively as "no."

Under certain circumstances the child's behavior is not as negativistic as it apears. He may not be objecting to doing what he is asked to do as much as he is protesting against having to give up something he wants to do. Bedtime is a case in point. While some children object to going to bed under any circumstance, many children originally refuse not because of a strong dislike for bed but because they are enjoying what they are doing and do not wish to stop. The battle that then ensues may result in a secondary distaste for going to bed. Parents who are successful in establishing a technique for winning the child away from his enjoyable activity complain less of the problems of bedtime at this age than those who scoop the child up, kidnapper fashion, because the clock says so.

During this period the child has another source of confidence in himself—he believes in the magical power of his thoughts. The origin of this concept is not completely clear. Certainly in his pre-thought period in early infancy he was seemingly omnipotent, since his basic needs had but to be felt to be relieved. An adult patient recalled very vividly in therapy the time when reality taught her the fallacy of her belief in her magical power. A treasured doll had been broken. She secreted it in an empty drawer, convinced that in the morning it would be repaired because she would think it so, but the next morning the doll was still broken. She felt her world collapsing as she recognized her own powerlessness against external forces. She recalled that her parents had played a little game with her. When something was broken that could be repaired, she would leave it among her toys and later discover it fixed. Until the broken-doll episode, she attributed this result to the power of her thought, not to the ingenuity of her parents. After the doll episode she avoided a continuation of the parents' game by insisting that any repairable toy be kept by the parents until the repair was accomplished. As an adult she always objected to anything being repaired. Something once broken could never be accepted again, and from her viewpoint should be immediately discarded.

The belief in omnipotence of thought does not completely disappear with increased knowledge of the causes of events. Many adults have experienced a resurgence of this belief in their own power. Angry with some loved person, they wish some disaster for him. Immediately, or as a delayed reaction, they are aware of anxiety and guilt as if the thought would produce the actuality. The relatively emotionally healthy person faces the absurdity of this and the intensity of the anxiety and guilt decreases. The less emotionally healthy person may protect his intended victim by developing a compulsive neurosis. The saying "the wish is father of the deed" is used with many implications not too far removed from the belief of the small child and that of the compulsive neurotic in the magic power of thought.

Whatever role the belief in the power of thought plays in making the small child's life happier, the effect it has in creating anxiety is quite apparent. A child of two cannot refine his responses of anger easily. If he is angry at a toy he throws it down with the aim of smashing it irreparably. When he hits his formerly beloved but now temporarily unacceptable mother, he may not have the strength to succeed, but his goal is to destroy her. His thoughts are equally destructive. He expresses them by telling his mother to go away, or that he doesn't like her. The implications of both statements are similar, for what the small child doesn't like he throws away. As the acuteness of the rage subsides, the possibility that his magical power may cause the fulfillment of his hostile wish frightens him. If anger can destroy a toy can it not also destroy a parent?

A child at this age reacts with a sharpness of black and white. When he is angry he is only aware of anger. When he feels pleasantly to others he is only pleasant. The idea that one can love and be hostile towards the same person is a philosophical truth beyond his grasp. He assumes the same blackness and whiteness from the parents. When they are cross he sees their reaction as solely hostility, unleavened by love. He fears the degree of their retaliation, a retaliation that may be physical attack or that may be desertion.

The child's concept of interpersonal relationships is often dramatically summarized in his behavior in a period of anger and immediately afterwards. His rage is complete and all-encompassing. It passes, either as the result of a check placed upon it by parents or because it has exhausted itself. The young child may then wish to be held by the very person towards whom his rage was directed or by the meaningful person who stepped in to curb the rage. His bodily and verbal responses indicate anxiety and the need to re-establish his security with the beloved person. An older child, more aware that his anger is not so destructive, will seek the re-establishment of a positive relationship more casually and with less evidence of anxiety concerning the consequences of his behavior.

This period of unreconciled ambivalence gradually resolves itself. The child learns to live within the limits of reality as defined by his parents. He finds some relatively simple but acceptable ways to express impulses that, unmodified, are denied expression. He learns he cannot bang a glass ashtray but that he can bang a noisy toy or a kitchen pan. A toy that fails one purpose need no longer be abandoned or destroyed. It can be put on the shelf until its real purpose fits into an interesting play or another game can be substituted in order to enjoy the toy. The child finds satisfaction in pleasing his parents by being toilet trained. He also finds increased confidence in himself because of this achievement.

The child's anger at the frustrations of reality decreases, first of all because he gains increased tolerance for frustration. Secondly, he has developed an ability to avoid frustration by substitute activities. Most important of all, he has, because of repeatedly reassuring experiences, realized that his destructive feelings do not destroy. He learns he can feel both hostile and loving to the same person. He has found that his parents love him even when they disapprove of his behavior. They will not desert him. His security with them is re-affirmed.

This resolution is brought about most effectively if the parents are willing to give the child time, experiences that guide him towards this resolution, and recognition for any positive steps he takes. To cover all the ways in which the parents can achieve or fail to achieve this end would take a volume in itself. Certain broad generalizations will perhaps guide the handling of specific situations.

Because during this period the child is so manifestly fearful that the parents' love will be withdrawn, parents sometimes in exasperation confirm the child's anxiety by either threatening to go away or by saying that they do not love the child. Sometimes the threat corrects the child's behavior alarmingly quickly. But this period of behavior *should* last awhile. When it is so effectively controlled with a few threats to his security, it is probable that the child has met defeat, not success, in mastering the conflicts inherent in this stage of development. He may therefore accept defeat in later situations before he even tries. An alternative to defeat would be for the child to abandon his dependency upon parental love. Some children do choose the alternative; but a person who does not wish for love is ill-equipped to make a socially constructive adjustment. Fortunately the child usually knows that the parents are deceiving neither themselves nor him with such remarks. Unless he has repeated consistent demonstrations that the parents will withdraw loving support, he reacts to the true situation rather than to the parents' false statement.

This ability to find the truth beneath appearances may prove disastrous when the truth itself is not favorable to the child's security. The effect of the inability of the parents to really function as parents often becomes evident at this age. Even though to an outsider the parents are performing adequately, they may be acting a role in a well-directed play. In such instances, no matter how insistently they verbalize their love, the child reacts to the underlying deficiency. Only gradually, if at all, does he profit from the minimal kernels of love he can separate from the chaff.

If parents press the child for a resolution of this period before the child is adequately equipped, the child, instead of submitting, may defeat the parent. Demanding as some parents are, the child may feel stronger. Parents can rant and rave, threaten and cajole, but unless they are very emotionally sick people, they will not carry out their destructive threats beyond the point of physical safety. Some children, intuitively knowing this, effectively defeat the excessive parental pressure by intensifying their negativism. The pleasure of achieving the demanding goal imposed by the parents is destroyed by the effort required. Mastery of the situation through negativism becomes more rewarding than the struggle to comply at a level beyond easy achievement. This parent-child battle is most clearly recognizable in toilet training. The parental eagerness may give the child a way to match the frustrations the parents impose upon him by frustrating them in return. A child can be forced to remain in bed by tying him in. He can be forced to stay in a room against his will by locking the door. (These are not recommendations!) He can be forced to give up throwing an ashtray by taking it away from him and holding his hands. There is no way in the last analysis to toilet train a child unless he wants to be trained. He alone has control of his sphincters. The parents' overzealous attempts at toilet training can bring frustration upon themselves. They can show the child a way to gain token control of the total situation through refusing to be toilet trained. This may become a substitute for achievement and mastery in more productive areas.

Overdemanding parents are not the only ones who cripple the child. The alternative response of complete *laissez faire* may create a different but equally difficult problem. A child needs help in taking the steps toward maturation; he needs to be shown not only what those steps are but also that eventually their achievement is expected. The adult is defining for the child one segment of reality. The effectiveness of this definition will color the pattern by which the child will eventually reconcile his internal impulses with the reality that has been interpreted for him. The definition is most effective when the timing is most accurate.

Ominous as this period may sound, parents and child usually survive it successfully. The degree of success varies. Certain adult character traits are traditionally traced to the conflicts of the anal period, but if we all had identical personalities, the world would be a much duller place to live in.

Some children grow into overmeticulous, overly cautious adults who save too large a portion of their income. Such people are needed in the culture since the details of social living should be neatly, cautiously and economically cared for if the machinery is to run smoothly. Some children grow into untidy adults because their toilet training has not been transposed to broader living patterns. Such people often add a zest to life that the tidy person cannot provide on his own. Most people will never come to peace completely with their mixed responses of love and hatred towards the same person. They can still live happily through their life span without a disintegration of their ego structure. The philosophical concept that if you think right, things will be right, can bring reassurance rather than disillusionment to the adult who sincerely believes it. The origins of both character traits and the neuroses are similar; the difference is quantitative. A neurosis may be only an exaggeration of a not-unpleasant character trait. The significance of the past is also weighted for good or bad according to the ratio between positive and negative experiences.

Furthermore, since the child needs time to master this period of physical and psychological growth, parents have time to find out how to help him. If parents can understand what struggles the child is indicating through his behavior, they may intuitively find an answer. They have time to change answers that, accepted in good faith, prove wrong. The best answers aren't conclusive or final; their usefulness may be exhausted and they may have to be changed as the child changes. Indications of difficulty in mastering the steps to maturity are not evidence usually that the house is going up in flames. They more often indicate that the house is inflammable and that precautions need to be taken against the fire that may destroy.

6 : The phallic or Oedipal period

AS THE CHILD FINDS AN EFFECTIVE WAY TO DEAL WITH THE CON-
flicts of the anal period, his relationship with the primary
members of his family undergoes a change. While the need
for emotional security does not disappear, he is surer of
himself. He has more confidence that he won't be deserted.
He does not cease to have mixed feelings about his parents,
but he finds those feelings easier to tolerate and to manipu-
late. The child now becomes more aware of his affection for
his parents. Earlier he hugged them in part because someone taught him to, then in part because of the reassurance
given by the response, but he now more frequently embraces
as an expression of non-anxious affection. At first his affection is directed to either or both parents, depending upon
the relationship that has been established. This changes and
the child turns with increased intensity of affection towards
the parent of the opposite sex.

The most severe criticism of the psychoanalytic concept of
human psychosexual development has been leveled at the
theory that at this early age the child responds to the implications of a bisexual world. However, it is interesting to note
that at the very time when Freud first postulated that sexuality did not come out of nowhere at the onset of adolescence,
educators were beginning to stress the importance of gratifying the sexual curiosity of children openly and construc-

tively. It was recommended that sex be revealed to a child as an essential and beautiful part of life. The same people who accepted that suggestion released a vitriolic attack upon psychoanalysis. It should dare to pollute the beautiful concept of mother–son love by introducing the idea of sexuality! That a child of four was not an "it," but reacting according to his biologically determined role in a bisexual world was frowned upon as a destruction of the cherished fantasy that childhood was a time of "purity."

Part of the difficulty arose from an inaccurate understanding of the psychoanalytic concept. In common usage "sex" was considered synonymous with mature heterosexuality if expressed in conformity with the cultural standards, or as pathological if not at least superficially in line with those standards. The psychoanalytic theory of sexual development was not directed only towards adult sexuality but was rather an attempt to retrace the steps leading to it. Adult sexuality was recognized as the end result of childhood development, to be traced not only through adolescence but from birth on. The oral erotic and anal erotic gratifications were significant in the final sexual pattern of the individual. So, too, were the child's experiences in dealing with his special feelings for the parent of the opposite sex, feelings that stem from what is called the *Oedipal Conflict,* derived from the Greek tragedy in which the son unknowingly kills his own father and weds his mother. Such a formulation could throw valuable light upon the disturbances and abnormalities in adult sexual behavior that previously could only vaguely and inaccurately be blamed on glandular imbalances or mental aberrations.

The resistance to this psychoanalytic theory was undoubtedly strengthened by the cultural heritage. The human species, in contrast to others, instinctively bans incest. This taboo seemed threatened by Freud's ideas, and the first response to such a threat is emotional rather than rational. Obviously, a knowledge of the psychosexual growth of an individual does not endanger the taboo against incest but only clarifies the problems the child faces in integrating this taboo into his behavior.

Before this age, personality differences between boys and girls are observable but they are not sharply outlined, and seem at times no greater than the contrasts between two children of the same sex. What sexual contrasts do exist may be in part inherent but are also undoubtedly fostered by the parental attitudes and expectations. These early distinctions are such that the basic steps in growth can be described without sexual differentiation. From the time the shift of relationship with the parents occurs, it is no longer possible to use an editorial "he" in referring to either a male or female child. The psychological changes, conflicts and solutions of the male and the female child during this period are different.

THE BOY

No matter how meaningful a little boy's father has been, the mother, by meeting the child's basic dependent needs through her maternal response, has been the most significant person in his life. That early significance, while not lost, now becomes overshadowed. The little boy does not shift his primary love object; his relationship to that love object is modified. As this new form of love for the mother evolves, the boy's father becomes his rival.

The desire to compete with the father leads to potentially dangerous and conflict-ridden possibilities. The father not only has prior rights to the mother, but is larger and stronger than the child. The father is not an antagonist with whom a little boy can safely join in battle. In such a struggle a child would inevitably lose. This does not prevent the child from wishing the situation were different or from being angry at this man who is the more successful competitor for the prized object. He shows his anger by irritation at his father, particularly in his mother's presence. He shows his jealousy by resenting any demonstration between the mother and father from which he is excluded. He tries to separate them when they are either figuratively or actually close together. Often he handles his competitor on a verbal level. When mother becomes upset because father says she is spending too much money, the child fantasies and often tells his mother that when he grows up he will make a great deal of money so she can have just what she wants. Rarely does the son assure the father that when he grows up he will make a great deal of money so that the father will have additional resources with which to woo the mother! The child daydreams of what he would do should the father die and be removed from the competitive field. In those daydreams his mother is quite adequately cared for.

Such daydreams often end on an emotional tone of anxiety. The boy, if his past experiences with his father have been happy ones, also loves his father. Both parents share the role of furnishing security to the small child. The father's very size and strength, so defeating in an antagonist, is a source of real safety in a protector. As much as the rival father is desired out of the way, the loving father is an important part of the child's life. The child resents and wishes to dispose of the rival father; he loves and values the power of the protective father. He is thus in conflict because he is hostile toward and loves the same person. During the war a boy of three acted out his ambivalent feelings towards his father who had just gone overseas. In his bath he played with a boat on which were stationed two soldiers who were identified as the little boy's daddies. One was a bad daddy, the other a good daddy. The bad daddy was always lost at sea, the other returned safely to join his son again. The reunion with the good daddy was verbally expressed as unusually happy, because the bad daddy was gone.

The child will often be the instrument that precipitates a

quarrel between his parents. Their manifest antagonism has many pleasurable aspects for him. It indicates that their unity is not as complete as he had feared. It permits him to dream that he can win his battle with his father by default; if the mother rejects the father, he can perchance slip into a valued place which the father really never occupied. He can also say to the mother like Little Jack Horner, "See what a good boy am I." But the apparent victory has a bitter taste. The pleasure is not complete. The quarrel disrupts a meaningful unity between the parents and the child fears he has destroyed it permanently.* In his fear and self-blame he may become quite upset, begging the parents to stop, or he may run away from the fiasco. Though the disagreement between the parents is in reality benign and soon forgotten, the child cannot evaluate it as such. His very wish to create it causes it to have unreal implications for him. He is frightened by the fantasied fulfillment of his wish. Many children, both boys and girls, are well aware at this age and later of the condition finally identified as divorce. They wish the parents separated and are frightened by the possibility of the fruition of the wish. A few years later, when father criticizes the roast beef because it is too well done and mother responds with irritation, the child inquires fearfully if they are going to get a divorce. The child has heard the word from his friends or other adults; the act, now categorized by a word, represents a wish and fear of the past if no longer of the present.

The child often considers himself to blame for disharmony between parents even though he has not consciously stimulated it. This creates real difficulty for him if the disharmony is chronic and severe. The child cannot identify the subtle incompatibilities in which he actually has no part. Particularly if the family is dissolved by divorce, the child may assume that he is responsible. His wish has become a reality. In such an event the child makes pitiful efforts to make up to

* See chapter on The Family.

both parents for what he believes he has brought about, trying to placate his own guilt as well as both parents.

The mixed feelings that a boy has for his father at this time create another anxiety. If he is jealous of his father he also fears his father will be jealous of him. He fears the father's anger if he recognizes the child's attachment to the mother and the child's desire to replace him. The child handles his hostility towards his father by fantasying many destructive solutions, and he assumes the father will respond in kind. But the father's superior strength will enable the father to translate his fantasies into acts.

The form of imagined retribution often relates to the organ that is of particular value to the child at this time, his penis. He fears the father will cut off or mutilate the penis. This will deprive the child of his most valued body part and also take from him the symbol of his masculinity, making him forever helpless in wooing the mother. During this period a boy may be very exhibitionistic, displaying his penis at any opportunity as if to defy danger, as well as reveal what to him is attractive. He may, on the other hand, make a great effort to hide his penis, as if to deceive the father by denying its existence. More typically he vacillates between the two, now flaunting, now hiding the prized symbol of his masculinity. It is difficult to question the validity of the castration anxiety of the little boy after the analytical material that an adult patient brings out is examined.*

Fear of castration used to be reinforced by parents and other adults. In the past parents warned children against masturbation by indicating that either as punishment for the act the adult would cut off the child's penis or that the masturbation itself would result in the penis dropping off.

---

*Were the only information concerning this obtained from patients with severe neuroses one might conclude that only seriously sick people would have such bizarre ideas. Many people who, within the limits of human frailties, are normal, such as physicians, teachers, psychologists, social workers, etc., are analyzed not because of severe problems but for their own professional growth. In the return of their repressed material the same anxiety is revealed.

Though this threat is used less frequently now, boys still indicate that they fear this consequence not only of masturbation but also of parental ire.

The content of nightmares at this period is revealing. A typical frightening dream is that a large animal or other destructive force is attacking the child. The attacking animal usually, though not always, represents the father! At the same time the child's conscious daydreams are of being Superman, a policeman or someone equally invulnerable. The child relieves his fear by temporarily living in a fantasy world in which he has the power to fend off any attacker. Again, with some exceptions, it is the father who is the terrifyingly powerful adversary against whom only Superman or a policeman can prevail.

It may be upsetting to a father that his beloved child sees him as such an ogre, but only half of him is seen in this light; the other half is a nice person. Anyhow, it can be rather reassuring to a man who may in most of his daily relationships, wonder if he is not Mr. Milquetoast incarnate, to find that in the eyes of his son it would take Superman to match him! Interestingly enough the little boy often values the feared ruthlessness of the father because it is evidence of the father's adequacy. A child of three and a half informed his mother, with a great deal of pride, that his overseas father wasn't killing Germans, he was really killing little boys. The only answer he would give concerning the motivation for this infanticide was that his father wanted to.

The mother is also a source of conflict to the little boy. She does not, if she is emotionally healthy, accept her son's wish to displace his father. Her son remains her child to whom she responds warmly, but not sexually or seductively. By her behavior she shows him that while she loves him, he cannot effectively rival the father who is not a child to her but a sexual love object. This response frustrates and angers him and confirms his worst fears about himself. It proves to him that he is an inferior person who can be loved only if he satisfies his mother by being a helpless, dependent baby. He is striving to give up the infantile role, to see himself and be recognized by others as a more adequate individual. She denies him the privilege of fulfilling this aim in the way he wishes.

A mother often reacts intuitively but unwisely to the son's conflict. Instead of giving him consistent acceptance of his present immaturity and gradual maturation, she responds with a denial of reality. She stresses that he is "a little man," over-evaluating, at least verbally, his adequacy and implying that he is the same as his father. But she doesn't accept him as a replacement. A boy must face the reality of his immaturity. To ask to consider himself "a little man" and thus be directly compared to the father is to face him with an incontestable defeat.

The intensity of the little boy's feelings at this time, especially if his mother or father respond unwisely, may be such that he can find no solution. Never fully satisfied in a relationship with his mother in which she always promises but never completely gives, or facing a too-formidable father, the boy remains tied to the mother and is unable in adulthood to establish a more mature relationship with a woman. The bonds formed in his early childhood period have checked his development as effectively as the bindings around girls' feet in the Orient have arrested their growth and caused deformities. Another possible solution is to try to placate the father by abandoning the childlike love for the mother and turning to the father as a mother substitute, but in so doing the little boy also abandons the possibility of further growth.

In some families it is not the father but the mother who is frightening to the boy and the attacking figure of his dream. Some women, for reasons which will be indicated in discussing the girl's adjustment to the Oedipal conflict, never overcome their jealousy of men. As her child passes from infancy to boyhood he arouses in her the antagonism all men arouse.

She wishes to destroy or imprison his masculinity. Figuratively speaking, she wishes to take his penis. Her resentment is communicated nonverbally if not directly to her child. He fears her anger will be expressed in her destruction of him. He senses her unconscious wish to destroy his masculinity out of envy, and his unconscious response is one of fright.

Even if the mother is not hostile to men, her failure to comply with the child's wishes may make her a temporarily fearful person, for to a child those who are not for him are against him. He is at this time especially sensitive to the mother's reactions. His periods of irritability are difficult to fathom and the mother may become irritated by his vacillation between a Dr. Jekyll and a Mr. Hyde. He may feel deserted by her failure to understand that which he himself doesn't really understand. He may fear her very ignorance, that unintentionally may be destructive.

The wise mother, who values her son as a male child, not as a "little man," helps him because she does not conspire with him to overthrow the father, a forbidden achievement. Her refusal to cooperate in the triangular situation reassures him that he probably cannot win out. Failure to win will insure the continuance of the child relationship to both parents, which he needs. His love for the mother is actually enhanced when she refuses to respond in the mode he wishes!

The mother who fails to maintain her maternal role with the boy during this period increases his conflicts in and anxiety over the triangular relationship in which he is caught. It appears to the child that she adds to the likelihood of the father's recognizing the situation. She justifies the father's jealousy. The father then becomes an even more dangerous person. She also arouses an intensity of feeling in the child that he cannot relieve except by escape, either into actual activities separate from her or into a less dangerous fantasy life.

THE GIRL

The girl child faces an even more complicated situation than the boy as she develops more intensive feelings toward the parent of the opposite sex. Just as with a boy, irrespective of the meaningful relationship that has been established with the father, the mother in the average family constellation has been the more important person. But when the nature of the little girl's affection changes, the object also changes. Her new feelings are directed toward her father.

This creates an ominous situation. If she allows her feelings full reign, her hostility and jealousy will be aimed at the primary source of her safety, security and dependent gratification. It is as if, in order to grow, she must uproot herself emotionally from the soil which she has so far found essential. There is no other adequate soil in which to take root again. Her father, desirable as he may be, does not represent, or indicate any real capacity for, maternal assurance and protection.

The girl has the same confused feelings the boy does. She fears retaliation from her rival, in this instance her mother. She loves her mother both because of her dependence, and because in the last analysis her mother is for the most part a nice person. She is at the same time angry at her mother for standing in the way and wishes her out of the picture. This is a frightening wish because of all persons she doesn't want to lose, her mother tops the list. She faces the same frustration in her father's refusal to recognize her as a sexual object that the boy does in relation to his mother. She is angry at her father for his failure to respond to her wiles. Nothing would terrify her more than if he did! The dilemma in which she finds herself has not two but many horns.

Her nightmares are often populated with dangerous people, animals and things, disguised portrayals of her mother. As one little girl stated it, "I think I know mother as she really is during the day; at night I dream of her as I am afraid she is." Another little girl, as a result of observing a loquacious though harmless mentally ill woman, being led in handcuffs to an institution, developed a real terror of her mother's insanity. If her father were absent at night, she could not sleep for fear her mother would go insane and choke her. As long as she could be with her mother and observe that her mother was sane, she felt not only safe but devotedly happy in the relationship. The striking factor in this case was that the child did not think of the possibility of anyone else becoming insane, only her mother. She intuitively knew, probably because of the handcuffs, that insanity indicated a loss of control, with a breakthrough of previously controlled impulses.

The fearful element of the nightmare may represent the father rather than the mother, just as for the boy it sometimes represents the mother instead of the father. To avoid this anxiety, the girl must be certain of the benignity of her father's response if she allows herself to accept a feminine role with him. She may see him only as a powerful person who will injure anyone displeasing him. If she observes behavior toward her mother which she interprets as cruel, she feels herself pulled hypnotically toward a whirlpool in which she cannot survive and yet which she cannot resist.

To add to these problems that must be solved in some way before further maturation will occur, the little girl faces a rude awakening. This is in part the result of the shift in primary erotic feeling to the external genitalia which occurs in both the boy and the girl. One reason the little boy prizes his penis and fears its destruction is because of the enhancement of its value by this erotization. With this anatomical shift, the little girl becomes aware that she has been deprived of an organ—she doesn't have a penis. She may fantasy that she had one and lost it. Some girls interpret the configuration of the external genitalia as a scar indicative that something once there has been removed. This fantasy is not unique to the little girl. The little boy may believe his fear of castration justified when he sees the female body.

Some little girls, on discovering the clitoris, assume that it is a sluggish penis and will eventually grow to normal size. A brother and sister acted out such a situation in a way which revealed various aspects of their confusion and anxiety. Jane, age four, two years younger than her brother, asked her mother how the doctor knew when you were born whether you were a boy or a girl. Her mother was surprised at the question. Jane was a bright, observing youngster and had daily seen her brother Donny nude. The mother pointed out to Jane that she had seen her brother undressed. Couldn't she tell the difference? Jane answered that she knew the difference at present, because he was different now, but she thought that "thing" had just grown. She thought it had come at the time Donny had begun to hide it when they were undressing together. From her story it seemed that she had ignored Donny's penis until he became modest. But Donny's modesty had its developmental story too. Donny had begun to hide his penis from Jane after Jane had wanted to touch it. Donny knew that when Jane wanted a toy she was apt to grab it away. It seemed to him wisest to keep temptation out of her line of vision. Jane had repressed one aspect of her awakening to the difference between boys and girls! She had forgotten she wanted to grab Donny's penis.

Little girls often verbalize disappointment in their own anatomical structure. They will wish to be little boys so that they can "wee wee standing up." Half jokingly, but with an implication also of longing to succeed, they will attempt it. Many times they "pretend" they have a penis by holding some penis-shaped object in the appropriate position. Again, it is done in jest, but with a touch of wish fulfillment.

Some little girls resign themselves to their fate reluctantly and continue to envy the boy who is more adequately endowed. "Penis envy" becomes a part of their psychology. They accept their fate as women, not because of the gratification it offers, but because it is inevitable. They feel permanently inadequate because they were not born men. They are jealous of men. They may compete with men in order to prove one can be a man even though one doesn't have a penis. As one little girl of seven, who insisted upon boyish haircuts and wearing boys' clothes put it, "If I dress like a boy, Mommy, Daddy and I are the only ones who will know I am not a boy. I want to be a boy. I'll fool everybody else and they will let me be a boy."

Penis envy leads to a conscious or unconscious wish to destroy men, both because of jealousy and because if men did not exist, the woman's inadequacy would not be revealed by comparison.

Resignation to their anatomical poverty may result in some women in a pervading sense of inadequacy rather than in the form of protest and denial. Only men are important in the world; women exist to make masculine importance possible. While this solution may be gratifying to some men, it deprives society of the contribution a woman who believes in women can make.

It is often questioned whether "penis envy" is due only to a recognition of the anatomical differences or whether it is also a cultural phenomenon. Many arguments on both sides can be offered. There is a tendency generally in this culture to overvalue the male child and undervalue the female. Giving birth to a male child is seen as an achievement. It is many times jokingly evaluated as evidence of the father's virility. The impact of cultural pressures is well illustrated in the problem of curly vs. straight hair. Races with curly-haired members often change their values on contact with a society that puts a premium on straight hair. The reverse is also true, when straight-haired people come up against a culture that considers curly hair a mark of beauty. (When races are mixed, as in the present civilization, the resultant cultural confusion finds straight-haired people having permanents, while those with curly hair use straightening devices.)

Whether or not cultural influences affect the problem, the response to the apparent deficiency in female anatomy is very real and has to be met. A little girl of four or five is after all rarely exposed to the full impact of cultural attitudes. In her own home she may actually be of the favorite sex, for reasons not related to cultural patterns. But it is a human characteristic to want what somebody else has that is different, and to fear the theft of something you have by those who lack it.

It would be theoretically possible to protect a girl child from knowing that little boys have penises. Realistically this ignorance could be planned with surety only on an island where females lived alone. The child's own curiosity about herself and others will guide her toward the information. The normal exhibitionism of little boys will expose her to it. The little boy's ease in urinating where he wishes, within the framework of toilet training, will unexpectedly, perhaps, reveal the facts! There is little to be gained and much to be lost at this time for the little girl to be unaware of these anatomical differences. She is in a stage of growth during which she will finally not only recognize herself as feminine but will find satisfaction in that recognition. Her progressive awareness of what she is will be facilitated if she also knows what she is not. It is important that parents be aware of the likelihood of the little girl gaining the knowledge of her difference so that they are prepared to handle it constructively. It is not a disadvantage to know the truth that an individual is a boy or a girl. The disadvantage lies in the false evaluation of the truth.

The difficulties of living with the little girl during the Oedipal period are similar to those felt with the little boy, though often more exaggerated. At one moment she is impossible to live with; she may at the next moment be delightful. She will vacillate between being cross at everyone, winningly flirtatious with her father and angry at her mother, conciliatory with her mother and ignoring her father, and trying to establish the triangle as a happy family of which she is a part. She will whine and cry like a caricature of a little baby; and later act like a caricature of a grown woman.

LIVING WITH THE CHILD

During this period, parents often pose a seemingly unanswerable question to each other. Father is fed up with the irritable children he finds at home when he returns after a hard day's work. Mother defensively points out that she can't understand it. The children were so good until father came home. One answer is obvious. The children are tired; mother is tired; father is tired. That is a bad combination at any age. The inexplicable aspect is that if father doesn't come home, the household may run smoothly in spite of the end-of-the-day fatigue. If mother retires with a headache when father comes home, the machinery again may run smoothly. One factor in this phenomenon may be that during the Oedipal period of conflict, the child can take on only one parent at a time. It's trying to handle both. To fuse them into a harmonious interrelationship is too much for the tired child.

This is perhaps a logical point at which to discuss the parents' response to the child of the same, and the opposite sex. Parents often say there is no difference in their love for the individual children in the family. That would be possible only if the children were made from a standard mold or cut out like a string of paper dolls from folded paper. Every child in the same family has a different personality. Why should parents be proud that they react the same to such different people? To say they love each child differently but equally is a questionable platitude. There is no scale that weighs love! One reason a child, jealous of a sibling, is not reassured by the parents' protestation that they have the same or equal love for both children is because the child knows that the first statement, if true, would make the love meaningless to him personally; the second is something that cannot be determined by anyone.

Parents react differently to the child of the same, and the opposite sex. Since parents have been told that this is inevitable, they have been freer in acknowledging it. It is not necessarily that the parents' love one child more than the other, but rather that they love them differently. A father, for example, may love his son because he likes men, enjoys companionship with boys and men, sees his son as a medium by which to relive his childhood, or sees him as a future companion in a man's world. His daughter may represent the potentially ideal woman whom he will never really understand but who will always be fascinating. It is well that parents do react in accordance with the sex of the child. If they accept and value their own role as man or woman, if they like others of their sex, if they like the opposite sex, and if they understand clearly that their feeling for their child will not be the same as for an adult of that sex, they then will love the child as a child, but according to the sex that the child is. It is when parents do not have a happy acceptance of the bisexuality of the species that their children suffer.

THE RESOLUTION OF THE OEDIPAL CONFLICT

When the significance of the Oedipal period was first recognized, much thought was given as to how the conflict could be avoided. The wish to avoid it was motivated not only by a desire to help the child escape tension and dissatisfactions, but by the realization that many later psychological illnesses could be traced to this period of development. Fortunately, no method was found to effectively circumvent the conflict. Studies showed that even in a sexually segregated orphanage with a staff of the same sex as the children, the other sex became available in some way. In one orphanage for girls the only available man was a janitor. He carried the burden, unknowingly in this instance, of being the Oedipal father to 100 little girls! The little boy mentioned previously who had imagined his absent father guilty of infanticide had thus kept his father a familiar figure. One result of his fantasy was that he could use his father as a part of the triangular struggle when the need for such a person arose.

The conflict is by no means unsolvable, and it is important that the child experience it. The later difficulties are not so much the result of the conflict *per se,* but stem from the nature of the answers the child finally finds. As we have stressed before, these answers cannot be expected to follow any logical or mathematical rules. They are psychological answers, and their success or lack of it depends on how effectively they further the child's present and future psychological growth. The child's resources lie in the multiple aspects of his relationship with his parents and the experiences available in his expanding world.

He explores a variety of solutions before he finds the one that has some effectiveness for him. He may avoid the adjustment task involved by at least temporarily arresting his psychological growth. He remains on a plateau, resisting the appeal of the vistas beyond. He may be frightened by the step forward that seems to expose him to potentially overwhelming dangers. Uneasy, he remains not on the plateau but retreats to an even more protected area, his earlier dependent, helpless relationship.

A third general pattern of solution offers possibilities. The child tries to substitute some individual for one or the other parent. The little boy may shift his love to another man—a neighbor, an uncle, the gardener, the policeman on the corner. Or, instead of choosing a substitute for his father, he may attempt to find a substitute for his mother. Often a sister, another female associate, or an adult friend becomes the object of his infantile sexual love, the mother retaining the historically earlier role of gratifying dependent needs.

A girl also frequently turns to someone else to provide the dependent security that she fears her mother may withdraw.

A maid, a nurse, a favorite aunt or grandmother may be turned to for a substitute mother-child relationship. She may as an alternative deny her father's meaning to her, and direct her attention to other masculine objects—an older man, an uncle, or a brother.

This shift of love object does not alleviate but rather often increases the child's tension. The child may fear that the parent will be jealous of the substitute, a fear which is not entirely unrealistic. Parents do not accept graciously their replacement by another. What parents have not at times said, "If you think Aunt Mary and Uncle John would be so much nicer, why don't you go and live with them?" The child does not always succeed in letting such remarks go in one ear and out the other. Even in the absence of manifest parental jealousy the substitutions do not usually prove satisfactory. Often the lessening of the rivalry problem by the substitution of an outsider for one parent or the other still results in the child's recognition that something is absent in his life. The little boy, for example, who has substituted another woman for his mother will wish the father to re-establish the triangle he himself has evaded. He suggests the father marry the mother substitute! The little girl, having turned her attention to another man to avoid rivalling her mother for the father, will then indicate a wish that the mother marry this other man! Unless the family configuration presents unsurmountable problems to the child, such as one or the other parent being too seductive, too rejecting, or in actuality too threatening, none of these solutions really answer the problem adequately enough to satisfy the child. He strives to continue his progress toward psychological maturation.

It is obvious that both for the individual and the species the sexual desire cannot be acted out in unmodified form. As the child faces the futility of his Oedipal response to the parent of the opposite sex, he utilizes the defense of repression to remove from consciousness the sexual aspects of the relationship.

As the intensity of the sexual response lessens due to repression, other defenses become effective. The most significant is the child's identification with the parent of the same sex. If the boy, for example, can repress the sexual rivalry with the father and yet have the characteristics of the father that the mother loves, he can be assured of the mother's nonsexual but loving response to him. His entire relationship with her can then take the more mature form of being a son rather than an infant. Furthermore, by employing the tactics of "if you can't beat them, join them" and becoming the type of masculine figure his father is or wants to be, he can retain the father's valuable love. The average father is obviously pleased as his small child develops characteristics the father considers desirable and masculine. Finally, the child, having discovered he is a boy and that his father is the adult counterpart of a boy, sees his father as a model to emulate. Since he respects his father and sees his father respected by others, he believes that this emulation will assure him of the same treatment as an adequate male figure. In his resolution of the Oedipal conflict he has clarified his masculine role in a bisexual species.

The little girl finds a parallel solution—she identifies with the mother and in doing so sets her sights for herself as a woman in an adult life. Her envy of the boy decreases as she finds gratification in a feminine role.

Some of the rewards of this identification must be anticipated rather than realized. The little boy is often impatient over the delay before his penis reaches the size of his father's, thereby proving his masculinity. He recognizes certain inadequacies in himself because he isn't like his father but only shows promise of being so. The little girl may find her inadequacy more intolerable. She not only, in general, is less adequate than the mother; she is unable to show the ultimate proof of femininity, pregnancy. The play of many little girls indicates the goal they are seeking. How often little girls put a pillow under their dresses so that they "look

like" grown women. All grown women are not obese, but all
pregnant women have enlarged abdomens! Girls find satisfaction in mothering dolls and pets or playing a family constellation with friends. Little girls can't be forced to play
with dolls; it isn't an ominous forecast of the future if they
do not; it is probably fortunate when they do find doll play
pleasurable. It offers a fantasy fulfillment of the feminine
role, a rehearsal for adulthood.

Observation of children suggests another tool they use to
find a constructive answer to the Oedipal conflict. The father
and mother lose some of their identity as individuals. Father, mother and child become fused into one family. It
would be unrealistic to attribute the development of the concept of the family solely to the necessity for it during the
Oedipal period, for undoubtedly many other factors contribute to its formation. It would appear, however, that during the Oedipal period the family rather than only its individual members becomes significant to the child. The use
of the family as a source of dependent security dilutes the
need to find that security in an infantile relationship with
the parents, particularly the mother. The family as a unit becomes a meaningful love object, thus decreasing the intensity
of the response to each individual member. Family loyalty,
in simple form, becomes a part of the child's reaction pattern. Family activities, in spite of frequent complications,
also have positive elements for the child. Parents should not
anticipate that, out of this shift, the child will manifest a
sudden delight in becoming a part of a story-book family in
which family gatherings, family games, family sings and un-
ambivalent love of each member of the family for all other
members, become the all-encompassing activity and aura. The
change is rarely that complete. It may be more evident in
what the child says away from home than how he acts at
home!

The child also relieves the impact of his intense relationship with his parents by less intense but multiple relation-

ships with people outside the family orbit. Some are with other adults, most evident in a child's acceptance of a relationship to teachers, neighbors, and frequent visitors in the home. More significantly he begins to relate meaningfully to his own age group. Embryonic signs of liking other children, or wishing to play with them, now gradually evolve into a real relationship. He likes or dislikes other children not solely because of the activities in which they will participate but because they are people.

In addition, as the Oedipal conflict becomes more solvable, the child directs much of his energy towards learning without, instead of primarily through, experiencing. His innate curiosity offers him a way to occupy himself, thus diverting him from the more personal problems with which he has been struggling. He is ready and eager for more formal education.

With the discovery of a way to handle the Oedipal conflict that is adequate at least for the present, the child enters a new phase of development, latency.

7 : *Latency*

WITH THE RESOLUTION OF THE OEDIPAL CONFLICT THE CHILD gradually passes on to the phase euphemistically referred to as "latency." This term originally indicated the supposed sexual latency from roughly five or six years of age to the onset of adolescence but it has today lost much of its meaning. First of all it is doubtful that real sexual latency occurs during this period. Secondly discussions in such terms have implied that no real growth, psychological or emotional, occurs from the end of the Oedipal period until adolescence. More careful evaluation of the relatively well-adjusted child of this age indicates that he is by no means psychologically dormant.

As indicated previously, some repression of sexual goals is probably essential if the child is to handle Oepidal problems effectively. Redirection of sexual energy is manifested in the child's eagerness to learn at school and in relationships with his own age group as well as with other non-family adults. The child takes what is, in effect, the long-term view —he recognizes that he must grow up before his direct sexual goals can be practical. He enjoys fantasies of what he will become, accepting with some reluctance what he is. The boy assures himself of his ultimate adult masculinity by participating in sports, acting to a greater or lesser degree "tough," courageous and self-confident. The girl prepares for her real adult life through her doll play, her reading interests and her own fantasies of the future. Tensions in both boys and girls that arise from unfulfilled cravings are discharged through interest in activities.

However, sexual interests and responses do not become entirely dormant. The little boy is not indifferent to the feminine aspects of his mother, the little girl continues a playful flirtation with the father. The flirtation in both cases is often very effective—the little girl is usually much more skillful in handling her father, the little boy in handling his mother. They have both found very practical ways to deal with a situation that was originally overwhelming. Some sexual feelings are also directed to other children of the same age but opposite sex. Little boys have "girl friends," girls have "boy friends." Adults are amused by this "imitative behavior," but there is more involved than just imitation. In many communities boys and girls are dating earlier than was formerly the custom. While this appears to be motivated by the wish to be like "everybody else" and these relationships may lack true depth of meaning, they cannot be so easily dismissed. What starts everyone doing it? It is often suggested that the parents start it by encouraging mixed parties and by reacting favorably to any interest their child shows toward the opposite sex. The first snowstorm often makes shoveling snow appear fun, but all the encouragement and favorable response in the world will not result in a group move among children to maintain interest in shoveling snow! Parents' attitudes affect child behavior but not to the exclusion of other influences.

The experience of children of the present generation is changing. In the past, for the majority of children, the resolution of the Oedipal period coincided with a cultural pattern of more or less segregation of the sexes. Boys and girls participated in a different play and work life. Girls that played boys' games or had interests assumed to be the prerogative of the males were called "tomboys," a benignly and tolerantly expressed criticism. Boys were supposed to be boys, which implied they were not to enjoy any activity a girl enjoyed. Today girls are not only allowed but encouraged to drain off some of their exuberance in activities formerly limited to the boys' domain. This no longer implies the denial of their femininity. Nor are these activities hidden behind the doors of a girls' gymnasium; they can be directly shared with boys on the playground, the street corner or in the back yard. With greater freedom in activity, less segregation of the sexes, less secretiveness imposed upon the child, and in most instances more tolerance for free discussion of sexuality and sexual fantasies the period is not one of complete sexual latency today, if it ever was. It may be that the behavior noted under earlier cultural conditions was the child's way of conforming to the demands and prohibitions of reality.

There are certain valid questions about the desirability of the present trend. It has been suggested that encouraging boys and girls to participate jointly in sports, school experiences and social activities hinders their evaluation of the sexual differences. This could result in greater difficulty in the ultimate selection of a suitable sexual partner. The individual himself may be more confused in his own self-identification if boys and girls are so similar in outward behavior. But while little girls and little boys may wear identical bluejeans, most little girls manage to look very feminine in them (and by adolescence know they do and enhance their femininity by the way they wear their seemingly masculine attire). Some little girls do act, look and talk like little boys. These little girls are probably those who would have been tomboys in the days when little girls were ladies.

Another possible effect of the changing mores of this age group is that, exposed to continued sexual stimulation, the children will have less urge to direct their energy to learning. It would seem that there is little evidence of this. Many of the activities children participate in represent in themselves the diversion of energy into and the release of tension through nonsexual activities. Where there is a more direct sexual implication, such as in pairing off at parties and movies, it still appears that this opportunity for some redirection of immature sexuality is more psychologically health-promoting than the complete repression of it would be.

If boys and girls, during roughly the pre-high school period, are encouraged to seek outlets in joint activities, interests and work, parents should not try to make of this a miniature adult world either sexually or nonsexually. Such attitudes may result in negative repercussions that are not inherent in the actual experience. For example, parents may, by their innuendos about their son's date with a little girl, stimulate the boy far beyond his own spontaneous response. They may also, under the guise of so-called parental humor (which is rarely humorous to the child), cause him to feel ridiculous and inadequate whereas, unexposed to parental ridicule, he would feel competent by the criteria of his own age.

Under the wise but relaxed observation of adults, children, if psychologically healthy, will find a structure for their interrelationships that is comfortable and constructive. Overt sexual play, which can be quite disturbing to the child because he is not biologically mature enough and which is also indicative of unresolved conflicts, can be expected to be at a minimum. Episodes of sexual play are common under any cultural regime. Most children have some such experience during childhood. Because it does not have adult meaning or offer adult gratification the activity is, under usual circumstances, abandoned after a few experiments.

The increased permissiveness for more active play between boys and girls offers two additional benefits. It may not be so difficult for a girl to accept a feminine role, if during childhood she can participate in physical activities that formerly were reserved solely for boys. Furthermore, playing and learning the laws of sportsmanship together may improve the later relationship between the sexes. During this period just prior to adolescence boys and girls used to have an antipathy for each other comparable only to the proverbial dog and cat enmity. This antagonism undoubtedly left a mark on later relationships. Perhaps if a boy who knows he is a boy finds he can enjoy playing with a girl and still respect her as a girl, the so-called battle of the sexes may lose some of its intensity. Girls and boys can learn how to enjoy each other in many areas of activity and their adult relationships can become less defensively belligerent. Sharing many activities is as important for the attainment of a happy marriage as is sexual compatibility.

The second reason why the term "latency" is ill-chosen is because during this age period the total individual is not "latent" and never was even in the era which encouraged sexual latency. During this age period there are tremendous strides in personality development. As indicated in the previous chapter, the child broadens his world in order to dilute the intensity of his immediate environment. Internal conflicts present fewer new problems. Reality expands as the result of increased contact with both people and things in the world outside the family. The child is rapidly developing skills with which to explore those wider horizons. The child's focus becomes the real world and the gratification it offers. This reality gives him additional means for handling unresolved aspects of the previous internal conflicts. Reality becomes not only a challenge to, but also a tool of, the personality.

One of the most characteristic developmental patterns during latency is shown in play. Earlier the child's play is to a large extent self-focused. He may like other children to play with because he likes others around, because others broaden the scope of play or merely because they don't interfere. Most children prior to latency reject a playmate if the other child is not interested in or does not conform to the plan of activity. Parents complain that the three-year-old doesn't play well with the other children. That is understandable. If other children do not fit into the particular plan, they are no more valuable than a telephone pole.

Gradually two changes occur—their exact sequence varies. The child may first begin to divert some of his interest in his primary love objects to others outside the home. He wants companionship and acceptance without the deep conflicts a close relationship to those in the family might reactivate. He likes children, not solely because of what he can do with them but because of who they are. The other closely related change is stimulated by the child's expanding interest in activities, activities which are more pleasurable if other children participate. The younger child may have begun to play cowboys and Indian with his own equipment, either carrying many roles or fantasying others in the multiple roles. He may use toy figures, manipulating all of them, or he may be a cowboy pursuing a tribe of Indians that exists only in his imagination. As reality entices him more, he finds it more fun to have his toy Indians manipulated by another or to have real people playing Indian roles.

Once these two characteristics develop, they fuse so quickly that they are often not discernible separately. The child has found the gratification in interpersonal relationships with his own age group, as well as the pleasure in combining fantasy with reality. The wish to like and be liked by another child proves more gratifying than always following his own whim and thereby risking the loss of the social contact. As elements of reality in the fantasy become important, the satisfaction from socialization is augmented.

During this early play two other characteristics can often be noted. At times the children may play together as a group attacking an imaginary enemy. They find strength in numbers and in a common danger or goal, even though the enemy exists only in fantasy. At other times the real group or individual may attack another actual group or individual cloaked in the fantasy of enmity. In the latter instance the wish to strike out aggressively is becoming closely linked to competitive urges that are being redirected into play.*

* See page 96, sublimation as seen in competition.

Fantasy play slowly turns more and more to reality. A ten-year-old boy invited to join a game of cowboys and Indians says with finality, "No, that's baby stuff." More realistic sports become dominant in the boy's interest. The development of an interest in sports brings new tasks and new satisfactions. Skill must be achieved by long practice, but once achieved, results in frequent but not inevitable success. Arbitrary rules established not by demanding parents or by the self but by an abstraction, the game, must be complied with. The hostile implications of competitiveness are relegated to the dimly-lit background. Competitiveness defined by protocol becomes one of the rules in the game. These characteristics are true of all games, even those for one alone. Consider, for example, the adult playing solitaire. The cards are real, judgment and skill are important but do not make winning inevitable, and certain arbitrary rules must be obeyed or the game loses its identity as a game. Competition has many aspects—the player is competing with the self, with luck and with the fantasied force struggling to defeat him. Finally, the satisfaction gained from winning is real.

When games involve more than individual prowess, an additional aspect enters; in games between two there is a real person with whom to compete, an individual who is, within the framework of the game, the Indian enemy to the cowboy. The hostility implied in competition is kept within the accepted framework of the game and is thus depersonalized. In team games the individual achieves that superficially paradoxical state of maturity in which he finds *himself* most completely as he becomes an importantly functioning part in something bigger than himself. He now, if he is sufficiently mature, handles impulses that are primitively destructive in a form that is constructive to his own team, to the opposing or enemy team and to the spectators. He has become "the ideal American boy," a person playing according to the rules of sportsmanship.

The psychological growth that must occur between the

time the small child in nursery school knocks down the blocks and the time when he is able to give up his place in a batting order for a pinch hitter is tremendous. It occurs healthily only if the individual is allowed time, is given support and is offered success and satisfactions along the way. Parents often complain that their six-year-old child is a poor sport. Aren't they expecting too much? Do they on their part ever get angry at bridge partners who play contrary to their wishes? Do they ever get tired of a bridge game when the distribution of cards is consistently favorable to their opponents? If adults, who should be able to adapt to reality more readily, often have difficulty, it is not surprising that a child needs a few years to learn patterns of sportsmanship. While learning he requires guidance, not placid indifference. He can learn best from those who are not angry at him, not afraid that because at six he knocks the blocks down, at forty he will throw his bridge hand at his wife. His parents should not be embarrassed that at six he doesn't act like a well-adjusted man of forty.

It has been suggested that the development of competitive sports puts an overemphasis on competitiveness in adult life. In reality, the current culture has accepted the validity of competition. There is evidence that many animals, and particularly humans, are inherently, aggressively competitive. It is certainly deep enough in our civilization to make it difficult to eradicate! I had an amusing experience in observing the program at a "noncompetitive" camp for adolescent girls whose director was a well-known protagonist for the theory that all the evils of the world stem from competition. Her camp was a monument to non-competitiveness. No games remotely competitive were tolerated; all activities were "creative." On the day of my visit a festival was to be held. The summer's creative theme had been "Indians." The girls had learned Indian dances, made Indian costumes and jewelry, learned the tricks of the Indian cuisine. A large bonfire was built, around which were circled the elaborately decorated tepees the girls had worked on all summer. Upon each tepee was an incongruous number. When the director questioned one of the girls about the meaning of the number, the response was enthusiastic and immediate, but very disconcerting. They had decided to give a prize for the most artistically decorated tepee!

Any characteristic which seems so rooted in the culture should perhaps be evaluated in the light of how it can be used constructively instead of how it can be destroyed. The goal may not be to forget childhood games, but to explore methods of translating their lessons into maturity. A boy who cheats in games, no matter how subtly, is not acceptable to those who share his activities. Once an individual becomes an adult, subtle cheating is condoned, only non-facile cheating is disapproved. The combination of the team, the opposing team, and pleasure from expressing competition within the laws of sportsmanship offers many constructive possibilities for facing the problems of adulthood.

The educational philosophy that all competition should be repressed in childhood was in part the result of adult misuse of the competitive drive in children. In many instances children were pressed into complex situations before they were ready for them. They were encouraged to play on teams, before they were sufficiently mature to find gratification in team cooperation. They feared the *loss* of their identity in the team because they were not ready to *find* their identity there. The competitive activities therefore caused additional hostility rather than serving to direct the competitively aggressive impulses into less personally meaningful outlets. Even though competitive sports now are accepted to be a chronologically later social development, the individual child may not be ready for them. Forcing him into a premature experience may make him a "poor" sport rather than teach him to be a good one.

Another situation formerly strengthened the conclusion that competitive sports were unwise. No other outlets that offered pleasant experience for the child were provided. Certain camps established their entire program on the basis of competition. The only pleasure in participation was winning. The schoolroom used competition to promote learning—not the subject but the grade that rewarded the work was important. This led to a discouraging situation for children. To have a winner, there must be a loser. Since the goal was not enjoyment of the activity, but victory, the need to win and the discouragement over losing became the only meaningful aspects. In the long run both the winner and the loser were deprived of the fun inherent in the activity.

Just because competition carried out within the boundaries of sportsmanship is valuable, it is not the only valuable experience a child should have. An enriched program at camp, school or during free play, offering both competitive and noncompetitive activities, provides the child with opportunity to express many sides of his personal interests and abilities. If the child is given reasonable choice he will vary his activities according to his stage of development.

A child may need help in hazarding games or competition in any area. If for some reason his skills in a particular area have developed slowly, he needs encouragement to gain the skill. If some inherent handicap limits the extent to which he can develop the skill, he may need help in finding other areas in which to succeed. It should be borne in mind that most people gauge success according to the achievement of others. That is one little quirk of the urge toward a relationship with others, colored by the competitive pattern. Even people absorbed in artistic creativeness are not immune to the critic's statement that the production is unique (thus indicating no one else has done as well) or comes closer to the master's touch than any of his other students have. The success is richer when the production is, by implication or more directly, evaluated as superior to that of others.

Success in comparison to others is gratifying only if the comparison is with a standard the individual accepts as desirable. A musician who aspired to Wagnerian turmoil in his creations would not be pleased if the critics enthused that his compositions came the nearest of any modern composer to the delicacy and melodiousness of McDowell. A boy, small for his age, delicate in body structure, may excel in activities requiring fine motor skills. He may be ineffective against a husky classmate who, unable to achieve any success requiring fine muscle coordination, can by his sheer bulk reach the goal posts on the football field. If the husky boy represents to the small one all that is desirable in a male child, the fact he can climb better than his idol is little solace. Forcing the smaller child to fight the bigger, brings little but increased discouragement. Urging him to give up his desire to compete with his idol in his idol's own field of effectiveness, can, if pressed for too early and too insistently, cause the child to reconcile himself to the loss of an image of himself as a masculine figure. This type of situation often has to be lived through, the child enduring the pain of what to him is his own inadequacy, until through greater maturity different criteria of success become available. The school and group leaders can help however. The adults should strain their ingenuity to find some masculine activity in which the smaller boy can excel! Fancy embroidery (or its more subtle equivalent), which he could undoubtedly do well, will destroy more than it will mend.

The child at this age, as indicated above, focuses most of his interests and activities upon reality. He enjoys doing things, making things, and exploring things. While the degree will vary from child to child, he tends on the whole to consider abstract ideas of little interest. He is not particularly interested in himself either, beyond the area of his own demands and wishes. Food, hunger and other realistic cravings are important to him, but he is not greatly occupied, either consciously or unconsciously, with their broader implications. An adolescent, for example, who is obese will describe a deep craving for food that has nothing to do with hunger. A latency child asked why he eats so much candy answers that he likes it, as if the answer were obvious and thus the question silly. The real reason for his overeating is the same as that of the adolescent, but the latency child is more unaware of it. The child's strongest urge is to know and live in reality. Introspection is usually minimal. Internal conflicts are answered through direct living in the reality world. While the internal conflicts are of real significance in determining the child's conscious behavior, he denies the causes for his acts with what to him are plausible explanations. Thus a boy who is stealing for reasons that are easily recognizable as neurotically determined, will be satisfied, and expect others to be equally so, when he explains that he wanted what he took. If it is commented that he really didn't need what he stole since he already had a similar object, he answers "I know." It's hard for him to understand why more should be said! This does not mean that the child is free of guilt or conflict, or has no standards for his own behavior. It only means that he would rather deal with real facts than with the vague outlines any introspection would reveal.

The child's acceptance by and of others in the same age group is achieved through conformity. Perhaps one of the most disturbing examples of this type of conformity is a change in vocabulary. The child comes home from school using expressions that cause the parents horror only surpassed by their embarrassment. Since the home is the primary influence on the child, people will assume the parents use such language, which they certainly don't! Well, at least they usually don't. Anyway they have told the child not to use such language.

Parents are often really embarrassed at this point because their own language has not been quite so pure as that they have wished to impose upon the child. On the other hand, the indignant mother sometimes says, "Why, I don't even know what some of the words mean." There would seem to be some justification in wondering why, if she doesn't know the meaning, the words disturb her so. But that would be a digression from the more significant meaning of the child's shift in vocabulary. The chances are that all he is doing is learning the language of the new country into which he has entered, in order to communicate with its inhabitants. When a newcomer moves permanently to the United States, the sincerity of his wish to become a real part of the nation is questioned if he doesn't learn English. Equally so, to be a part of a social group, the child has to use the language of that group, even though it may not coincide completely with his native tongue.

Parents often give the child an additional reason for using the acquired language. The use of words that are so disturbing to the parents gives him a fuller sense of emancipation. He, backed by his group, dares defy authority. Furthermore, it should be remembered that many words children use at this time are not too well understood by them, that the parents' knowledge of the correct definition is often more accurate. The parents' horror indicates to the child how brave and what a dare-devil he is in using the words and they thus come to have even more value. A group of children who were using many "four-letter" words were asked by a friendly adult what the words meant. In this particular instance not one child knew!

Just because these words have constructive value to the child in his progress toward socialization does not mean the parents should sit back and enjoy such language. Nor is there anything to gain by taking up the intercommunicative language of the child world, or enriching that particular type of vocabulary for the child. The aforementioned immigrant would revert to his native tongue upon return to his own country; so the child can be reminded to speak his native language with adults. Though they can both be expected to let some of the new language accidentally slip in during conversation, they can also be encouraged to utilize the chronologically older language when it is appropriate. In contrast to the foreigner who learns the new language and retains both, the child and his group gradually slip back, with maturation, into using the accepted speech. Parents just need to take a long-term view of the problem. The school also takes over some of the responsibility for the child's vocabulary!

Eagerness to learn about the world is characteristic of the latency period. One of the mechanisms for dealing with the Oedipal conflict is to divert interest from parent figures and their emotional implications to more objective learning goals. An urge to learn is not born with latency, however. It is traceable through the entire life of the child. The small infant explores within the range of his ability to coordinate and comprehend. During the first few months of life he begins to explore his toys, his own body, and the outlines of other people and things. The wider his reality, the greater his capacity to understand, the more resources he discovers for finding answers; the more eagerness he shows to learn, the more he learns.

When the child can walk and talk his urge to explore and to learn becomes quite evident. He may at this time ask the questions that are so baffling to parents. Other parents may have a longer period to enjoy the illusion created by the very young child, that they know everything. Sooner or later parents must face such questions as "What is a sky?" "Why is dirt black?" "How does a balloon stay up?" The theory that in order to assure a child's gratification in learning, the parents should always answer questions honestly and in a language the child can understand is beautiful and constructive. Practice on the above questions to see if your knowledge is adequate enough to simplify your answer so that a child can comprehend! If you can, write a book about your answers and the many others you will make. Parents, psychiatrists, pediatricians, and your well-meaning friends need such a book.

If you can't answer these questions it is understandable. If you reply that the answer is something the child will be able to understand when he is older, your very lack of answer may give him the incentive to develop the tools to find out for himself. He is more apt to find the parental response stimulating if the parents do not try to hide their inadequacy by being irritated at him for asking the question, contemptuous of him because he is too inadequate to understand or disapproving of him for his interrogation.

It is important to answer those questions one can and give the child the gratifying experience of finding out what he wants to know. This implies to the child that curiosity is an acceptable characteristic, as well as a hunger that can eventually be relieved. Curiosity is after all the stimulus for all learning. If it is constantly unsatisfied, it may atrophy from disuse or may express itself in excessive exploration. A child whose curiosity has found acceptance by others will do a great deal of exploring with a specific goal in mind. A child who has had his verbal or other curiosity frustrated sometimes will explore frantically, not in order to understand something, but as if he were trying to find and understand anything, he knows not what. He frequently is so frantic that he does not pause to understand what he does find, but rushes on to new fields. Another child similarly frustrated may be apparently lacking in curiosity. Defeated in early attempts to find answers, he reacts as if it were not worth while to inquire further.

During the Oedipal period, sexual curiosity comes to the fore as the child seeks to understand this phase of living. His questions involve the origin of himself and of other children. Many times he cannot press for the answer he really seeks because the deeper question would relate too closely to his own emotional confusion. He will ask the questions he can tolerate having answered. It is for this reason that parents are advised to answer the questions in regard to sex that the child consciously asks, not the questions that may be disguised behind those verbalized. It is for someone more objective, less involved in the child's family relationships and more experienced in satisfying childhood curiosity to answer the underlying questions, if they are to be answered.

As the intensity of the Oedipal triangle decreases, the child's eagerness to learn becomes even greater. He can set a goal for his learning to which he can direct his energy. He is eager to learn to read so he can find things out not only by asking questions but by the more formal method of the printed page. This will give him additional means to satisfy his curiosity. There is a real enjoyment in questioning and then finding the answer. Once curiosity is gratified concerning one area of interest, new questions arise to provide again the anticipatory tension in not knowing and the pleasant feeling of satiation when the answer is found. The child is intrigued by a new method of communication—writing. He is ready to assume more initiative in learning. Additional knowledge will make him more the equal of his parents and also more independent of them. His ability to delay gratification and concentrate longer before an end result is achieved makes formal education more tolerable as well as intriguing to him. At the same time, his mental development is such that he is able to acquire the formal skills of reading, writing and arithmetic as taught in the classroom. Latency thus becomes a time of learning facts. During latency a child masters many rudimentary concepts that are the basis for the more complicated learning achievements of higher academic levels.

STEPS AWAY FROM HOME

One of the highest hurdles a child has to vault is the enforced separation from home when school starts. Some children take it with facility—they are comfortable away from home and mother and easily accept the classroom régime. Some may find the first few weeks of school a difficult time because of the forced separation from the old environment. Although they may not show it, they feel lonely and fearful away from the protecting mother, and suffer all the pangs of homesickness until school becomes part of their life. Another child may be quite comfortable away from home but find the demands for conformity to the group under the guidance of a stranger difficult to accept. He has been used to parental control. He knows what parents do in a given situation, what they permit, what they forbid, how they respond to violations. He also knows when they will protect and when they won't. He is uncertain of the expectations and responses of the new adult in charge, the teacher. Until he knows the framework of this new world he will be uneasy in it.

Frightened by the separation from home, the demands of the group and the idea of a stranger's care, some children are more than uneasy; they object forcefully. If the parents are not too embarrassed, too upset, or too convinced that the problem will go on forever, the difficulty is usually mastered. The mother can remain at school for the first day or so without having to anticipate attending college classes with her child. The teacher needs to establish a relationship with the youngster before the mother discontinues her trips to school. With this type of child, the teacher plays an important role in establishing the child's confidence in a world in which he is not sheltered by the mother. Often during this transition period the child will not play actively with others. He has regressed to his presocial level of adjustment. Once he is secure in his new environment, he will play with his own age group again.

After the child becomes familiar with the school environment, he may concentrate more on attaining friends than on attaining knowledge. Teachers of the first few grades know well that the eagerness to learn, verbalized and sporadically put into effect by the average child, succumbs readily to a glimpse of another's activity, or to a conversational word from across the aisle! The teacher has an important task in finally establishing a wise balance between the urge to learn and the urge to socialize. Modern educators are attempting to develop techniques to facilitate the expression of both, but anyone who has followed the various educational theories will know that no complete answer has been found. Fortunately most children get educated anyway.

Parents may discover a different side of their child once he attends school. The teacher may complain that the child is impudent, defiant and nonconforming, though at home he is quite the opposite. The parents have never had any trouble with him and they therefore assume that it must be the teacher's fault. It may be. There is, however, another possibility. The child may have been too well-behaved at home. Through fear or love of the parents he may have complied with demands that were actually in excess of reasonable limits for him. The teacher cannot impose the severity of punishment the parents can and her love is not as important as theirs. The restraining bonds are off and the child acts out in the school situation what he dare not express at home.

On the other hand, a child may be over-conforming, too "good," in the classroom because instead of contrasting the parents and teacher he equates them. The alert teacher, no matter how much she may enjoy one completely compliant child, may recognize the child who goes too far in being good. Parents should appreciate particularly the teacher whose intellectual honesty requires her to inform them that the child who adds no burden to her teaching would be a psychologically healthier child if he did present more of a problem to her. Both teacher and parents should bear in mind, though, that a child can be obedient, cooperative, and quiet when quietness is required, and still be psychologically healthy! An apparently well-adjusted child is not *per se* a maladjusted child!

On the whole the child cooperates with the educational system. Gradually he learns that security as well as gratification of his curiosity lies in his adaptation to school. He finds pleasure. at least to a limited extent, in satisfactorily treading the academic path. By the time he reaches fourth or fifth grade,* he conforms within reasonable limits to the clossroom routine. School-wise, life becomes serene.

The home may bear the brunt of the undesirable side effects of this conformity. The child may, with irritating frequency, growl at a request with "Aw, I don't want to," or "Leave me alone." Parents should be able to understand this response. The tired father who all day has conformed to the rules of the working world may feel the same way when his wife indicates that the kitchen faucet needs fixing. The mother who has had to iron the clothes, fix the meals, make the beds, and leave a bridge game just as the gossip was getting interesting, may want to say exactly the same thing when her husband needs a button sewed on immediately. They may with great dignity find a means to duck the request— father may suggest calling the plumber the next day, mother may suggest that father wear another suit tomorrow. The child does not have a facile way to politely avoid the parents' demands, nor are the parents as willing to allow the excuse to get by as they are when the question involves each other.

This leads to a very realistic problem, that of the child's duties in the home. Should children dry dishes, make their own beds, take out the garbage, or fulfill any other "little" responsibility that parents wish to delegate? It is pleasant when they do. It isn't doing the child any damage. When he doesn't do it willingly, tension between parents and child often reaches a destructive level. An understanding of why the child resists may help parents handle the tension either by gaining the child's cooperation or by abandoning the attempt to get the task performed.

First of all, adults often fail to realize the intensity of the child's "working day." The typical child leaves for school at about 8:30 A.M. He has the responsibility of getting to school on time in spite of the temptation of chasing a vagabond

---

* There is nothing wrong if it should happen earlier.

dog, examining the progress on the new building, and playing ball with a similarly tempted buddy. He arrives at school to face the demands of the classroom routine. From nine to twelve he must obey the dictates of his teacher, not of himself. During that time he must "work" at his learning. No matter how skillful or how wise in child psychology the teacher may be, how enjoyable the subjects studied are, it is work. A businessman may love his work and find real gratification in the tasks he must perform. Yet he will come home complaining of fatigue because he "worked hard" at the office that day. His child has a parallel experience in the classroom.

To return to the school day, at twelve the child is free from the classroom, but how free is he? Again little tempting devils line the route home. The child must get home, wash his hands, eat lunch, and return to school before 1:15 P.M., or else face disapproval. Spending an hour and fifteen minutes conforming to the clock and to parental admonitions, resisting Satan, and at the same time having some fun, is not the most relaxing experience. Then the child again meets the school demands for two more hours. There are a little over six hours in his working day, a working day that has many pleasant moments, but which is still a required period that may be modified only in small details by the child himself.

Now is the time for parents to do a little mathematics. It has gradually been established in the present culture man should have eight hours of work, eight hours of self-chosen activity, and eight hours of sleep.* The child is supposed to have ten hours of sleep rather than eight. He has six hours of work imposed by the compulsory education laws of the State or the parents' concern. These two requirements add up to sixteen hours, allowing eight hours of free time. If an adult needs eight hours of free activity, why should not a

* The housewife hasn't usually been so successful in establishing a fair-labor practice, but that is for her to work out.

child? Is it surprising that many children resent impingement upon that time?

"But," comes the protest from parents. The man of the household does not ignore all tasks during his free eight hours. He wipes the dishes, he usually does fix the faucet, and at least occasionally cleans the basement. Why shouldn't the child have tasks? There is no reason, but the psychological situation is different. The man does all of those tasks by his own choice. He may hate to wipe dishes, but he realizes his wife's fatigue, or knows that he can share the day's news with her as he helps her. He can also refuse to dry the dishes. His wife may be angry, but his son will not order him to his room as discipline because he refused. In contrast, the assigned task of drying dishes is to the child nothing over which he has control.

Parents often complain that their husky son objects to mowing the lawn. It is his home too! Why doesn't he get pleasure out of carrying some of the responsibilities for it? Of course it is the child's home too. But many considerations important to the parents are of minor significance to the child. If he had an honest choice between mowing the lawn and having it a weedy overgrown jungle, the chances are he would choose the latter. What the neighbors would say and the violation of his own esthetic tastes would be insignificant compared to the effort required to mow the lawn. A dirty basement, a mussy room, unwiped dishes, and an unmade bed would not seriously disturb his serenity. If it is his home too, he wants the privilege of accentuating what he likes about it and ignoring what is not important to him.

Tasks about the house delegated to a child are often those the adult does not like to do! Why then should a child gracefully accept them? With due apologies to one of the author's favorite fathers, who is probably about as successful a father as one could hope to be, the following story should be told. Several years ago when George Smith (a typical occurrence deserves a typical name) was 12, guests arrived at the

Smith home for dinner. During the day it had snowed heavily. Mr. Smith came home just in time to greet the guests and to find the sidewalk unshoveled. His son had failed to carry out his share of the household management. George had what was, to him, a good excuse. He had arrived home in time to clean the sidewalk, except that he had had to call some of the boys about plans for the weekend and the conversation had lasted too long. Mr. Smith was irate. After all, the important part of the sidewalk wasn't more than 6 feet long and wouldn't take more than five minutes to clear. George would be able to see the boys he called next day at school. The really alarming aspect, and what worried Mr. Smith, was not the sidewalk, but George's character. Would George ever assume any responsibility?

Some years later the same guests arrived for dinner, again after a day of snow. Son George was now at college; the sidewalk was not shoveled. Mr. Smith apologized. He had arrived home in time but tired. Furthermore he had to call his bowling partner about a game, and they got to talking. As it happened his bowling partner was also his business partner, whom he would see the next day. The significant part of the sidewalk was still only 6 feet long, and could be shoveled in five minutes. Mr. Smith acknowledged finally that he just hadn't felt like shoveling the snow. But no one would wonder if Mr. Smith, the reliable businessman, would ever assume responsibility.

Another problem related to household tasks is when and how they must be done. A husband may choose to clean the basement before he plays golf, but it is his choice. If he never cleans it, eventually his wife, with all the secondary joys of martyrdom, will clean it herself, hopefully putting some of her husband's tools in the wrong places. If the dishes are ready to be dried, and her husband wants to finish the chapter he is reading first, she will wait a reasonable period of time, and when she suspects that another chapter has proven equally interesting, she will dry the dishes herself.

If she treated her husband as most parents handle a comparable situation with their child, she would be condemned as a shrew. Her husband would be encouraged to rebel against her henpecking. A child who reacts in this way would in contrast face a barrage from both parents and the neighbors would agree that the present generation seems characterologically deficient in their behavior.

A child wants time to play with others and time to be by himself. He is sick and tired of people, teachers, friends, parents, saying "do this, do that." He wants to relax before the TV screen, to read his books, play with his own equipment, or make what he wants to make. When, into this world of his own, there suddenly intrudes a voice saying that the dishes are ready for drying, it is discouraging and irritating.

There is nothing fatal to child development in the request that the child "do something around the house." Certainly those tasks should not occupy all the time left over after a full day of school. It is better that the tasks be done by someone else, than performed only in an atmosphere of resentment by the child and anger and discouragement on the part of the parents. Parents often use more energy getting a child to dry the dishes than they would use drying them themselves. As for responsibility, the chances are that the child is learning to assume it by meeting the demands of the classroom and his own social group. There is nothing magical about washing dishes, picking up clothes, or making beds that develops a sense of responsibility.

There are other characteristics common to the child of this age group. On the whole he does not like to brush his teeth. He knows the medical truth that dirt on the hands and neck does not necessarily imply an overwhelming concentration of fatal bacteria. He feels that baths can safely be infrequent. He is not convinced that it is important to pick up clothes. His mother can do that efficiently, and if she wishes clothes picked up she can use her talents instead of imposing the task upon him. Above all, the child feels that the game on the corner lot, the turtle hunt, the exploration in the park, and the outcome of the TV program are more important than household tasks, clean hands or a prompt appearance at the dinner table. Within reasonable limits the child is correct. The parents and the child require time to gradually find out what "within reasonable limits" means. They need to experiment, make mistakes, and correct the mistakes. They have, roughly, six years to find the answers. They have no reason to be discouraged if they don't find them in one day.

This period is predominantly a pleasant time for both children and parents. When dishes, piano practice, and straightening the room are not involved, the child is characteristically responsive, interested, and fairly free of mood swings. He has a growing ability to use his own judgment, comply with the demands of the culture, and at the same time enjoy himself. Latency is on the whole a time of lull before the storm of adolescence.

Serious problems requiring special attention during this age period are usually the result of unsolved conflicts of the pre-latency period which may not have been recognized until now. Conflicts unsuccessfully handled in the earlier stage of development may color the child's adaptation to the demands of latency. When this occurs professional guidance is indicated before steps to correct the situation are taken.

8 : *Adolescence*

FROM LATENCY TO ADOLESCENCE

IN A MUSIC CLASS WHICH WAS SINGING "WINTER IS OVER (MUSI-cal pause insisted on by the teacher), Springtime is near," a curious child once asked an interesting question: "What comes between winter and spring?" The teacher, being musically literal, answered "A pause." A comparable "pause" is often discernible between latency and adolescence, a betwixt and between period that doesn't quite belong to either phase. Physically, this period is characterized by the sudden spurt in the body's growth rate which occurs, on the average, at about ten in girls and twelve in boys. This growth continues and when its pace is most rapid, between twelve and thirteen for girls and one or two years later for boys, this period of physical growth overlaps the onset of the psychological patterns of adolescence.

Earlier, with the first evidences of the acceleration in growth, a similar acceleration in personality development is shown in an increased urge toward maturation and a greater adaptability. At this time, the child approaches the social group with confidence and participates in games that involve skill and team cooperation. He plays and studies, he argues with parents and friends, he enjoys pleasant experiences and protests against unpleasant ones with a minimum of conscious anxiety and guilt. He assumes responsibilities within the framework of his reality, though his evaluation of reality may differ greatly from that of his parents. To him it may be important to finish a game, to his parents it may be more important that he go to bed. It may be more worthwhile to him to make a model airplane than to shovel snow from a sidewalk, a conviction that the parents do not share. Such difficulties between the child and the parents may reflect differences in values. They are not necessarily indicative of deep conflicts in the relationship.

A child at this age attempts to circumvent undesirable aspects of reality if he can; if he cannot, he makes what is to him a realistic adjustment to them. He is less apt than a younger child to succumb to unhealthy solutions to the problem he faces. Not that no child ever does so at this age, but generally he has relatively greater adaptive power. If the pressure is too great, however, unfortunate defenses may develop.

Episodes that inevitably have deep emotional significance are frequently handled, at least for the time being, with surprising facility. This is well illustrated in the adjustment a child at this age makes to the loss of a parent or sibling. The child appears to meet the tragedy realistically by accepting it and by readily turning to other activities and interests. Later, if the individual undergoes psychoanalytic therapy, it becomes clear that the emotional implications were muted, repressed or denied, that the threatened disintegration of the child's world was mastered by a flight into reality. At the time the traumatic event occurred, the adjustment was such that the underlying conflicts were completely hidden not only from the observer but also from the individual himself.

Parents now become most aware of the change in boy-girl relationships. The interest in the other sex shows a marked acceleration in the latter half of grammar-school days; girls and boys begin dating, having mixed parties, and verbalize an interest in each other not only because of shared activities but because of sexual differences. At first glance this seems to imply an early sexual maturation. Careful observation reveals that to a large extent they are playing a game of having sexual interest in each other which they are not quite ready for emotionally. This behavior is to them evidence of growing up. It has a value not only because it is meeting an internal but immature sexual need but chiefly because it implies leaving childhood behind and taking on the patterns of an older age group.

The wish to be grown up creates a problem for the child. He realizes consciously that he is only playing a part and feels how inadequate he is. His attempts to fulfill a role for which he is not prepared result in a caricature of adulthood. The pseudo-maturity is even more striking in contrast to the total behavior which is still characteristically that of a child living in the day-by-day child reality of school, play, friends and home.

On the whole, however, this interim period is one of relative peace both for the child and for the adults responsible for him. Parents are reassured to find their child a reasonable, reliable and independent individual, a state they were not sure he was ever going to attain. Schools recognize the change with an enriched curriculum and with emphasis on discussion groups in literature, art and political science. Society assumes that the child has accepted certain mores. Stealing now is considered delinquent behavior whereas at an earlier age it was looked upon as an understandable sign of immaturity. The child is expected to go to school on time and to come home at a reasonable hour. If he fails to do so he is told that he is old enough to know better. The attitudes of the home, the school and the other social groups imply that the child is expected to have made a successful adjustment to the demands of reality.

ADOLESCENT STRESSES AND STRAINS

This peaceful state is of short duration, for the transition to adolescence is anything but smooth. The child becomes increasingly more sensitive, difficult, and irritable; the valued reliability and conscientiousness diminish; the boy or girl demands the privileges associated with adult living, at the same time continuing to behave in many ways like a baby. By these signs adults know that the latency child has metamorphosed into an adolescent.

The interrelationship between physical and psychological changes at adolescence is more complex because the changes are more complex, but a description of the physical side of the picture will inevitably clarify the psychological pattern. The acceleration in growth already mentioned continues, becoming most rapid when the girl is between the ages of twelve and thirteen, the boy one or two years older. Statistically, girls will tend to be taller than boys from the ages of eleven to fourteen, the boys tending to pass the girls in height by the time they are fifteen. Weight also increases more rapidly during adolescence than during latency, though this change is less startling than that of height and extends over a longer period of time. It is in part related to the changes in height and in bone structure as well as to the increased massiveness of individual bones. As the rate of growth subsides there is for a time a continuance of growth in the muscles which accounts in part for greater weight. The increased growth rate usually occurs when the secondary sex characteristics begin to develop, the primary sex organs start functioning, and the glands of internal secretion start working. Therefore, in addition to more height and weight, the body contour changes from that of a child to a physically adult male or female.

The sequence leading to the mature body structure is in general orderly. In the girl, breast development is one of the earliest signs of sexual maturation. This begins before the appearance of pubic hair. Axillary hair develops later, and often grows only after the first menstrual period. Pubic hair is the first masculine secondary sex characteristic to appear, coming shortly after the primary sex organs, the penis and the testes, show evidence of increased size in comparison to the total body. Axillary hair and then facial hair follows. At the time of development of axillary hair, there is often some breast enlargement in the boy. This typically disappears after some months but may cause concern to his parents and the boy unless they are aware of how frequently it happens. Voice changes in the boy have traditionally been the criterion for determining the onset of adolescence, but actually this occurs relatively late in the period and usually indicates that the typical bodily changes are fairly well advanced.

While the growth picture of the "average child" will follow this pattern in early adolescence, as always the "average" person is more statistical than real. A healthy girl of twelve or boy of fourteen may not show a rapid spurt in growth but only gradually become taller. A boy or girl may shoot up much earlier than the average without indicating some abnormal phenomena. A girl may menstruate at nine years of age or earlier without any further significance than an early physical maturation, or she may not menstruate until she is seventeen. Different ethnic and social groups vary; even climactic conditions may modify the usual growth rate. The evaluation of the growth period characteristic of early adolescence is more accurate if it is based upon the physiological rather than the chronological age of the child. When there is some question of abnormal physical growth, a physician who knows and is equipped to use the various tests available for determining physical age should be consulted.

One observation at times offers some reassurance to parents and children. When the spurt in growth occurs earlier than the average age, the child tends to stop growing earlier and therefore does not reach the final height of the child when more rapid growth occurs later. This particularly helps two groups. The little girl who early faces the threat of growing taller than her girl friends and of towering over "the little boys" in school, may find in a couple of years that she has dropped from the rank of tallest in the class to being just average. The boy who sees his status as a potential man threatened because his boy friends suddenly soar above him may have the later consolation of becoming a six-footer. It should be borne in mind however that a child with tall parents is more likely to become a tall adult, while a child with parents of small body stature will tend to be smaller than the average.

The common fallacy in parental attitudes toward the adolescent as well as in his attitude toward himself is the assumption that the glands of internal secretion related to sexual functioning begin to work with adult effectiveness and balance overnight. Thus the onset of menstruation is considered evidence of physiological adulthood in the girl. This is not true. At the time of the first menstrual period the ovaries usually have reached about 30 per cent of adult size. The glands of internal secretion have attained a sufficient level of functioning to bring about the changes in the uterus that result in menstruation, but there is considerable evidence that most girls are sterile during the first year or two. Likewise mature spermatozoa, capable of fertilizing an ovum, are typically not present in appreciable quantity until the boy reaches the age of fifteen or sixteen, although there is an increase in sperm formation at about thirteen. That these observations are valid only statistically, is indicated by the cases of pregnancy at a much earlier age than these generalizations would allow.

Entirely aside from their more subtle affects, the discernible physical changes contribute to the overall problems of adolescence. During the period of rapid growth the child's body becomes unfamiliar to him. As one boy said, "I don't think that I'm really awkward, it's just that my feet are so far away from my head these days." In addition to the actual change of stature, the growth of pubic hair, the modification of the childish contours, the development of the breasts, and the change in the external genitalia all add to the feeling of body unfamiliarity.

This feeling may explain an apparent discrepancy between actual clinical tests of motor coordination and casual observations of the child in his day-by-day living. The young adolescent is usually described as awkward. He does not know what to do with his feet or hands. He bumps into furniture, shuffles over the scatter rugs, falls over his little brother's toy car on the floor as if it were an object at least three feet high and invisible. Clinical tests of motor coordination at this time indicate that there is an increase in manual dexterity and muscle control! This contradiction may not be as great as it appears. It is possible that, when movements are directed to a defined goal within a limited framework, the individual is able to function well. When movements are not so purposefully determined but have to do rather with adaptation to sudden stimuli or impulses, awkwardness appears. In the latter instance, the individual attempts to handle a body which has become unfamiliar, without the assistance of a learned pattern. As a result, the adolescent boy may be an extremely graceful swimmer because he has learned to swim. When he does not know what to do with his feet he is awkward with them. This may also explain why the awkward adolescent girl responds so quickly to training in postural control. The metamorphosis that a modelling school can effect in her reflects the potential coordinating ability of the individual, an ability which becomes evident whenever a pattern for using the body is learned.

During adolescence the child may complain of many physical symptoms and show a great deal of concern as to what these symptoms mean. His complaints are often ill-defined. He has become a "hypochondriac." Before it is assumed that these complaints are groundless, a careful medical study should be made. It is important to bear in mind that during periods of rapid physical growth a child has greater need for certain specific foods and his diet may therefore well be inadequate. As a result, some of the physical symptoms about which the adolescent complains may actually represent a relative, sub-clinical malnutrition. No one except a physician who has made a careful study of his patient should assume that these complaints are psychological rather than physical.

Frequently, true hypochondriacal symptoms do develop during adolescence, for reasons which may be applicable to hypochondriasis at any age. In certain instances, however, the physical discomforts have always been present but the adolescent reacts to them with renewed sensitivity. His responsiveness resembles that of the very young infant, a responsiveness which faded during childhood as the individual became familiar with and therefore ignored many mild discomforts. At adolescence the keen awareness of bodily sensations returns and may account for many "hypochondriacal" symptoms observed at this time.

In other instances, the unfamiliarity with the body discussed earlier undoubtedly plays a part in the complaints. The "hypochondriasis" expresses the anxiety aroused by the physical changes. An example is the temporary breast development in boys during the early adolescent period. Boys often show considerable concern about this, feeling that it indicates effeminacy. Similarly, girls frequently complain about abdominal pain a few months before the onset of menstruation. The exact basis for this pain is not too clear. Girls themselves often associate it with the coming event. While a frank discussion of menstruation often relieves a certain part of the conscious concern, the basic anxiety is not relieved in a large percentage of girls. The period ahead is that of the great unknown. The anxiety that this anticipation creates may express itself in physical symptoms.

The physical complaints may be symbolic representations

of a basic anxiety concerning adjustment. The adolescent feels uneasy and attempts to pin down the uneasiness by relating it to his physical well-being. Physical concerns are easier to face, easier to expose to others, and easier to find reassurance for than are the ill-defined, nebulous, psychological sources of anxiety.

Acne at adolescence presents a specific problem. The reasons adolescents develop acne are multiple—the physical changes and the resultant glandular imbalance are factors; the adolescent's poor food habits often cause an exacerbation of it; emotional problems certainly accentuate the difficulty in many instances. The acne in itself is disturbing and a vicious circle, psychologically, is established. The adolescent often associates acne with being "dirty," a feeling based upon reality as indicated by the doctor's insistence upon cleanli-ness. The adolescent may feel, however, that this concern relates not only to external "dirt" but also to his own internal, concealed "dirtiness." In the past the adolescent frequently associated acne with masturbation; the association is probably less frequent now because of the more tolerant attitude taken toward masturbation. Acne still, in many instances, means to the child that his otherwise secret sin, of whatever nature, is being shown to the world.

The revolutionary changes taking place in the body, particularly in the glands of internal secretion, have a bearing not only on physical development and functioning, but also have a direct effect on the psychological responses of the individual. Clinical observations suggest that these changes occur not in mild ripples or gradually increasing volume, but actually with the intensity of breakers that flow over the individual and overwhelm him. There are waves of new feelings and an intensification of old ones. The average adolescent lives through a period, sometimes of fairly short duration, sometimes much longer, in which he seems to have lost a good part of his capacity to deal with reality. His emotional state borders on panic. In the relatively normal child this period is not too striking. He appears somewhat anxious. He may relate dreams of nightmarish quality in which his panic and disorganization are more discernible than in his waking hours. In school he may seem to study but not be able to learn; he may have difficulty in concentrating. He may be extremely restless in his activities. He may appear to be basically confused, a confusion partially disguised by a veneer of adaptation.

Gradually the individual mobilizes his defenses. Probably this process really begins after the glands of internal secretion have established a new interacting balance. Although the reproductive glands will continue to grow for some time, with a resulting increase in hormonal secretion, the change is in quantity, not function. Relative physiological stability has been attained. Any attempt to build a psychological structure before this time is made on shifting sands, but it can now be based on the firmer foundation of physiological integration.

The task is not easy. Old defenses prove inadequate and new ones must be established. An appreciable period, months or perhaps years, is needed for the individual to find solutions both to earlier underlying problems that now have increased in intensity, and to problems newly acquired.

It is important to stress that the onset of activity of the reproductive glands not only results in a heightening of the sexual responsiveness of the individual and an increased body sensitiveness but also in a general increase in sensitivity. During the entire period of adolescence, the individual is more responsive to all stimuli. The sunset, which before adolescence was only a signal to return home for dinner, now becomes an esthetic experience, beautiful, depressing, or stimulating, according to the mood of the beholder. Trees, previously of value only for climbing, now take on symbolic meanings. Music is now associated with all the emotional turmoil of the individual. Thoughts previously accepted or discarded on the basis of their practicality now take on poetic coloring. If the individual may be compared to a musical instrument, we could say that what seemed previously to be a cigar box strung with catgut appears suddenly at adolescence to have become a Stradivarius. It sometimes responds as if played by a concertmaster, at other times as if by an untalented amateur. At times it refuses to produce music at all.

Adolescence is a stage of emotional growth which cannot be avoided if adulthood is to be attained. It is a period in which many conflicts dormant since childhood return to be solved. It is a period also of new problems, problems created by the physical changes that have occurred in the individual, and the resulting emotional responses.

The psychological structure of the adolescent has much in common with a jigsaw puzzle. In early adolescence the pieces of the puzzle lie in a chaotic heap with no part fitted to another. As the reconstruction of the picture is undertaken, matching pieces are found. Several groups of three or four pieces are assembled but their relationship to the total picture is still obscure. Ultimately these sections can be interlocked and finally the total picture is produced. For the adolescent the completed picture is his adult personality.

If the early adolescent personality can be thus compared to the unassembled pieces of a jigsaw puzzle, it is little wonder that parents are confused by the multiple shapes and colors they see jumbled together, never quite making sense, sometimes suggesting combinations that may work and that may not. So often, just as a possible interrelationship between two pieces becomes evident, the colors or shapes shift so that what appeared related becomes obviously completely impossible! The young adolescent's personality is characteristically contradictory and inconsistent, predictable only in its unpredictableness. But there are certain common elements in the chaos that most parents recognize as they try to comprehend this individual their adolescent son or daughter has turned into.

THE PARTS OF THE JIGSAW PUZZLE

The adolescent struggles for independence, verbalizing vehemently his protest against the protective ruling of the adult group. He does not want to be told what clothes to wear, what hours to keep, what food to eat, what political party to respect, or what ethical or moral formula to embrace. On the other hand, he is unable to handle his independent activities as adequately as he did in the immediate past. He is impulsive in his behavior and confused about his goals. Not only does this disturb the adults who are interested in his present and future adjustment; it also disturbs and frightens him. As a result, he is apt to make demands for dependence which he has not made since he was a small child and seek the very advice he has so strongly spurned.

The adolescent's own group dominates his thinking and his behavior, a group composed of individuals of approximately the same emotional level of development. Its membership is not primarily determined by chronological age or intellectual ability, although both play a part. While superficially its influence may seem to be wielded by its key members (for example, Mary is a "big wheel," John is a "big shot"), the deeper cohesive force is the mutual emotional empathy that exists. Excessively insecure individuals may seek membership in an incompatible peer group, but they imitate the members in order to gain status and they tend to remain on the fringe. True members are a more inherent part of the group.

The carving on the escutcheon reads: "One just doesn't do that." The motto supplies the answer to almost any question, whether it involves wearing a hat to town, straightening bobby socks, wearing blue jeans that still retain their original color, being sexually promiscuous, or cheating in examinations.

In spite of the iron control of the group, membership is not lifetime. Exclusion will occur if the member proves recalcitrant. A member may also withdraw voluntarily if his rate of emotional development varies from that of the membership as a whole. During periods of marked fluctuation in the individual's degree of maturation, he may have loyalty for more than one group. He will then use the standards of the particular group that is at the moment most compatible with his emotional state, swinging with little hesitation to another group as the rise or fall in his maturity level influences his needs and his capacities.

Parents may complain that their son is easily influenced by a particular group. They will frequently say, "Our son has a group of friends who are such nice, mature boys. When he's with them he's fine. Then he becomes interested in some other boys for a few days, boys who are rough, coarse, and unreliable. When he is with them he acts just like they do." Actually, their son is controlled by each group with whom he is sharing an experience and it must be remembered that he has some empathy with each, temporary as it may be. He vacillates between contrasting peer groups because his needs vary.

The adolescent's behavior toward the opposite sex is extremely confusing. A boy may appear excessively preoccupied with his relationship to girls, neglecting all other responsibilities in his attempt to fulfil what he sees as the demands of that interest. Then he may suddenly change his point of focus, centering his interest on boys; girls then either do not exist or are unworthy of his time. He is either occupied with seemingly purposeless activities with other boys or is engrossed in organized athletics. He may become devoted to a very desirable girl, at which point his parents relax because "he is finally showing some sense." Suddenly he may lose all interest in this desirable love object and choose a girl who is in complete contrast to the standards of his family and of the community. He may explain his abandonment of the first love object by stating that she is too nice. He later explains his abandonment of the second by indicating that she is not nice enough. His loyalty to his group does not necessarily include a girl with whom he has temporarily been compatible. He may talk freely about her in an extremely derogatory way, exaggerating her faults and denying her virtues. The problems created by the relationship may have been of such intensity that they neutralized the strength of his usual pattern of loyalty.

The adolescent's relationships with other people are extremely hard to classify. One moment he hates intensely; the next he loves with equal intensity. The object of his emotional seesaw may be the same person or it may be a different person. The intensity of the response is not always consistent with the actual episode that aroused it. He will forgive a boy friend who steals his girl friend but swear everlasting enmity for the person who disparages his necktie. He may accept a severe and unjustified reprimand with graciousness and tolerance that embarrass his harassed teacher, and the next day show extreme rage because the same teacher asks him very patiently to try to write more legibly.

What the adolescent says and what he does are in frequent contradiction. On occasion he verbalizes ideals, but any similarity between these ideals and his actual behavior is purely coincidental. Or he may verbally deny all ideals, at the same time behaving in complete conformity with socially acceptable standards. The philosophy he approves of today is followed tomorrow by a slave-like devotion to a completely contrasting approach to the problems of living. At one time he rigidly adopts a code of conduct which, if really followed, would deny him all human gratifications. As if by a sudden metamorphosis he then violates, or more often talks of violating, every acceptable code of behavior. To add to the confusion—but also to introduce a more optimistic note—it should be pointed out that the average adolescent, while never as angelic as he talks of being in his angelic moments, rarely acts out the extremes of antisocial behavior he often praises.

In no area is the dichotomy more evident than in his relationship to his parents. At times he rejects his parents as if they were lepers in a community of healthy people. They dress too well or not well enough; they talk too loudly or not loudly enough; they know nothing or they know too much. In almost the next breath he reveals his idealization of them, picturing them as more holy than the saints, more learned than the sages, more omnipotent than God. When he is in this phase, parents can do no wrong. Parental mistakes are met with sympathetic tolerance. Then parents have the gratifying experience of finding someone who seems to understand what a hard life they have had as parents and as adults. It is all the more confusing for them when the child who has shown gracious understanding of their whim to indulge themselves in the use of the family car for pleasure, later responds with a vitriolic attack when they plan to use the car for a necessary errand.

The adolescent characteristically is secretive about himself and his feelings. Most of the time it is extremely difficult for him to express how he does feel. Furthermore, even if he can put his feelings into words, he is reluctant to expose himself to others. Again, however, this pattern is not consistent. Suddenly he may bare his soul (or so it seems), revealing his ambitions, his feelings of guilt, and his conscious awareness of the nature of many of the conflicts with which he is struggling. Sometimes this revelation is a frank one, though limited by the degree of his own insight. At other times it is probably consciously or unconsciously distorted.

Adolescents frequently reveal in therapy some of the ways in which they distort the verbal picture of their feelings, especially in dealing with their parents. Alice expressed this rather interestingly. She stated that she often confided in her mother and discussed her problems with her. She felt, however, that what she discussed was carefully selected, that certain stages preceded her verbalization to her mother. The first stage was a feeling of general confusion, in which she found herself thinking such contradictory thoughts so rapidly that she was unable to formulate them sharply. During this period she remained silent. Gradually some of the contradictions took on sharper form so that she was able to develop from them a definite point of view. During this period again she did not talk to her mother because she did not wish to be influenced by her mother's attitudes. Finally, things became clear enough to her so that she could find her own definite answer and know what concepts she wished to abandon in order to accept others. In other words, in a particular area of conscious conflict, Alice had developed a philosophy of approach. She would then discuss her particular question with her mother but would not present her own conclusions. She would instead review the various possible solutions. If her mother suggested a solution other than the one she herself had found, she attempted to evaluate it frankly and test her own solution against it. If her mother's solution seemed sounder, she might change. More frequently she either would win her mother to her own point of view or become angry at her for her obvious stupidity. Alice's mother was extremely proud of the close relationship she had with her daughter, being quite certain that she was the recipient of genuine confidences from her daughter!

Joan, another adolescent, gave a slightly different version of what confiding in parents can mean to some adolescents. She had given some advice to Mary, a friend of hers, and wished the psychiatrist's opinion of its soundness. She then told the following story. About two o'clock in the morning, Mary, in tears, had called Joan. Mary had gone to bed after returning from a date but was awakened by her mother's crying. When questioned, the mother said that Mary did not love her, that she could not bear living because she felt that Mary was indifferent to her. She was planning to commit suicide. Mary had attempted to console her mother by assuring her that she did love her. After a tearful scene, she finally persuaded her mother to go to bed. Later she called Joan for advice.

Joan pointed out to Mary that she was directly responsible for this episode, that she had made many mistakes in the way she handled her mother. For example, when she came in from a date she did not awaken her mother. When she mentioned her date to her mother, she never went further than to say she had a good time. She never talked to her mother about things that girls might be disturbed about. Joan had quite different recommendations for the proper management of mothers. She suggested that when Mary came home she awaken her mother for a talk. If the mother refused the invitation, Mary should find an opportunity to tell her mother that she was hurt by the rebuff, that she wanted to talk over some things that were worrying her. If necessary, she should force her mother to listen to a tale of woe. Mary should describe her worries about some feelings she had—for example, that she was frightened by the feelings she had when a boy kissed her, or by the implications of getting married.

Mary had demurred at this advice; she didn't want her mother to know her true feelings; she felt her mother would only be horrified or would irritate her by platitudinous advice. Joan's answer was, "But Mary, you don't see the point. You don't talk to your mother about the things that really bother you. You mention things that don't disturb you. Then whatever she says won't make any difference to you. Your mother will feel happier and reassured that you love her; she won't commit suicide. You know, lots of the things that people expect girls our age to be bothered about don't worry you at all. These are the things to talk to your mother about." It would certainly appear that Joan herself had worked out an approach to her mother that ensured both her mother's happiness and Joan's privacy.

The adolescent is not only confused about and confusing in the present, his dreams of the future are equally unstable. Although he spends hours chatting with his parents about his ambition to be a lawyer, his grades suggest that he won't be able to enter college. Yet the high school psychologist indicates that he could easily qualify if he would study. He dreams of being an experimental chemist and cuts chemistry laboratory at the slightest excuse. He outlines his future as a concert pianist and refuses to practice. He plans a successful business career and then wishes to leave high school and work as an unskilled laborer.

It is equally typical for the adolescent to change his goals frequently. He finds many possibilities intriguing but he feels unable to choose any of them permanently. Little wonder many parents question whether they can survive the present, and if there is any hope for their son or daughter in the future. Will he or she ever settle down? Most of them do.

ASSEMBLING THE JIGSAW PUZZLE

As the adolescent attempts to deal with the world in which he had formerly felt at ease, he finds it vaguely different. Because of his increased psychological responsiveness—to the external environment as well as to internal needs—many things previously casually accepted or ignored become strongly charged emotionally. In addition, the drive toward maturity and greater independence causes the adolescent to expose himself to unfamiliar situations that make new demands on his capacity to integrate his world.

DEPENDENCE VS. INDEPENDENCE

In the past, he was more or less willing to permit his parents or other adults to determine the situations to which he was exposed and to give him the support of their guidance. Now he often refuses guidance or seeks new experiences without the parents' knowledge. When he is challenged by situations he is unable to meet, he becomes frightened and turns again to his parents or to other adults for support. If the situation is not too terrifying, his dependency upon others is no greater than the actuality demands. Frequently, because of the deeper emotional significance of the circumstances, he does not gain the reassurance he needs from a mature dependent relationship. The resultant panic brings about a return to the familiar pattern of infantile dependency. He does not "act his age" but rather acts like a small child, seeking the solution that earlier proved helpful in mastering anxiety.

If the adolescent is given the type of support parents give a small child, he feels increased internal strength and can abandon the more immature temporary solution. Were this the only effect of the episode, he would proceed happily on his way. But as the panic fades, he sees himself as having lost his struggle to become adult. This is a real blow to his pride and confidence. In order to maintain his own self-respect, he must protest against this immature flight into childhood. To protest against himself, however, is to acknowledge his own weakness. He must seek a victim outside himself upon whom to vent his rage and yet avoid admitting his disappointment in and anger at himself. He chooses for his attack those who know of his defeat—his parents or other adults. He protests angrily that they will not let him grow up; they treat him as a child. If, on the other hand, parents do not respond to the adolescent's immature demands, his anxiety mounts. He may then turn upon the parents, angrily accusing them of expecting too much of him. Again the parents are accused of failure so that he may avoid his own sense of defeat.

Undoubtedly, it is true that many times the complaint an adolescent makes concerning his parents is valid; they may not give support when they should and may refuse freedom of choice when they should grant it. It is important, however, that the situation be evaluated carefully. Average parents of the average adolescent inevitably are frequently in the opposite phase from that which the adolescent desires. If his parents are fulfilling one need, the opposing need often becomes dominant. If they are meeting his dependency needs, he will sooner or later gain the security that makes possible a rebellion against that dependency. If his parents are giving him adequate freedom, he will expose himself to frightening situations that will cause a return to a childlike relationship for a time. He will usually save his self-respect by blaming his parents for advising him either too much or too little. Parents can perhaps console themselves with the knowledge that even as scapegoats they are fulfilling an important function for their child.

A situation fraught with danger to the ultimate maturation of the adolescent is one in which he cannot express a need for both dependence and independence and thus gain gratification in transient phases of each. This danger is present if the adolescent is unwilling to indulge himself in dependent gratification or to expose himself to experimental independence. Dependency may be too tempting and thus to be denied; or it may be denied because past experience has taught him that he will either be rebuffed or permanently engulfed by adults. Independence may, in contrast, be too overwhelming because his past experience has not given him confidence in his own resources or in his ability to use them. If he is quite willing to accept gratification of his contrasting longings for freedom and protection, his environment must be willing both to accept his desire to be free at one point or to satisfy his desire to be protected at another.

A chronically frightened adolescent is a disturbed adolescent. Broadly speaking, either his earlier experiences have not given him enough security and tools to deal with the present reality, or else the present reality is, for some reason peculiar to him and his surroundings, too overwhelming.

On the other hand, in the author's experience, the adolescent who does not indicate some conflict over his strivings to become independent should be studied carefully. Perhaps he has found a way through adolescence that has not been too frightening. It may be that the struggle is there but is carefully hidden. It is also possible that the problems presented at the onset of adolescence may have been too overwhelming and, under a thin façade of growing up, he actually has remained at an earlier, more comfortable level of adjustment. Just as it is impossible to go from one place to another without crossing over the intervening distance, one cannot go from childhood to adulthood without being adolescent. Either he stays in childhood or he weathers adolescence.

Ultimately, during the years encompassed by the term adolescence, the individual learns to deal with the broader world he has found. His anxiety decreases and the return to the more immature relationship with parent figures is no longer necessary. With the resulting increase in self-respect, he is not so threatened when he needs support from others. He can accept a mature, dependent relationship with others because his independence is more confidently maintained. This particular section of the jigsaw puzzle is put together.

LOVE AND HOSTILITY

The adolescent's ambivalence toward people to whom he is close has many of the characteristics of the anxiety-ridden ambivalence of early childhood. There is also considerable similarity in the causes of this behavior.

At adolescence the surge of new impulses and reinvigorated older ones places the individual in a difficult situation. Parents and the social world limit many types of gratification, limitations which are frustrating but which are more or less obeyed in order to avoid the anxiety that parental or social disapproval would cause. The adolescent has a great deal of disorganized energy which adults would like him to put toward constructive goals. He, having not yet determined his goals, wishes to express the energy impulsively. He is noisy, rushes around aimlessly, laughs loudly, is often clumsy, talks too much, sings too often, and forgets his manners. He wants the car right now, a new suit right now, something to eat right now. The logic behind a restriction seems irrelevant and unimportant when stacked against the strong emotional force behind the impulse.

Adolescents make many illogical demands and wish to carry out plans of action that are incompatible with the social mores. Parents return to saying "no" and "don't" with a frequency that has its closest counterpart in parental behavior during the very early, toddling age of the child. The adolescent, his energy restrained and his whims not gratified, resents the immediate source of his discomfort—the adults. His feelings are too raw and too intense to be handled with diplomacy enough to gain external acceptance, or with rationalization to achieve internal peace. He hates his parents.

This hatred is no safer than it was in childhood. The need for parental love is as intense as it ever was. Moreover, the child is afraid to deny his very real love for his parents and his need for love from them. The resultant anxiety and guilt make hatred untenable. He reverses his emotions, loving his parents with the intensity with which he has hated them.

The sudden inability to handle love and hostility toward the same object is reflected in his relationships with his friends. At times his need to be reassured that his friends like him, is dominant. He accepts their behavior toward him as if that acceptance were the price he pays for security. At other times he feels angrily that the restrictions they impose upon him destroy him as an individual. His answer is to hate them, hoping thus to be free of his need for them. Friendship with a peer often has an obscure component— that of substitute parent. As such, the friend may be exposed to the same ambivalent feeling that the adolescent expresses toward his parents.

Since the adolescent's feelings are too intense to be kept in balance by compromises, renunciation, and substitute gratifications, under stress he reveals the several facets of his emotional relationships with people as if they were separate entities. Under less stress he will respond with the reasonableness of his preadolescent days. Frequently, however, the intensity of his emotional response to a particular situation is of such magnitude that his formerly established pattern for dealing with ambivalent feelings breaks down.

Gradually, the average adolescent, if he finds he has not provoked a totally hostile response from his environment, will again find patterns of behavior with which to avoid chronic frustration. He finds substitute gratification for impulses that, in unsublimated form, cannot be expressed. The panic created by forced inhibition of his impulses is allayed by rationalization and by acceptance of overall goals for himself. He again becomes master of his ambivalence. His energy, recently expressed so explosively, once again becomes channelized. He settles down to school work, organizes his social life, systematizes his living in the present, and recognizes and follows the guideposts that lead him to future goals.

As the adolescent develops a capacity to harmonize his multiple impulses, he again sets up his own controls. This is a recapitulation of the earlier developmental period when he learned to say "no" to himself before his parents said it, thereby facilitating his adjustment to his internal demands and external restrictions. When the individual's behavior gradually becomes determined by his own judgment rather than by controls imposed from outside, his parents and friends are less frustrating and his hostility toward them diminishes. The storms in interpersonal relationships, so frequently observed during the early phase of adolescence, decrease in frequency as the individual approaches psychological adulthood. Another section of the jigsaw puzzle is assembled.

THE STRUGGLE FOR SEXUAL ADJUSTMENT

While the adolescent strives for security in the more broadly stimulating world around him, and while he flounders in the sea of ambivalent feelings and disorganized impulses, a major and more significant struggle, on a relatively unconscious level, is taking place within him. Additional ambiguities in his behavior, an intensification of his fight for independence, and further confusion in his responses to his parents develop. This struggle has its basis in the difficulties he faces as he tries to reach a heterosexual level of adjustment.

The physical changes of puberty bring an intensification of the biologically determined sexual drive. The mechanisms of repression utilized earlier fail and the established barriers threaten to dissolve. If the renewed feelings sought a new love object, the problem would be less severe. They do not do so. Although the pathway established for earlier sexual impulses has become covered with camouflaging undergrowth, it still is the only familiar road to follow once the barrier is down. The sexuality of early adolescence reactivates the family triangle, and the boy's mother, the girl's father, become the focus of sexual feelings. Expression of this is forbidden by previously determined prohibitions; yet the need for expression is intensified. New defenses must be established. The defense most likely to have the strength to combat the newly intensified impulses is that of denial. The adolescent boy denies the appeal his mother has; the girl denies her father's attractiveness.

The boy's need to avoid an affectionate relationship with his mother is easily recognized. Although he had in the past enjoyed his mother's physical shows of affection, he now refuses to accept them. His mother, he insists, not only must refrain from kissing him; she must avoid all physical contact with him. Verbal expressions of affection on her part are met with annoyance. If she praises him, he protests that she is treating him "like a baby."

If the mother hazards a suggestion as to how her son should act, he responds with irritation even when the suggestion coincides with his own plans. Not only is her suggestion met by refusal, but it often results in behavior of an opposite nature. This rebuff is necessary to reassure himself that he is capable of independent action, free from the dictates of his mother. He can then prove to himself that he not only is not a child but, equally importantly, that he is not the sort of person his mother wishes him to be. Accepting the mother's ideal of a man as a model for his own masculinity entered into his original solution of the family triangle. But it was safe only so long as the sexual implications of the relationship were repressed. With the weakening of his defenses against the sexual nature of the relationship, identification with her concept of a man becomes too dangerous.

The part of the child's ideal formerly colored by his identification with his father now becomes equally hazardous. If he is like his father, he is again the type of man of whom his mother approves and thus comes the danger of winning his mother's love in competition with his father. This need to deny the sexual significance of identification with the father is also related to the boy's need to achieve independence and dignity. Mimicry of his father means to the boy that he himself is inadequate; achievement of mature behavior patterned after his father's represents only a shell that covers fundamental weaknesses. While he has an exaggerated feeling of inadequacy during this period, the urge toward maturation carries with it an implication of his own potential worth. On the one hand he fears he cannot achieve maturity on his own, but he also cherishes the contradictory conviction that he can. He does not wish to lose his hope through mimicry. Thus, he wishes to prove himself an independent individual by abandoning his imitation of his father.

Feelings of fear and incompetence, which were aroused in the earlier period of competition with his father but remained dormant, flare up in the boy with the reactivation of the triangular emotional constellation. He must deny his father's strength and attractiveness in order to conceive of himself as a more powerful male figure. He establishes his own self-respect by denying the virtues of his adversary—he belittles his father in thought, in action and in words. But, his mother's refusal to accept him as a mature person may again confront him if he over-extends himself. In order to avoid the feeling of inadequacy that this fantasied rebuff would bring, he must deny the sexuality of his mother. She fails to accept him, then, not because he is inadequate but because she is incapable of sexual response. His father is a nincompoop, his mother a hag.

With a brave gesture the adolescent has stripped his parents of their powers to obstruct him and has cleared the way for his own sexual and social maturation. He is free, but his sense of freedom is short-lived. In disarming his parents, he finds he has inadvertently disarmed himself as well. Instead of finding adequacy he has increased his own inadequacy. The bricks that fitted together to lay the foundation for his character were molded from forms designed by the parents. Removing the individual bricks now threatens to destroy all he has built. By accepting, as his own, the standards of behavior acceptable to his mother and father, he felt safe in the world of his family in early childhood. The application of these standards proved relatively effective in his broader social world. Emulating his parents provided a comfortable, successful, and reassuringly consistent pattern of reaction to life situations. Abandonment results in a deep sense of loss. He then no longer has the assurance that he is able to deal comfortably, automatically, and successfully with the demands of the world. He has stripped himself of tools that he had learned to use. He has exchanged relative sureness for complete uncertainty.

If the adolescent boy seeks to fill the vacuum by returning to the security inherent in being like his father, he then must face the significance of the denial of his father's strength. If he is like his father he will be as inadequate as he wishes to believe his father is. Identification with his father can no longer cause him to feel adequate in the world, for he has convinced himself that his father is weak. In attempting to enhance his own relative strength, he belittled his father. Now he finds that in doing so he has belittled that part of himself which contributed significantly to his sense of security. If he is not like his father, he has no standard to follow. If he is like his father, he is, by his own definition, a nincompoop.

His denial of the role his mother has played in his life adds further to his confusion. If his relationship with his mother has been a satisfactory, though asexual, one in the past, his ideal of femininity is based on his relationship with her. Thus, his ultimate image of a heterosexual love object would be someone like his mother. In order to win such a love object, the most obvious way is to become like his father, with the modifications suggested by his mother's picture of the ideal man. He cannot abandon this composite idea of a man if he is to gain the love object he seeks. Also, if he denies the sexual power of his mother, he equally denies that of his ideal love object. How can he be sure of gratification for his total love needs if he accepts the serious limitations he has placed on his ideal man and ideal woman?

Day by day patterns of behavior indicate this confusion. In one phase the adolescent boy refuses his mother's affection and renounces her concepts of masculinity. He ridicules his father and struggles to be indiscriminately "different." His parents' concepts of how he should dress, what he should believe politically, and how he should act socially are of value only negatively; they indicate what one should not believe or do. The parents dress wrong, have embarrassing table manners, act wrong, and talk wrong; they are completely impossible. In the alternate phase he seeks the mother's response provocatively, flirting with her as if she had suddenly lost her scars of age and had become an attractive adolescent herself. He accepts his father as an oracle and treats him as if he were the exceptional man he always wished him to be. The boy seeks advice on every move, as if he were incapable of independent judgment; he is again the helpless child of infancy.

The adolescent girl faces an identical struggle. While she feels drawn toward the father, she must deny this attraction. Yet she cannot judge other men with confidence except by standards based on her concept of her father. She does not dare to be like her mother; she must deny her mother's virtues in order to assure herself of her own superiority. Yet her clearest definition of femininity is that with which her mother has acquainted her, and which she has accepted as a model for herself. She vacillates between contempt for her mother and father, idealization of her mother and father, contempt for her father and idealization of her mother, idealization of her father and contempt for her mother.

Ultimately the girl or boy becomes confident in the role biologically determined for them. Their progressively maturing sexual drive is directed toward a heterosexual goal in which the loved object is someone outside the family and of an appropriate age. Parental figures lose their dangerously intense meaning and a third section of the jigsaw puzzle is put together.

THE INFANTILE CONSCIENCE

A major psychological struggle in the process of maturation which occurs in adolescence is rebellion against the infantile conscience. The infantile conscience was adequate for the adjustment of a small child; its structure was determined by the needs and requirements of childhood. The same standards of adjustment are not satisfactory for adult living, and because the conscience is a part of childhood, it becomes a barrier to maturation. An adolescent feels he must free himself from infantile modes of behavior; he rebels against his own conscience.

This rebellion contributes to two characteristics of adolescence which are often alarming. The adolescent flaunts his new freedom from his conscience; he verbalizes his contempt for its demands and acts out token proof that he is free of it. In seeking a symbol of his conscience against which to strike, he most frequently chooses the persons who were the original pattern for his conscience—his parents. A significant part of the adolescent's rebellion against parental control is actually a symbolic rebellion against the no longer serviceable part of his own unconscious demands upon himself.

If the structure of the infantile conscience is considered in detail, it becomes obvious why the adolescent must escape it. Heterosexuality is forbidden by the infantile conscience. It was the need to find an efficient means of repressing parent-forbidden impulses, especially the early sexual impulses directed toward the parent of the opposite sex, which resulted in the crystallization of the infantile conscience. The early sexual feelings were, in embryonic form, the beginning of ultimate adult heterosexuality; they must be freed of the chains by which they were bound in childhood before mature heterosexuality can be attained. In other areas of development the conscience has imposed unwarranted restrictions. As the child moves into adulthood, activities, drives, and impulses that were forbidden to him now become permissible. But to the infantile conscience, that which was once bad is always bad. It protests against any act that was forbidden in childhood and is deaf to the approval expressed by a more flexible reality world. This is true because of the nature of the repression that took place. It is characteristic of repressed drives and feelings that they remain unconscious but unchanged in structure and in power. The repressing force therefore tends also to remain unchanged in structure and in power.

The rebellion against the conscience is frightening to the adolescent. Previously he had a sense of ease with himself. He felt assured that his impulses would not be expressed in a form that would jeopardize his security since the pattern was molded by internal standards that mirrored the demands of the external world. Impulses now strengthened by new energy are difficult to hold in check by former methods; whereas to abandon the protection of the former methods is to invite chaos. As the anxiety mounts, the adolescent tries to strengthen the old defenses. The conscience then becomes more alert and more rigid than before. The adolescent becomes overly severe toward himself—a swing in the opposite direction from his earlier abandonment to impulsive behavior. He suddenly becomes a prig.

In one phase the adolescent may be frighteningly free of inhibitions and, in the alternate phase, he may be deprived of all normal spontaneity by unrealistic, self-imposed prohibitions. A girl was referred to a psychiatrist because of her unconventional behavior which had resulted in her being branded as the "bad girl" of the community. Her dress, her mannerisms, and her verbalization seemed to flaunt her defiance of all conventional standards. When the psychiatrist, in a comment, implied that he thought she permitted boys to kiss her, she left treatment. As an adult she recalled this episode. She could remember her horror at the thought that the psychiatrist had so little respect for her decency that he would believe it possible that she behaved in this manner —a manner completely unacceptable to her.

The adolescent often handles this conflict between the wish to be free of the conscience and slavish devotion to it by expressing defiance but acting with complete compliance to its standards. Sometimes, however, the defiance is not only verbal but is acted out, with serious consequences. The acting out that occurs during the phase of defiance results in an overwhelming guilt reaction when the conscience is again in control. Although the conscience did not succeed in prohibiting the behavior, it uses all its force to punish once the act is committed. Such behavior is difficult to evaluate in adolescence. It resembles the clinical picture of adults who act out impulses in order to be punished, and of those who, by their chronic defiance, provoke retaliation. With adolescents, the need for punishment plays a part in their acting-out behavior, but it is questionable whether it is usually a dominant factor. The adolescent acts out his defiance of his conscience in order to have a sense of freedom from it, not chiefly to gain punishment. Frightened by his freedom, however, he abandons his defiance and submits to his conscience. The conscience then behaves as parents do when they punish a child for an act committed in their absence. Once the conscience is back in control, external punishment is sought or self-punishment is administered.

The rebellion against the infantile conscience does not remain internal. The pattern of the conscience was determined by the parent-figures of infancy, and this close relationship between internal and external forces makes possible a point of focus for the revolt. Parents may serve as a symbol of the conscience and thus part of the struggle can be externalized. The adolescent rebels against the parents and parent-surrogates not only because parents are restrictive but also because they are symbols of the infantile conscience from which the child must be partially free in order to reach maturity.

The adolescent's behavior toward his parents is as confused as it is toward his own conscience. At times he resents his parents' authority and flaunts his contempt for their beliefs and their pattern of living. At other times he seeks their controls and blindly follows the family mores. He often violates the most logical restrictions, knowing that he will be punished. He is using them as an excuse for rebellion, trying to free himself of chains that are invisible but can be symbolized by the parent. At the same time, he values the restrictions since they assure him that external restraint against unfettered freedom exists and that punishment will follow if he oversteps the rules.

The importance of justifiable family restrictions and the punishment resulting from their violation was clearly shown in the following incident. Henry was fifteen years old. His general behavior was characterized by constructive conformity both to the demands of his family and to those of his environment. The parents had only one major complaint, concerning the use of the family car. Henry was allowed to use the car at any time it was not needed by his mother. Frequently she would allow him to have it when she was aware that she would need it later in the day and although ordinarily he was very reliable, he sometimes failed to return it on time. The parents finally punished him by refusing him the use of the car, but he did not "learn his lesson" and failed again to return the car promptly the subsequent day. When his mother decided to handle the situation by completing her errands first and allowing him to have the car afterwards for an unrestricted period, a perplexing reaction developed. Before he would use the car he insisted that his mother set a time for his return. He was able to verbalize a feeling of uneasiness and dissatisfaction if he drove off without having a limit put on the time that he could be gone, even though he had repeatedly exceeded the limit.

Peggy, who was fourteen, created a somewhat similar situation. She was also very reliable. Her mother had overheard her, on several occasions, complain to her girl friends that her mother was too strict—that she made Peggy come home from parties at a certain hour instead of allowing her to remain until the parties broke up. The mother decided that she herself undoubtedly had been unreasonable. One night as Peggy, on leaving for a party, asked what time she was to return, the mother suggested that they not set a definite time but that Peggy use her own judgment. Peggy immediately rejected her mother's liberality. She asked her mother to state a definite time, explaining that even though she fussed at this restriction, actually she would feel uneasy if it were not imposed. She could not decide with any conviction what was the right time to leave and preferred that her mother carry the burden. She even admitted that the restriction served a further purpose—the time that her mother set usually coincided with her own wishes. If she should tell her friends that she wanted to go home they might criticize her. If she said that she had to go home because her mother made her, she could save face with her friends by blaming her mother and at the same time carry out her own wishes. She also confessed that sometimes when no restrictions had been imposed she invented them—if her group wanted to do something that she did not wish to do she would say she was not allowed, even though this placed her mother in an unpleasant light. By this subterfuge, Peggy consciously avoided the responsibility for failure to follow the group, transforming her distaste for an activity into a prohibition by her mother.

Although, in this instance, the subterfuge was used consciously, it can also be used unconsciously. When the adolescent wishes both to obey and to defy the conscience, he often externalizes the conscience by using the parents as its symbol. Such a use may lead the adolescent to report some strange interpretations of his parents' wishes. He may say that a certain act would be prohibited by the parents when actually they have no objection. His statements may indicate a simple misunderstanding of parental attitudes but in other instances, they reveal how the adolescent acts as his own censor. He does not feel comfortable in carrying out an impulse and projects the disapproval on to his parents.

Reassurance that his parents do not disapprove may lead him to decide that the act is proper and therefore should be done. On the other hand, unless he understands his own role in the prohibition, reassurance may only add to his anxiety and confusion.

The complex interaction of the role of the conscience, the role of the parent *per se,* and the role of the parent as a projection of the conscience, as well as the satisfaction that lies in revolt, is illustrated by Jean's reaction to a rather simple situation. Jean's parents were well aware that high-school girls and boys smoked. In discussing the matter with her, the parents expressed their opinion that while there was no convincing proof that smoking was either injurious or undesirable for young people, it was probably wise to delay smoking as long as possible. They added, however, that since she was shortly to find herself with friends who smoked, she might like to try it at home. They told her there was no need to hide the fact that she was smoking but that she might join them in an after-dinner cigarette. She did not accept the invitation, though eventually her parents became aware that she was smoking in her room. One evening after dinner her father passed her a cigarette, suggesting that since she was already smoking she might as well smoke with them. Jean blushed, very self-consciously took a cigarette, and smoked it briefly. It took several days before she could smoke relaxedly in front of her parents. She herself later described her feelings. She explained that she felt that she was doing something wrong in smoking in front of her parents even though they had not forbidden it. Smoking prior to their knowledge gave her a gratifying feeling of doing something prohibited, but when she no longer had to keep it a secret she noticed the enjoyment in smoking was much less. The simple episode revealed her own unconscious prohibition against smoking, which she identified with her parents and against which she secretly revolted.

THE INFLUENCE OF THE GROUP

During the period of early adolescence, when rebellion seems to threaten all previously accepted standards of behavior, the modification of the conscience by the mores of the group becomes apparent. Security in the group is extremely significant at adolescence; it helps handle the panic resulting from unresolved conflicts at this age. The average social group, wishing to be accepted in the social structure, does not abandon the more important standards imposed earlier upon each individual by parents. Frightened by his own impulses, and by the hazardous choice between complete repression or free expression of them, the adolescent turns to the group for support and for answers to his questions. He can there discuss his mixed feelings and find solace in the identical suffering of others. He can test tentative answers to his perplexities against the equally tentative formulations of his friends. Most important, he can participate in the development of restrictions upon his behavior. This will assure him of protection from a chaotic expression of impulses without risking the dangers inherent in the restrictions outlined by the parents.

Adolescent groups frequently have seemingly ridiculous rules of conduct, to which the average adolescent is a slave. There was, for example, a period in which an adolescent girl would have preferred walking down the street in a bathrobe to appearing with a cardigan sweater worn with the buttons in front. The group had decreed that to be "proper" a cardigan should be buttoned in back. Although the absurdities of the group-imposed restrictions frequently provoke ridicule or censorship from the adult world, the value of the group control is not always properly estimated. The group not only determines how a cardigan should be worn, but, more important, it tempers the effect of the rebellion against the infantile conscience. As a result of the mutual soul-searching by the individuals in the group, standards concerning more basic concepts of living crystallize. Attitudes toward questions of morality, ethics, and social customs take form. The standards are rigidly held to by the individuals in the group and gradually become part of the "conscience" of each member. The character of the group attitudes is influenced to a large degree by the past experience of its members. If these have been generally satisfactory, the resulting group attitudes will not be strikingly different from parental standards. The group structure serves as a relative island of security in a tumultuous world. It protects the individual from becoming lost in the possible blind alleys of the psychological maze of adolescence. The formulation and acceptance of the more mature, more realistic conscience brings another section of the jigsaw puzzle together.

THE SOCIAL STRUCTURE

It is important to give proper weight to the social structure to which the adolescent is exposed. In our culture, society makes heavy demands upon the adolescent but fails to provide him with a carefully outlined pattern to help meet those demands. By contrast, primitive cultures provide definite rules of behavior for both childhood and adulthood, and initiation ceremonies to mark an arbitrary line between the two. Within a framework of taboos and customs the individual personality develops. It is not for the young person to decide whether or not he will obey; failure to do so results in arbitrary punishment while compliance results in acceptance. The standard not only is unquestioned by the older adults but is also accepted by his own age group. If he obeys, he can be secure, secure not only in his relationship with his social world—his superiors, his peers, and his inferiors—but also in his own conviction of being an adult. Quite an opposite situation for the adolescent exists in our culture, particularly in a country that stresses democracy and the rights of the individual. We believe, at least in theory, that one has the inalienable right to develop as an individual so long as other individuals are not jeopardized. It is believed, moreover, that both adulthood and the culture are enriched if the individual is allowed to grow into adulthood without being forced into a mold. The lack of something like an initiation ceremony increases the confusion and anxiety. The adolescent is told in effect to grow up—but no one defines that state, or tells him how to reach it.

Although in principle our culture places value on the individual's right to choose his own pattern of self-development, in practice it penalizes those who do not recognize the difference between license and liberty. Certain controls on behavior are essential for the maintenance of society, but they are difficult to define and do not have the rigidity of the taboos of a primitive society. The concept of acceptable behavior is therefore a confused one. The adolescent keenly feels the impact of the social confusion. Unsure of his own goals, he seeks an answer outside himself, both in his own family group and in the world beyond his family. Neither source can give him rules of living which are without contradiction.

It is not only in the broader areas of ethics, politics, business, or international relations that social confusion exists. The adolescent faces an equally significant confusion in his own home. The typical parent's attitude toward dating is a case in point. The boy who is not dating girls is a source of concern to his parents. They feel that perhaps he is not maturing correctly. They press him to date girls, tease him about his self-consciousness, and imply that he should be more tolerant of his natural impulses. Finally he does date girls. The parents then become concerned because he is staying out late, or not studying as much as he should. They fear that he may not have sufficient understanding of the risks involved in his relationship with girls; they warn him of the dangers inherent in his own natural impulses.

His parents keep reminding the child that he is growing up. They say he should be able to assume more responsibility, think more for himself and be less dependent upon them for guidance. When he attempts, on the other hand, to be more independent they remind him that after all they are still his parents and that he is too young to know what is best for him. They have a right to control him until he is of age. Often, what they actually mean by independence is that he should take more initiative in doing what they wish him to do. But what they wish is rarely very clear. They expect him to be "grown up" in the sense of possessing all the virtues parents value, and yet to lack all the vices usually tolerated by adults in one another.

The parents of an adolescent are often frightened people. They sense his confusion. They also sense the impact of biological urges with which the adolescent as yet cannot deal constructively. In looking back upon their own adolescence they recall it as a time of stress in which they were apparently in grave danger of ruining their lives. By some miracle they were saved from destruction but they fear that the same fortuitous circumstances may not be present to save their child. On the other hand, they may have forgotten (or repressed) their own turmoil, or perhaps in their own adolescence they were unaware of their struggles. Both possibilities make the task of handling the difficulties that arise even more frightening. Yet most parents do want their child to develop into a heterosexual adult, although they are fearful that he cannot avoid the pitfalls of that development. They wish him to be independent though they fear that he cannot handle independence without their guidance. Most parents, consciously at least, wish their child to grow up to be a happy adult. They are awestruck by their own roles in this process.

It is equally true that many parents, while they consciously wish their child to grow up, actually resist this process. Perhaps they cannot face the vacuum that will exist when the child is no longer dependent upon them. Sometimes they are jealous of the child who is entering early adulthood with all its apparent glamour when their own adulthood seems tarnished. Many reveal their own maladjustments as they try to direct their adolescent son or daughter. The father may unconsciously fear that his son will be a greater success than he and thus point up the father's inadequacy. In other instances the father may fear that his boy will be as inadequate as he himself is. The son's failure will be his own failure and thus he tries to delay the evil day when he will be doubly exposed. A father may be so emotionally tied to his daughter that he cannot give her up to another man. He may strive to keep her a child to avoid this threat to his own happiness. Whatever the hidden or open conflicts in their relationship with the child, parents as well as the adolescent are confused, and each adds to the confusion of the other.

The dilemma of the adolescent is increased by the half-truths told him in good faith during childhood. Usually they represent the ideals to which adults wish to cling; the truth, which they evade, is that they themselves have made compromises with those ideals. The concept of democracy is an illustration of this point. The child is told that people should be valued for what they are, regardless of their race, creed, or economic status. However, as he leaves the playgrounds behind and he approaches the time for choosing his permanent social group and his life mate, he is confronted with a different set of values. He is then told that it is wiser to make these choices from persons with backgrounds and beliefs similar to his own. What he has been taught is not what his parents really expect of him. This seeming contradiction is probably unavoidable as long as the struggle to reach true democracy continues. It is important to recognize its impact upon the adolescent who is trying to find some stability in a consistent point of view.

Acceptance of the value of sex education for children has resulted in another half-truth. Sex information is given with an implication that sex is desirable, acceptable, and to be recognized without guilt as a part of living. It is mentioned, of course, that sex is something that finds its most complete expression in marriage. To the small child such a statement seems parenthetical, and probably has little significance to him. With the maturation of his sexual drive he faces an attitude incompatible with that implied when, in childhood, he was first told about sex. He is told that he should not gratify his sexual impulses; sexual freedom is now frowned upon. He must wait. He is likely to consider this a contradiction of the earlier parental attitude rather than to recognize that now he is learning the whole truth whereas before he learned only half of it.

The educational system creates additional burdens for the adolescent. Up to the junior-high-school level, he has had his teacher as a parent-substitute to guide him in his learning process. Because of the continuity of this relationship, his teacher has had meaning as an individual. The junior and senior high schools are geared primarily to subject matter and the teacher becomes a mere instrument for teaching the subject. Personal contact with the teacher is limited. The school system attempts to meet this problem by providing advisers, deans, and vocational counselors, but usually such specialists are not an integral part of the everyday school life of the child; he views them as persons set apart, filling a special role. He may find a member of the faculty who will serve as a guide and support, but this usually occurs as a result of his own seeking or through the initiative of a particular teacher, not because it is any longer inherent in the educational program.

Such an impersonal setting is obviously more characteristic of large schools than of smaller ones. But the growing tendency to increase the size of the high schools in order to broaden the curriculum is depriving the adolescent of the support he might obtain were he in a smaller educational framework. The advantage of subject teaching is negated unless the high school faculty has an understanding of and an alert interest in the total personality of the adolescent. Many high-school teachers interpret the adolescent's indifference to a subject as a personal attack upon themselves. Their resulting hostility widens the gulf between teacher and child at a time when the latter may badly need support.

The stimulation the adolescent receives in his free time adds further to his confusion. The movies have been so condemned that one hesitates even to mention the possible implications they may have for the adolescent. It should be noted, however, that movies, radio and television programs, novels, and plays are actually a source of education to the young person, not only about practical world events, but also about the way people live and feel. Most of the portrayals of life shown by these media represent only caricatures; but frequently they reveal raw human emotions and human fantasy, stripped of many of the social defenses. As such, they appeal to the basic human strivings of people.

To the adolescent these portrayals may be both frightening and overstimulating. He may be afraid of the feelings that are aroused because of his unconscious worry that his own controls will break down. On the other hand, the dramas may force the adolescent to face emotions that actually need to be freed from too severe repression if he is to mature to healthy psychological adulthood. The effect of the stimulation is not entirely unfortunate so far as the ultimate development of the adolescent is concerned. It may, however, contribute to his confusion.

Other social pressures have particular repercussions for certain adolescents. As has been indicated, adolescence is not wholly chronological, but represents a physiological and psychological span of time. Because of variations in rates of maturation, it is impossible to establish an arbitrary chronological age for the onset of a particular individual's adolescence. Two persons of identical chronological age may be at very different stages of psychological maturation—one may be struggling with the full impact of psychological adolescence, while the other may still be handling his life situation with the responses characteristic of the latency period. Our society, in spite of its theoretical respect for individuality, tends to judge individuals by statistical norms. As a result, both the child who matures early and the child who matures late may be considered maladjusted if they do not meet the criteria used to judge "normal" development. Actually, their behavior may be quite "normal" for their level of emotional maturation.

Variations in growth patterns create problems for the individual not only because of the standardization of our cultural program, but also because of his relationship to his own age group. The child whose rate of growth is markedly different from that of most may find himself alienated from his chronological peers. If maturation occurs early he is aware that he is becoming different from his friends. He has difficulty in finding a common ground with them because his feelings, his tensions, and his needs are not like theirs. Not only does he sense that adults often frown upon him, but he finds no support from children of his own age. He feels drawn to those who actually are, from the standpoint of maturation, more truly his contemporaries. Because these individuals are chronologically older, however, they are not too accessible to him. They may also refuse to accept him because young people as well as adults consider chronological age the real indication of the level of maturation. Furthermore, while those in this older age group may from many standpoints be his true contemporaries, they have had a longer period of realistic experiences. Their intellectual development will be greater, since it follows chronological age more closely than emotional age. Their athletic skills, their academic background and the social activities they are permitted to participate in place them in a different category from that of the chronologically younger person. As a result, the individual who matures early often finds himself out of step with his chronological age group and excluded from an older age group.

The opposite problem arises when the child's development is slower than the average rate. Then, instead of failing to provide enriched experiences, the environment exposes the child to demands that he is not yet ready to meet. His own age group, too, is emotionally alien to him; he does not feel as they do. In no area is this more manifest than in the developing interest in the opposite sex. Often a girl of thirteen will see her friends interested in boys, enjoying dating, and in the throes of the confusion resulting from physiological sexual maturation. The girl who has not reached this stage has no genuine empathy with the girls who have. If she turns to a younger age group, she may be subject to this group's rebuffs, since they do not consider her a true peer. Furthermore, her attempt to find satisfaction in social relationships with the younger children who are psychological equals will be frowned upon by adults and will lead to contempt from the chronological peers with whom in the past she has found her social acceptance. This may mean to her that she is abnormal—that she is queer. The resultant anxiety may be quite overpowering. She may succumb to her own sense of inadequacy, accepting the rebuff and the implied opinion of her former friends that she is an inferior person. She may attempt to deny her inadequacy and by imitation play a role that requires greater maturity than she really has. Often this acting-out behavior not only further alienates her peer group but also brings severe criticism and rejection from adults.

Although, in theory, the solution to such a situation is to gear the social experiences of the individual to his level of emotional maturation, in practice this ideal is not easy to attain. The practical solution at the present time probably is a recognition by adults of the individual differences in the rate of emotional maturation, and in their support of the child who varies from the norm. Unless deep emotional problems exist, these children, if given adequate support during the period of being "different," will eventually find themselves in a world no longer alien. The child whose maturation has been rapid will find that his chronological peer group finally catches up with him. The child whose emotional maturation has been slow will still reach maturity; it simply takes him longer to get there. The problem can become complicated if parents fail to accept the variations and do not give support to the child struggling both with his "alienness" to his peer group and his inability to comply with the demands made by a society that equates "average" with "normal."

Differences in the average rate of maturation between boys and girls creates another social problem. The girl of fourteen is usually psychologically more mature than the boy of fourteen, as she herself is well aware. The freshman high-school girl does not usually find the freshman boy interesting, but is interested in older boys. The sophomore high-school boy prefers to date the freshman girl rather than a girl in his own class. Parents become alarmed at these choices and press the young people to be interested in their own age group. Left to his own devices, the adolescent will seek the companionship of the opposite sex in terms of his emotional rather than his chronological age. It is not alarming if a girl chooses a boy chronologically older than herself unless there is other evidence that this choice is motivated by unresolved conflicts. But it should also not be assumed that, because a boy and girl of the same chronological age are interested in each other, there is some emotional disturbance. It may only be an indication that the boy's rate of maturation has been more rapid or the spurt of growth has occurred earlier than would be anticipated from the statistically established norms.

The adolescent faces a confusing world. The confusion is

not necessarily unfortunate in the light of the goals our culture has set for the development of human personality. Since the degree of confusion may be too great for the individual adolescent to handle wisely, it is important that those interested in him recognize the pressures to which he is exposed. It may be possible to lessen the traumatic impact by alleviating the pressures or, if the pressures are unavoidable, by supporting him through this period. Most confused adolescents ultimately find a way to clarify the confusion, entering adulthood with an acceptance of reality and constructive ideas of how the reality can be modified. From their new perspective comes cultural and social change, creative research, and a philosophy toward others that make the world a better place. The unrealistic dreams of the adolescent, mellowed by age, form the core of the constructive changes of the next social era. The average adolescent at last brings some order into his chaotic relationship with the society into which he was born. He finds some way to conform to the "tribal" demands without destroying himself or the "tribe." The jigsaw puzzle nears completion.

SUGGESTIONS FOR JIGSAW PUZZLE ADDICTS

It is not surprising that parents find adolescents challenging and irritating, baffling and obvious, charming and crude, stimulating and dull, frustrating and gratifying. The average adolescent has at one time or another any or all of these contradictory characteristics. He will retain them until he either gives up the struggle and returns to a preadolescent psychological structure, or masters the conflicts and finds a satisfactory, adult resolution for them.

The adolescent needs to experiment. He cannot be protected from all the dangers that lie in exploration. Only by trying his strength can he test his adequacy. Only by experiencing some of the frustrations and hazards of maturation can he learn to deal with the real world as separate from his fantasies. Only by knowing the satisfactions of independent activities can he resist the lure of permanent childhood.

On the other hand, he is apt to expose himself impulsively or through lack of perspective to situations beyond his capacity. Freedom exceeding the individual's knowledge and ability to deal with it leads to license or panic. The young person is not prepared to face the intensity of internal drives and the pressure of external demands without assistance. His experiences with freedom should be within a framework of wisely determined limits. What these limits should be differ from individual to individual and from one situation to another. They should be flexible, broadened as the individual shows a capacity to handle the problem, and narrowed when the capacity narrows. Rules established by parents for the adolescent can be designed to strengthen his impulse toward mature behavior rather than to bind him to infancy. Such rules give the adolescent the assurance that outside agents will prevent him from carrying his exploration to the serious point of harm to himself or others.

There is a tendency at present to be too permissive with adolescents, perhaps as a reaction to a former trend to handle all children too rigidly. As a result, high school students are often given too much responsibility for controlling their own behavior and making their own decisions. Victorian concepts of guidance may have been crippling to the development of maturity, but the complete absence of control leaves the young people at the mercy of impulses they cannot handle. Too great freedom is discernible in two diametrically opposed patterns of behavior. On the one hand the individual may be so frightened by the responsibility placed upon him that he is unable to express his impulses in any form, desirable or otherwise. He acts paralyzed. On the other hand, the individual may accept the freedom as tacit permission to act out his impulses whenever the pressure is sufficient. He may drink excessively, be sexually promiscuous, keep late hours, refuse to study. Although in some instances such behavior is the result of deep underlying conflicts, it may frequently represent an immediate expression of impulses that have no constructive goal. They are being expressed in these forms because of the absence of external guidance at a time when the internal mechanisms of control are inadequate.

While limits are important, it is equally important that they not prevent the adolescent from successfully carrying through a part of his revolt. The protective devices of childhood become shackles that must be thrown off if maturation is to occur, but the revolt against them causes a sharp sense of guilt. If this guilt becomes too great, the revolt will be abandoned. The adolescent needs reassurance from others on this point, though he need not be freed of all guilt. Guilt, if reasonable in intensity and caused by violation of healthy standards of behavior, is an important stimulus to integration. A tolerant parent does not have to condone everything completely!

One of the most difficult problems for parents is the establishment of a relationship with their adolescent that enables them to give him the freedom he needs while assuring his acceptance of guidance. Without this basic relationship, supervision leads only to defiance and counter-behavior. An adolescent needs parents who are not afraid to play the parental role. He may be critical of his parents but he still needs them. And often his criticism makes sense—it should be heard and carefully evaluated. Parents are neither always right nor always wrong.

Adolescents, with their limited experience of life, are frequently idealists. The boy brought up to wealth suddenly finds that life unacceptable and refuses to participate in activities from which some are barred because of economic or social status. He decides that the kind of position his education and family background will open for him is intolerable since that position is not open to everyone. He would prefer to work in a factory. The girl condemns her parents for not feeding the beggar at the door, and dreams of doing an heroic one-person job of cleaning up the slums. The idealism of the adolescent is almost as difficult to guide, preserve and yet not encourage beyond the limits of reality as is the rebellion! Yet, unless parents can empathize with the idealistic philosophy, they cannot help the adolescent to temper it with realism!

It is important that adults realize the extreme sensitiveness of the adolescent. His state is comparable to that of an inflamed nerve. Slight stimulation may result in a vigorous, undirected response. He takes seriously remarks that were intended as friendly teasing or a bit of humor. Parents will often comment in a derogatory way about the adolescent's appearance, his ability, or his behavior. Even a casual reference to an incident of the moment is often a verification to the adolescent of his own suspicion that he is not attractive or adequate. A teasing approach is therefore not wise unless the adolescent is quite confident that he is basically accepted by the teaser. Such confidence does not result from verbal reassurance but comes only from experience, an experience provided by the adult's sympathetic but casual tolerance for the irritability, moodiness, impossible ambitions, and unrealistic sense of failure revealed by the adolescent. Teasing always carries some implication of hostility, rejection or belittling, and thus is a questionable tool.

Ponderous, pontifical seriousness is not the only alternative to teasing. Frequently the adolescent is reassured if parents reveal a sense of humor, particularly if the adult is not laughing at the adolescent but is helping him to see the humorous aspects of a situation. The very fact that the adult is not overwhelmed reassures the young person. A too consistently solemn approach may be frightening by its implication that the multiple difficulties of life are all uniformly serious and weighty. The adolescent often knows, too, that the reality is not as serious as parents' solemnity would imply. The obvious lack of perspective on the part of the older people can invalidate their conclusions.

Many parents unnecessarily lose hours of sleep because of an over-identification with the unhappiness of their adolescent son or daughter. Meanwhile their child sleeps contentedly, his misery forgotten. He has confided his uncertainty about himself, his future, his acceptability by his classmates, his intellectual ability or his seemingly peculiar fantasies; at the time he is seriously concerned. But with the resiliency of youth, the concern, once expressed, is soon displaced by other interests, or erased by a pleasant experience. The next day the child cannot understand his parents' worry about his supposed problems. He is irritated when his parents seem to feel there is something wrong with him.

The adolescent may turn to someone outside the family constellation for the adult guidance he seeks. This substitution for the parents may be the result of experienced or expected rejection by them. More commonly it occurs because a relationship with an outside person can be more specifically defined, limited and idealized, than a relationship with parents. Parents by definition play many roles, while a person not of the family can be limited to selected roles. Parents on occasion feel unnecessarily threatened when their adolescent son or daughter obviously prefers to confide in or seek advice from a relative stranger. Such a relationship may actually be very valuable to the adolescent if his choice is a wise one.

Frequently the description he gives of his mentors appears to have about as great a relevance to actuality as a character in fiction does to a real person who by coincidence bears the same name. But the adolescent is often not seeking a *whole* person in these relationships but rather some aspect to meet a particular need. These people may represent what, to the adolescent, are ideal parents, because while providing emotional support and tolerant guidance, they have no real jurisdiction, feel less anxiety, and can be pushed aside if they fail in their roles. Whether they have them or not, they are often endowed with all the idealized characteristics the adolescent wishes to have himself but feels he lacks. He may therefore imitate their mannerisms, dress or behavior with awkward intensity. If the objects chosen are of the opposite sex, they represent either a comfortable substitute for the parent of the opposite sex or the embodiment of the ideal prince charming or fairy princess. On occasion these adults are used as intellectual sounding boards on which the adolescent tries his mental exercises, hoping to have them echoed back to him in harmony.

The adolescent group exerts a stronger constructive influence on the individual than does any one adult. It is easier to accept the attitudes of one's own peers than the teaching offered by individuals who are older and thus from a more psychologically alien world. The relationship to the peer group, confused as it may be, is less charged emotionally. The group can offer limitations, freedom, and standards in a more palatable form. Because of the adolescent's anxiety, he seeks the protection of conformity; to the group he rarely violates seriously the standards it imposes. If its behavior can be guided to constructive patterns, most of the individuals in it will develop the same patterns. Group psychology has a more direct and immediate effect on individual psychology at this age than at any other time in life.

Group experiences offer many learning opportunities for the adolescent. In establishing a satisfactory role for himself among his contemporaries, he is laying the foundation for his future role in the adult social world. His ultimate fulfillment, after all, will not be in the world of his parents, but rather in one that he and his peers will construct. Through sports, especially those involving team play, he learns of the individual satisfaction that can be gained as part of a social structure, a structure which not only is greater than he, but which cannot exist without his individual contribution. He experiences the satisfaction obtained through reaching a goal by mutual cooperation. In day-by-day contact with his age group in every activity, he learns the gratifications in and limitations of a realistic social world.

While the psychological picture of adolescence I have presented may seem rather bizarre and a figment of the imagination to an adult reader, the adolescent himself is often closely in touch with the raw materials from which these conclusions are drawn. Parents, particularly those who accept the psychoanalytic thesis of development, often foster excessive introspection in their child at this time. This may lead to an orgy of self-examination which takes the individual nowhere. A girl, for example, may reveal to her mother that she feels inadequate to compete with her for the attention of the masculine half of the world. The psychoanalytically unsophisticated mother who answers that such an idea is nonsense will often help the girl more than she would were she able to discuss the Oedipal conflict! Parents can be understanding without being their child's psychiatrist.

How does one know if a particular reaction of an adolescent is "normal"? The answer to that question would lie in an accurate evaluation of the level of emotional maturation of the particular adolescent. Unfortunately, there are no techniques for such an accurate evaluation. Normality can only be approximated. Chronological age should not be the only yardstick; careful study of past history and present actions is probably the best means of judging the significance of behavior at any given time. The reactions of one day or to a particular situation are not enough; detailed observation of an adolescent, covering all situations in one day, must be combined with the consideration of his reactions to these situations at other times. A proper study of an adolescent must show him, not in a static portrait, but in action projected onto a movie screen. If there is any doubt about the composite description that results, a professional opinion should be sought.

With all the current publicity concerning adolescents who are acting out their difficulties asocially, too little is said of the remarkably good adjustment most of them are making. Throughout history, adults have always seen the "younger generation" as composed of serious misfits. Statistics would suggest that at the present there is an increase in the number and seriousness of crimes committed by this age group. Those statistics do not reveal how deserving the average adolescent is of praise instead of condemnation. High-school boys plan a future for themselves which they know will have to be postponed until they have completed a period in military service. They have no assurance that that future will ever be, since war is presented to them as imminent and probably inevitable. Yet they appear to accept the present more realistically than do their parents. Considering their own personal difficulties in growing up, and the superimposed complications of a chaotic world, the degree with which they are meeting the demands placed upon them without giving up the struggle should bring more laudatory publicity to them than they have. The average adolescent of the present day gives one reason to renew faith in the human species!

PART III

THE GROWTH OF THE EGO

9 : Why behavior becomes sensible— or doesn't

BEHAVIOR IS THE RESULT OF MULTIPLE IMPULSES, ORIGINATING within the person himself, and finding an expression in action directed either toward a short- or a long-term goal. This organization into a pattern of behavior is not inherent in the multiple impulses themselves. It appears justified to assume that impulses in their primary form press for expression without relationship to other impulses, or to time, logic, morals, ethics or the limits of reality. The primary psychological structure is chaotic.

If every impulse found immediate and direct expression the individual's behavior would resemble what would happen in a world without roads, if cars ran across country haphazard, oblivious to the existence of other approaching cars or obstacles. Some people do behave somewhat in that fashion much of the time—they are described as impulsive or impulse-ridden people. And everyone at times follows an impulse without stopping to check it. This is indicated in the common cry "I did it on an impulse," implying that no rational thought or premeditated goal controlled the expression of the impulse.

All through life impulses are experienced toward goals that would be satisfying to the individual but which contradict the goals of other impulses. In many instances these impulses are not even consciously recognized but are checked before they take discernible form. If the impulse does become conscious, the adult, rejecting it, manifests "common sense" in denying its gratification. A salesman may comment that he wanted to play golf but he had promised Mr. S. he would discuss some business with him. Going back on his word would jeopardize his good relationship with Mr. S. Furthermore, if the sale went through he would get a good commission. He denied fulfillment to his impulse to play golf because its goal was incompatible with the need and desire to earn a living. The impulse to succeed took priority over the impulse to play golf.

The chaotic nature of the internal impulses and their natural tendency to fight one another could be expected to be manifested most clearly in observations of the newborn. Though the psychology of the newborn child is still to a great extent unexplored, it would appear justified to say that the very small infant, because of his limited development, does not have many impulses. Those that do exist are the result of physiological needs, and their goal is the maintenance of physical well-being. Even during this early period there is a priority list established that is a forerunner of the later psychological organization that brings order out of chaos. Consider, for example, the handling of hunger and fatigue in the newborn. Both of these conditions are physical. There is an "impulse" to eat and also to sleep. The two cannot be done at the same time. Thus the infant wakes from sleep because of hunger, eats enough to lessen the hunger and then returns to sleep. One might speculate that one impulse, physiologically determined, wins out momentarily, to be replaced by the other when some of the intensity of the first impulse is lessened. Another step in this development is seen in a slightly older infant. Overpowered by a desire to sleep, he seems to be experiencing a dream phenomenon—he moves his lips in a sucking motion. The "dream" attempts to serve two purposes by permitting the gratification of the physiological impulses to sleep and to eat at the same time.

The incompatibility of unmodified impulses can be observed in certain types of disturbed children who are unable to "concentrate." The child may want to make a model airplane and to play with a toy car at the same time. Both impulses take over, each interrupting the progress of the other toward gratification. It is readily recognized that such a struggle between contradictory impulses is normal in the toddler. He shifts his focus of interest from one toy to another, from one bit of activity to another. He responds to the stimulus of the moment, abandoning one goal when another offers a fresh appeal. It is in the older child that such behavior becomes significant. In such instances the child is indicating that he is still unable to reconcile multiple impulses. He has remained at the psychological response level of the toddler.

The sense of frenzy that develops when several unreconciled impulses clamor for release is familiar to everyone. The housewife decides to make the beds. She then realizes that the dishes are unwashed and that Mrs. J. may drop in for morning coffee at any moment. (Mrs. J. would greatly disapprove of her unwashed dishes and her unmade beds.) But the laundry should be soaking in the washtub. The groceries should be ordered so as to arrive in time for lunch. Mrs. Housewife should really call Mrs. B. to assure herself a ride to the bridge game for which—final straw—a dress must be pressed. Madam Housewife will accomplish little and will feel pretty harassed unless she can collect herself and direct her activity to "one thing at a time." This, in effect, is what happens in the struggle between multiple internal impulses. Chaos and emotional tension will inevitably result if impulses are of equal weight; if no checks and balances develop; if no compromise in goals enables multiple impulses to be expressed in one action or a few integrated actions. Luckily, this frustrating situation is generally avoided—even though the housewife above may wonder in a panicky moment if the chaos of irreconcilable demands has not arrived.

The avoidance of chaos is one of the roles of the "ego." The ego is a differentiated part of the psychological organization. It may have its origin in one primary urge, an urge for harmony. There is an adaptive tendency observable in every living organism. Plants attempt to adjust to the environment in which they are found. The physical adaptive mechanisms of various species of animals are well known. This adaptive drive may be an inherent characteristic also of the psychology of animals, reaching its most complex form in man. As a result, in spite of the chaotic nature of most of the impulses, there is an inherent urge to bring harmony. The ego integrates the demands of the internal impulses with those of the external world, and later, when the conscience develops, with its demands as well. The ego tests and evaluates reality. It determines the kind of adaptation the individual makes to internal and external pressures; its strength determines the individual's ability to master a situation; its way of handling the pressures requiring adaptation determines the personality of the individual. It effects the compromises necessary to avoid a chaotic psychological state. If it fails to function adequately as a coordinator, disintegration occurs.

In a sense the ego functions as a traffic policeman at the gates to a ball park. The policeman allows one lane of cars to enter, holding the other back for awhile. The other lane then is allowed to enter while the original lane is held in check. If a man drives up without a ticket his car is permanently forbidden entrance. So the ego directs the traffic of the impulses. It temporarily holds in check an impulse that is opposed to the one that is given the go-ahead sign. It attempts to hold back the impulse that is irreconcilable to reality or forbidden by the conscience. In such an event, just as some people without tickets will attempt to crash the gate or sneak through a hole in the fence, impulses intolerable to the ego will often find "illegal" ways of expression.

On the other hand, the ego accepts a role traffic policemen are not so willing to assume. If a selected lane toward a goal is barred to an impulse, the ego may permit and aid a switch to an unblocked lane. Thus if a businessman in his exhaustion would like to hit his bald-headed boss, his ego will not let the impulse come into existence. It will however, not only allow but encourage the man to seek his first opportunity to hit a golf ball, not even making the well-behaved businessman consciously aware that the golf ball does indeed resemble a bald head.

The ego plays a part in helping solve the difficulties of the frantic housewife we left earlier, facing so many tasks. It is her ego that will organize her morning's work rationally. She will recognize that it may be wiser to call Mrs. B. early for that ride because Mrs. B. does not like to gossip before her own housework is done. An early conversation will be brief. If Mrs. J. arrives for coffee before the dress is pressed, perhaps she'll be willing to stand by and chat while Mrs. Housewife irons. Since the children's clothes are very dirty and really need to be soaked, the most important immediate task is to get those clothes into the washer. This leaves the dishes and the beds, with Mrs. J.'s arrival coming closer and closer. Now a certain selectiveness comes into the policeman-ego's role. Mrs. Housewife decides that she has time to do the dishes, but probably not the beds. So she will close the door into the bedroom. Mrs. J.'s manners should prevent her from opening a closed door. If she does she is a snoop, and Mrs. Housewife could relieve her tension by quietly being very angry with Mrs. J. Otherwise, Mrs. Housewife will enjoy the visit and fit in the bedmaking sometime before the children are home for lunch. If, in spite of an honest use of her time, the beds are not made, Mrs. Housewife will not be too severe with herself, because reality made it impossible for her to accomplish all the tasks she had outlined for the morning. Mrs. Housewife's ego has functioned well.

However the ego does not always function this well. It may break down when the situation is too frustrating—either because of excessive demands or because of too limited acceptable ways to express the insistent internal impulses. Mrs. Housewife's ego may break on this hectic morning if a little additional strain is placed upon her—if, when Mrs. Housewife tries to call Mrs. B., the line is repeatedly busy; if when she goes to put the clothes to soak she discovers that her son has used up all the soap flakes for a Halloween prank; or if Mrs. J. arrives before the dishes are done, or sees by chance the disheveled bedroom. About that time Mrs. Housewife may have the impulse to smash all the dishes and throw them in the garbage pail. This her conscience forbids, and her ego bows, apparently, to the demands of conscience. However, Mrs. Housewife may find that in the process of washing the dishes, she drops them, nicks them against the faucet and stacks those that remain whole without adequately drying them. An impulse, unacceptable in its primitive form to the conscience and as a consequence forbidden a direct outlet by the ego, has found a way to sneak under the fence and get into the park anyway.

Whether or not Mrs. Housewife answers her problem by dropping dishes, she may feel harassed, tense and angry at everything—an anger which she could turn on Mrs. J. or any thing or person who happens along, either in reality or in fantasy. She may come to an apparently irrelevant conclusion. She may decide she is sick and tired of picking up her husband's socks and would like to divorce him. The years of happy marriage they have had are as nothing compared to the dirty socks on the bedroom floor. Were he home at the time, he would be completely baffled as to why she should become "hysterical" and reveal previously unknown feelings. His whole concept of their marriage might collapse. He might not understand that it is not the marriage which has collapsed but his wife's ego, unable satisfactorily to deal with the situations pressing upon it.

A breakdown of the ego is not unique to Mrs. Housewife. Mr. Businessman experiences the same phenomenon. He awakes in the morning to be told by his wife that she was up too late the night before to get up and fix his breakfast —it won't hurt him to eat on the way to town. He shaves cheerfully even though his razor is dull and he has forgotten to buy new blades. As he rides the train to town he finds the stock market has dropped. This is a little alarming but he assures himself that after all the sun is bright, and stock markets have dropped before. He then remembers that he has a rather difficult letter to write as soon as he reaches the office. As he drinks a cup of coffee at the corner drugstore, he mulls over the wisest way to write the letter. He formulates it pretty well—if he can only dictate it as soon as he gets in.

When he reaches his office he finds that his secretary has not yet arrived. On his desk is a note from his superior suggesting that there is an urgent matter to discuss, which he had thought of minor significance. He wishes his boss didn't nag quite so much. Finally his secretary comes in and after her usual attempts to improve her appearance, sits down to take dictation. He wishes that she wouldn't chew gum in the office. Sometime he must point this out tactfully to her. This morning, however, the letter must be written. He starts to dictate. An idea that he thought he had formulated very smoothly seems hard to express. As he is trying to think of the word, his secretary snaps her gum. With it snaps his ego. He may show it by angrily attacking her for her gum chewing, for her lateness, for all her sins of omission and commission since she first came to his office. This attack may be so severe that she bursts into tears and deprives him, at least temporarily, of anyone to take down the letter.

Moreover, it is not only the secretary who suffers. He thinks over the morning and his resentment mounts over his wife's failure to get up. Why should he live with a woman who doesn't love him enough to fix his breakfast? The stock market is crashing. His family values him only for the lovely home he has built for them; that will dissolve with the stock market. He will be left without love. His superior is an impossible person to work for. This brings the grim possibility that maybe his superior recognizes that the work is not being done right, that he himself is a failure and his superior knows it. At that point a married daughter calls him, saying that she is to be in town that day to shop; she'd love to see him and have lunch. Usually such an invitation would have made the whole day perfect. Today he tells her that she shouldn't expect him always to be at her beck and call. After all he has work to do. He won't have lunch with her. She faces the possibility that the father to whom she has always felt so close, whom she could always count on, whom she thought loved her dearly, who found real gratification in her maturity, her marriage and her children, really has no true affection for her.

Fortunately for the survival of interpersonal relationships, most of us recognize that this breakdown of the ego is a common phenomenon. Thus the husband of the housewife recognizes that his wife is fed up with housework. He decides he had better take her out to a movie to cheer her up. The daughter knows that her father must be worried about something because this behavior isn't like him. Mothers often say to a child, "Daddy is tired tonight and feels irritable. Why don't you go out instead of playing your game here in the house. Outside you can make all the noise you want." The mother is only saying in common-sense language what the professional person says in the ominous-sounding phrase "an impending breakdown of the ego."

A temporary breakdown of the ego is not only reserved for adults. It is equally an experience and privilege of children. A child who ordinarily is a happy, responsive youngster may awake cross one morning and meet every experience of the day with tears, whining or irritability. He will be demanding and uncooperative. He too, like the housewife and businessman, has found his internal and/or his external world too much for him. Perhaps the proverbial backbreaking straw is physical illness or fatigue. Perhaps just too many impulses have demanded expression or too many frustrating experiences have existed. The child's ego is not up to the task of adaptation. Unfortunately a child with an overtaxed ego also overtaxes parental egos. Too often parents, as a result, are unable to say the counterpart of "Daddy is tired tonight." Irritability or punishment by the parents further taxes the child's ego. Only night and the child's retreat to sleep break the vicious circle established by the exhaustion of the ego of both child and parents. Parents, with a sigh, thank heaven that Johnny, who had been so trying all day, is asleep. The child, if he were more articulate, might counter with a comment on how trying the parents had been all day.

Many transient disturbances in children are no more significant than the businessman's irritation at his adoring and adored daughter or the housewife's dish-dropping. The child, like the adult, has had to adjust to too many situations at once. But he may also be adjusting to new demands caused by his development rather than to familiar ones, and his equipment to deal with multiple demands is less adequate than that of a mature adult.

10 : *How does the ego grow*

CHILDHOOD IS, IN GENERAL, A PERIOD OF GROWTH. ONE OF the significant developments during this period is in ego strength. As suggested in the previous chapter, the origin of the ego is controversial. It may be an inherent part of the psyche, becoming recognizable when the functioning of the sensory organs and of the intellect—with the accompanying capacity to think and be aware of the external world—reach a degree of effectiveness. Some authorities believe it becomes a specialized part of the psyche at this point, implying that it grows out of the impact of developmental aspects upon one another.

Regardless of its origin, its role in psychological functioning is reflected in behavior after the first few months of life. If a hungry baby stops crying when he sees his bottle approaching, his ego is functioning. The strength of the ego determines how much and how effectively the internal impulses, the demands of the conscience and the pressures of reality can be integrated. During childhood especially, the capacity of the ego to deal with multiple demands increases—this is part of the process of maturation. The goal for child care can be stated in terms of ego development. The end result parents seek for their child is an ego strong enough to adapt effectively in adulthood. No child has an adult ego—too many adults have egos no more adequate than that of a small child.

A prescription indicating a daily dosage for the promotion of ego growth would simplify the entire problem of helping children reach psychological adulthood successfully. There is no way at the present to write such a prescription. There are certain conditions that foster healthy maturation, others that frequently inhibit it. None of those conditions can be described in any but annoyingly general terms. It cannot be dogmatically stated that those experiences that are often disadvantageous are always so. At times what in theory might have a negative effect may appear actually to have had a positive one. At other times the best-laid plans fail to bring the anticipated positive results.

An adult, for example, may have had childhood experiences that would appear overwhelmingly negative. He may have lived chronically at an economic level near starvation. Paralleling his physical hardship, he may have had alcoholic parents, a broken home, a social environment of delinquency and immorality. Such a background would justify any picture of either social or psychological maladjustment. Yet his adjustment to his total life situation may for all practical purposes be excellent. He may appear not only to have avoided the possible bad effects of his past but actually to have benefited from it. In contrast, biographical data on some maladjusted people portray a childhood that does not clearly indicate why they failed to achieve healthy adulthood. Because no one has a childhood free of difficult situations, some causative factors can always be found. The question arises as to whether they are sufficient to explain the later picture.

The material gleaned from these latter biographies has led to undue anxiety on the part of parents and others dealing with children. A spectacular crime is committed by a man from a "good" family. There is speculation as to why this man committed such an asocial act. Studies of his background reveal a domineering mother and an ineffectual father, though to their friends these parents were "nice" people.

Other parents then are apt to take stock of themselves. Is there a parallel configuration to which their child is exposed? Confusion is compounded when the next publicized crime is committed by a man whose mother was too gentle, his father too aggressive!

The interaction of emotional elements is not as clear as is the interaction of chemical elements. Hydrogen and oxygen under defined conditions always combine to produce a predictable volume of water and it is possible to express what happens in a formula. The interaction of two emotions is not so predictable. This is true in part because the emotions are not sufficiently understood to isolate the *elements* comparable to the chemical *elements* of oxygen and hydrogen. Furthermore, conditions paralleling an uncontaminated chemical experiment are not, at least at present, feasible. Therefore an emotional formula of reaction falls far short of the scientific requirements for an adequate chemical formula.

Many biographical sketches of successful and unsuccessful people justify some skepticism concerning what we can predict of child development. On the other hand, the fact that everything is not known does not warrant an assumption that nothing is known. In spite of gaps in knowledge concerning the factors leading to ego growth or ego crippling, certain generalizations appear to be valid. Understanding the pattern of ego growth and the constructive and destructive circumstances that usually affect it is one approach to the problem of personality development.

It appears that the ultimate strength of the ego is dependent either upon certain inherent potentialities or is determined very early in life. It has been suggested that it may be influenced by intra-uterine experiences* and by the process of birth. Whatever the consideration given to these other factors, few students of personality development fail to emphasize the significance of the first few months of life to ego development. Further, the entire childhood experience—with

* Not that sitting on a strawberry will cause a birthmark.

its increasing number of internal impulses, its greater exposure to, and increased ability to deal with reality—affects the development of the ego. The child's interpersonal relationships with his family and later with those people at its immediate perimeter are of great significance in determining what the ultimate ego strength will be.

Ego growth is related to the growth of the other aspects of the physical and psychological person. Reality has to be known before it can be mastered. It cannot be known until it can be seen, heard, and experienced, and not then until there is the intellect to identify it and evaluate it. The development of vision and hearing in the infant and of an intellect to perceive what it sees and hears, and the development of a capacity to comprehend other bodily sensations— all contribute to the growing ego. Organized body mobility and the ability to communicate verbally offer further stimulation and nourishment to the ego, as well as increasing the demands on it. The capacity to store away experiences as memories and to recall them in new situations, a function of the intellect, increases the effectiveness of the ego. The ability to reason, to bring into synthesis experiences, observations and feelings not spontaneously in focus, help the ego deal more adequately with the pressures to which it is exposed. These factors are all important to the orderly growth process leading toward adaptation.

The effective functioning of the sensory organs, the development of purposeful mobility and speech and intellectual ability are part of the normal growth of the individual. But they form only one facet, even though a significant one, in the growth of the ego. They would be meaningless unless there were reality to see, to hear, to think about and to move in. Vision would be nothing to an individual brought up in total darkness. For sensory organs to possess ego value, they must be stimulated. Ego growth thus is dependent not only upon certain tools the individual possesses but also upon their use. It is nurtured both by stimulation from internal impulses and by real experiences. The neurophysiological growth of the child is of particular value if that growth is utilized by exposing the child to external stimulation at a level compatible with it. Even though he has adequate vision and intellect, a child does not learn to recognize a person unless he has contact with that person. A child will not develop an ability to handle the uneasiness a stranger creates if he never sees a stranger!

11 : *Security in love and ego growth*

THE INDIVIDUAL WHO EXPERIENCES REAL SECURITY IN HIS INTER-
personal relationships is more likely to attain optimum ego
growth than an individual who does not. Security is important—this concept has become axiomatic in our political, economical and philosophical thinking. Security allays anxiety,
and permits the energy otherwise exhausted by anxiety to be
directed toward solving the tension-producing problems. If,
to reach a destination, it is necessary to cross a frozen river,
fear that the ice may be too thin to support weight creates
tension and hampers muscle function. Assurance that the ice
is solid enables the crossing to be made with comfortable
coordination of the muscles. Insecurity about the ice decreases the efficiency of muscle-response patterns; security increases it. This familiar experience has its counterpart in all
the psychological ice-crossings that are required to reach
adulthood. In an environment offering security, the child's
capacity to meet and constructively adjust to the multiple
demands placed upon him is maintained most efficiently.

A sense of insecurity is primarily emotional, not intellectual. To be understood it must be divided into two broad
categories. Insecurity may be the result of an actual threatening life situation. In contrast, it may be rooted in early
and deeply imbedded uncertainty an otherwise diffuse sense
of uneasiness, to which the unpredictability of the external
world is only a point of focus. A sense of security or insecur-

ity experienced by three individuals may have quite contrasting causations. One man may feel insecure in his job because he *is* insecure. His employer may be about to reduce the number of employees. As the last man hired, the employee's sense of insecurity is rational and has its origin in a reality situation. On the other hand, another man may feel insecure in his position for deep-rooted emotional reasons for which the real situation offers no justification. A third man may be actually in a situation resembling that of the first, in real danger of losing his job. Until this possibility had arisen, he was comfortable. The threat of losing his job touches off a chain of reactions far beyond that required by reality. Each man will react differently to the situation.

The first man will be stimulated to explore other possibilities of work, will see if his money can tide him over a period of unemployment, and will consider other resources available to him. He will deal constructively with the reality as long as his belief in his own talents remains intact. Only when this overall secure feeling is destroyed will panic paralyze him. The second man will be unable to meet his uneasiness rationally because an all-encompassing security is not a part of his emotional pattern. He is "an emotionally insecure" person, in contrast to the first man. The third man, faced, like the first, with the loss of his job, will react as the second, revealing that his basic insecurity was only hidden by a thin veneer as long as the reality offered safety.

An intellectual evaluation is effective if the security or the insecurity is related to the actual situation. Realistic insecurity stimulates a rational solution to the problem if one is possible. On the other hand, primary emotional insecurity is only transiently relieved by intellectual concepts or reassurances. The roots of such insecurity lie in the internal psychological structure of the individual. The reality only brings it into the open. Frequently in adults it can be observed that as long as reality offers security, the deeper feeling of insecurity remains in abeyance. When things go wrong, the insecurity that results is a product, both of reality and of the underlying unease that had previously remained relatively dormant.

A prominent society woman had an acute anxiety attack, when, at the beginning of the war, her chauffeur was drafted. At no time in her life had she ridden on a streetcar, train, bus or taxi. She had never driven a car. Her anxiety aroused little sympathy from those around her—she was just one of the "pampered rich." It was really not that simple. Her parents had been too busy to bother with her and had delegated their role to a series of nursemaids and, later, to private schools. No one in her past had given her a consistent, durable relationship. She could not recall a single nurse, teacher, cook or chauffeur whom she could describe as a person or associate with some happy or painful experience. In her childhood, security lay only in material comforts. Chauffeurs changed, but a chauffeur was always there. In spite of the absence of any security other than that which money bought, she was able, up to the time her chauffeur was drafted, to have an essential sense of safety. The loss of a chauffeur, who could not be replaced because of the man shortage, completely destroyed this security. It left her exposed to panic. A real but superficial fear became the fuse that caused a deeper, primary anxiety to explode. Her ego, deprived of an essential support, could not master the situation.

While this is an extreme example of an event activating a deeper, more diffuse anxiety, it is a rather universal experience. Most people respond to uneasy situations with a feeling of impending danger that is not entirely justified. So common is this response that a person who is too optimistic, too confident of himself during unusual times is considered unrealistic by his friends. If his optimism in time proves correct, his friends decide he is just lucky. In most cases they are probably right, since his optimism may have been an effective technique for denying the existence of fears that, had he become aware of them, might have overwhelmed him. It is questionable whether any one knows complete security. The practical consideration is the degree of basic security the individual has attained, a security established primarily through his emotional experiences in childhood. If this has been adequate, his ego has had a valuable growth stimulus.

The difference between actual and neurotic insecurity and the fusion of the two in anxiety-producing situations is seen in children. One child may have experienced many physical changes in his environment, may live under circumstances of real material deprivation and still may feel fundamentally secure. Another child may have lived in a materially stable, even luxurious environment but acts as a frightened, uneasy youngster terrified by undefined dangers. A third child may appear to feel safe and free of anxiety in familiar surroundings only to manifest overwhelming fear when shifted from that environment to another.

In children as in adults, a rational explanation relieves rational fear—if the child has confidence in the explainer and if he can intellectually grasp the explanation. An intellectual evaluation of a seemingly frightening situation is helpful only when it can be comprehended. Telling a twenty-month-old child that his mother will be back right away will often enable the child to stand a brief separation, if the child's past experience has indicated that the mother does return in a short span of time. To tell him that she will return in two days is beyond his intellectual grasp. He will feel safe then only if he can turn to another source of security [to replace that which he has gained through his confidence in his mother].

Too often parents fail to account for this limitation. They go on vacation, leaving a small child, whom they think to be "secure," with an efficient, responsible but aloof person. On their return they find their child uneasy in his environment. They assume they have failed to provide earlier experiences that would have given the child a more solidly secure feeling. Maybe they have only failed to recognize that the child is not yet old enough to tolerate such a long separation without an adequate substitute parent. He cannot yet call upon his fantasy life to fill the gap and the coldly efficient nurse, though she provided actual physical safety, did not play that role. The parents felt secure on their vacation because they trusted her, but she failed to give the child that which the parents usually provided. He could not value her reliability and, with confidence, hibernate emotionally until the vacation was over. An older child, basically secure, could.

The failure of reassurance to overcome anxiety is seen in the reaction of certain children (and many adults) to thunderstorms. Lightning comes out of nowhere, followed by the ominous roll of thunder. There is mystery involved. Lightning and thunder can be explained in simple, non-anxiety-producing terms, and thus the anxiety is sometimes allayed. Some children (and adults) will persist in being frightened at a thunderstorm. Yet they will watch a display of fireworks as brilliant, as sudden and as noisy as any thunderstorm, without fear! Fear of a thunderstorm is usually only in small part rational; most of it is deeper than thought can touch.

In some situations the uncalmed fear of the child is a result of a persistent anxiety in the adult. Children are extremely sensitive—they can detect the true feeling underlying the acting of even some extremely talented adults. The surface calmness of a frightened adult is not always convincing; the child responds to the real feeling underneath. This was graphically demonstrated in an observation of a three-year-old child. He appeared to enjoy thunderstorms until one day he shared the experience with a grandmother who had always been frightened by storms. Wishing to protect the child from a similar anxiety, she talked, seemingly calmly, of the light and the noise, apparently sharing the child's pleasure. Very abruptly the child showed extreme anxiety. Subsequent storms brought only tearful clinging to some adult. Only after the grandmother left did the child return to his former acceptance of thunderstorms. Actually this response is not unique with children. Anxiety is contagious. Adults frequently respond to underlying anxiety and feel uneasy because another person is uneasy. Children are just more astute in recognizing the hidden feeling of others. Anxiety so aroused does not indicate that the child feels unloved. It is in part derived from past experiences where fear was created by the anxiety of an adult.

It is repeatedly pointed out that a loved child is a secure child, implying that if a child feels *really* loved, he will never experience any but rational fear. But whether a fear is rational or not must be judged from the child's point of view, not the adult's. Parents many times count too readily on the elasticity of the child's sense of security. They employ a strange baby-sitter and protect themselves from the child's protests by having him asleep before the sitter arrives. They assure themselves that it is all right to leave the child asleep. If he does awaken later, it won't matter because he makes up quickly to strangers. The girl is reliable, likes children and knows the important telephone numbers. They forget that the child may not look at the situation in quite as reassuring a way. He may wake up and, uneasy about the dark, call for a parent. A stranger appears. While strangers may be nice people if nothing is expected of them, what assurance has a child that they are as effective as parents in an unhappy situation? The telephone numbers have no meaning to him. The child is not asking for the doctor, the fire department, the police or to have his parents know he is awake. He wants comfort and wants it from someone he knows, not someone who arrives from the unknown. At that point he is not necessarily manifesting a fundamental insecurity when he cries lustily for his parents. His response, within the framework of early childhood, is rational.

When a frightening episode leads to behavior indicating fear far beyond the actual event, the child's response is easier to understand than when the source of anxiety is more ob-

scure. Oftentimes then its roots are related to the interaction of the child with meaningful adults, particularly parents. The parents are confused; they know they love the
child, with a love that could not be destroyed by any behavior. If the child is so sensitive to the anxious feeling of
an adult, why is he not sensitive equally to the all-pervasive
love of the parent? To a large extent he is, but not always
completely so.

Perhaps this response on the part of the child can be understood and empathized with if it is compared to similar
responses in adults. At the present time adults face daily the
anxiety that comes from the unpredictableness of world
events. This unpredictableness destroys the security felt in
the past. There is a reality situation that is fear-arousing. Because of the possibility of actual physical danger in the
future, precautionary steps are being taken, but they are not
allaying the mass anxiety as much as one might anticipate.

The insecurity of the present is not only a response to
actuality. What the additional factors are will vary according
to the individuals involved, but there does appear to be one
common denominator. Everyone is aware of the conflicting
ideologies in the world. The battle between these conflicting
ideologies implies many dangers. There is the danger of being injured as a result of hating as well as being hated by
others; there is no assurance of loving those of opposing
ideology and no assurance of safety in loving them. The
very uncertainty as to what and where the danger is and
where it lurks is frightening. Where is real safety, a safety
symbolized by much more than food and shelter? Where
lies freedom, freedom with safety? Where lie beliefs that
are not only satisfying to the individual but acceptable
even though not held by others? Where lies the ability to be
one's self—to be loved or safely disapproved of by others? All
these dangers revolve around interpersonal relationships.

Anxiety is not decreased when the individual with an alien
point of view assures that he will not attack. Past experi-

ences seem to justify suspicion. An earlier confidence in the reliability of interpersonal relationships has been destroyed by a series of significant episodes. As a result, a mass anxiety has developed, relating not only to manifest dangers but to ill-defined hidden ones. There is an uneasiness with former friends as well as with known enemies. Because suspicion about some people has proven to be justified, there is an uneasy distrust of all who do not share accepted points of view. This combination of rational and irrational fear makes it much more difficult to achieve a world in which people feel safe. Rational fear can be met by rational plans. Irrational aspects of anxiety paralyze.*

Similarly the child may have experiences with an adult that cause him to suspect that adult's motivation. These experiences are by no means always avoidable. A small child wants to smear his feces on the new wallpaper. The parents say he can't, and say so with a great deal of disapproval. It is obvious to the adults that the child must learn to respect the prohibition. Perhaps to the child this prohibition reveals the parent-wolves hiding underneath sheep clothing. His suspicion of parents may spread far beyond the actual episode. He in turn may have all the unanswered questions of the insecure adult. Interestingly enough, the parents' own security with the child may be undermined at this point. Does the child love the parent if he reacts as he does? Has a loving baby turned into a hostile, attacking two-year-old? A temporary loss of faith in each other may occur. The insecurity of the child with the parent, the parent with the child, nurtures the anxiety of both.

It is not unusual for a child, in spite of theoretically ideal situations, to have phases of ill-defined anxiety resulting from the temporary collapse of his own belief in his emotional security. As he grows up, he has to master many situa-

---

* Only the future will reveal how much of the current fear is justified and how much is not. In the meantime, we will probably continue to treat it as real.

tions that have frightening possibilities. His ego cannot deal with those situations with maximum effectiveness if he is unable to find relief from his fear. If he is secure in his world in general, he will deal most effectively with a specific uncertainty. Under such circumstances interpersonal relationships have a great deal of significance. If he feels secure about those relationships he knows that his world is not just made up of fantastic or real dangers. It is also inhabited by stable predictable people. They will show him that some situations that appear dangerous are safe and that real dangers can be avoided. He will accept their guidance because he knows from experience that they are trustworthy. This is not a lesson he can learn once and never forget. He learns it only after repeated proofs.

A child learns to trust or mistrust his world and those who people it through his relationship with his parents. Always telling the truth is not enough. Just because a parent debunks the Santa Claus myth does not establish the child's trust. Verbally assuring the child that he is safe and loved, and that the world is not a completely bad place does not convince him of the invalidity of his fears. The child's trust or lack of it stems from the reliability or unpredictableness of the interpersonal relationship with his parents. Parents determine to a large extent the nature of this relationship. It is an emotional, not an intellectual, experience.

The most valued component for promoting security and ego growth is the love the child feels emanating from his parents. He first experiences it in his first few months of life, in his complete dependency on his mother or mother substitute for physical comfort and safety. As he grows out of physical dependency the nature of the love changes somewhat. His needs are then met not only by what others give to him but also by what he can achieve by himself. Being loved no longer is represented only by being fed and kept warm—it becomes more intangible, more diffused into other areas of living. It can be gratified by more people. Assurance

lies in the father's love, the love of other relatives and finally
in the less intense love from beyond the family orbit. As he
passes from infancy to childhood, he will enter into and
value the less personal contacts of the world beyond the
family if his first experiences in interpersonal relationships
with his parents have inspired confidence. From his confidence in the love, first of his parents and ultimately of those
outside the family, comes emotional security that not only
sustains but increases the capacity of the ego to deal with the
multiple demands for adaptation that press upon it.

12 : *The child's ego and his reality*

THE GROWTH OF THE EGO IS NOT ONLY FOSTERED OR CRIPPLED
by the child's security in relation to other significant people.
It is also affected by his success in meeting the demands of a
real world. Mastery of a situation results in self-confidence,
which in turn encourages the individual to meet other challenges. This is evident in many physical attainments. Until
one learns to swim, deep water is dangerous. With the mastery of swimming comes self-confidence, and the danger
fades. Having gained the ability to suspend the body in
water, the individual is ready to try the intricacies of diving.
The steps in psychological mastery are not always as traceable as in the techniques of swimming. Much of psychological growth goes on as if behind closed doors. But as each step
in maturation is successfully integrated into his expanding
relationship to his world, the child develops increased confidence in his own ability to face new situations.

There is a corollary to the story of successful mastery. If a
child is pressed to tackle steps in development before he is
ready, his confidence in himself will be in jeopardy. He may
by great effort succeed but only with painful anxiety. Such
frightening efforts carry an implication that subsequent
paths will be equally difficult and might even prove to be too
much. Perhaps those paths should be avoided if possible.
Pressed too hard for adaptation, the ego attempts to avoid
the increased demand. The child in observation appears to

remain immature, fearful of taking the steps ahead that would seem compatible with his age. They are much more terrifying to him than they should be.

This is no unique concept having bearing only on the subtleties of child psychology. To return to the example of swimming—an individual learns to swim in the protective surroundings of a tank. Later, while rowing on rough water one hundred feet from shore, his boat capsizes. Mobilizing all his swimming capacity, he battles waves and distance to reach shore. If he has met the situation adequately, he will have increased confidence in his ability to swim. If however, he nearly loses the struggle and achieves the shore exhausted, he may fear water and hesitate to place himself in jeopardy again. He may prefer to avoid a boat until he can swim better. He may overestimate the dangers of a boat on a calm day.

When a situation is beyond the child's ability, his lost confidence does not remain limited always to the particular experience, but often results in graver doubts of his capacities. Parents may press a child for a level of behavior that is beyond him. As a result of the failure, the child cannot believe in himself. He cannot judge the implied or expressed expectations of his parents, and realize that they have made a mistake. He only knows that he is unable to live up to their demands. His parents may have expected him to catch a ball before he had the muscular coordination to handle the complexities of that maneuver. They may have timed wrong his separation from home, believing he could deal with the problems of nursery school before he was ready to take that step. The child experienced defeat on each occasion because he did not have the tools for success. Later, when he actually has the skill to catch the ball, or the internal resources to face separation from the family, he may remain fearful of trying because of his earlier failure.

At times, it is not so much that a new experience *per se* places too great pressure upon the child—it may be well within the child's adaptive capacity—but in addition to other demands still only precariously mastered, it proves too much. Often under such circumstances the child (and adult) not only fails the newest test, but also loses control of previously mastered challenges. Acute examples of this were illustrated in the previous stories of the harassed housewife and the businessman with the gum-snapping secretary. Both could have mastered many aspects of the situations they faced. Given an additional problem with which they could not deal, the total structure collapsed. A child may have learned to comply with the demands of toilet-training. He also may have adjusted to the baby-sitter who arrived for the parents' evening out. But it is the week before Christmas. The anticipation, the endlessness of the days and nights until the great event, are beyond the philosophical scope of the child. He becomes unpredictable. He may wet the bed. He may be upset and fearful over the parents leaving. It is nothing that won't be cured by the arrival of Christmas, unless parental irritation weakens the essential ego props that parents had formerly provided. If Christmas were always a week off, the resolution of the difficulty would not be so spontaneous.

Both the general capacity for adaptation as well as the ability to answer the immediate demands are fostered when an individual faces one problem at a time. The businessman faced with a serious problem at work will handle it more effectively and with greater ease if he is not also struggling with a sick wife or child at home. How often adults say they wish to deal with one thing at a time! It is simply a question of utilizing available energy on one problem or splitting it among two or more problems. The fewer major strains an individual is under at a time, the more effectively will his ego deal with each one.

It is easier to learn any subject if all attention is focused on it. No wise student would try to study algebra and American history by alternately reading a line in the history book and a line in the algebra book. It is easier to learn a more advanced subject after the basic knowledge is mastered. If the essential data of a subject is in a foreign language, it is easier to learn the subject if the language becomes familiar.

The same conditions affect the child's success in dealing with the increasing adaptive requirements that psychological, physiological and social maturation impose upon him. He will more easily handle the complexities of adjustment to the requirement that he control his excretory function if at the same time he does not have to become familiar with a new nursemaid. He isn't then reading a line at a time in unrelated textbooks. Furthermore he will integrate this new demand to be toilet trained more readily if he has already achieved in his interpersonal relationships a comfortable awareness of himself* as a person differentiated from the rest of the world, and is convinced that he has emotional security. He will know the language before he attempts to learn the subject.

A nine-year-old child may present a picture of poor social adjustment based upon a general feeling of insecurity. This insecurity may have its roots in ungratified dependency needs. The child will achieve social adjustment with his own age group with more facility if he can first experience the gratification of which he was deprived in infancy. In this way he will learn the language before he attempts to know the subject matter. Social adjustment will also come easier if he is not required at the same time to expend unusual energy in maintaining contact with an irascible teacher.

The mastery of each step in psychological maturation involves a modification or extension of the adaptive pattern of the individual. It is more readily attained if other strains are minimal. The child can then utilize most of his psychic energy in meeting the immediate challenge without having to divert some of it to another purpose.

* See page 44.

The child learns to deal with reality by experiencing it. His ultimate adulthood will be in a real, not a fairy, world. He will feel secure in that world if he has, throughout childhood, gained familiarity with it. Even though the known may have alarming aspects, it is the anticipation of the unknown that is more sinisterly frightening. On the other hand, experience should be dosed if possible to the child's capacity to integrate it into his limited field of knowledge. A small child, for example, often feels that darkness represents desertion by the parents. Such a child may find it difficult to overcome his fear of the dark if the parents leave him alone to face the darkness, an action which to him equals desertion. Thus reality to the child may be, by adult standards, distortion.* Only gradually can the child, as a result of experiences, correct the distortions that stem inevitably from his inability to comprehend the total reality.

An interesting example of a child's distortion of reality comes from the analysis of an adult patient. Her father had died when she was two-and-a-half years old. She had a surprisingly vivid memory of his death and funeral. In adult life the death of a meaningful person aroused normal grief plus an incomprehensible conviction that another important person would also die. It finally became clear that she believed her father's death was accompanied by the death of someone else, significant to her father but also very important to her. The mystery of the second person was solved when she learned through relatives that her mother had suffered a severe depression after the father's death and for two years had ignored the small child. As far as the child was concerned, two people had died. Death to her, even as an adult, meant the disappearance of two emotionally essential persons from her world.

While some parents fail to understand how a child interprets reality, others, in their zeal, expose them to over-

* Night terrors, page 295.

whelming doses of it. They encourage the child to accept
their way of life long before the child can really grasp its
meaning. They will refuse a small child a ten-cent-store present with the excuse that they can't afford it, rationalizing
that it will teach him that he can't spend ten thousand dol-
lars for a yacht just because he happens to want one. The
child may not learn this lesson, but he may know enough
about money to conclude that ten cents spent unwisely will
destroy the family's financial security. An adult told the author in the course of treatment that, in spite of a palatial
home and a large staff of servants, she often worried in her
childhood about what she would do when all the comforts
would disappear. Her parents had answered most of her re-
quests for inconsequential things with the statement that
they couldn't afford them. Only in adulthood did she discover that not only were her parents wealthy but had, as a
source of income, one of the stablest industries in the country.

If the parent wishes to curb the child's insistence upon
buying something every time he enters a store, it is preferable to have the child face the fact that he cannot have every
whim gratified, even by loving parents. A wisely planned
allowance later in childhood will teach the more abstract
concepts of economics.

Some parents use harsher methods for facing the small
child with reality. They deliberately expose him to the dark
side of life before he is sufficiently familiar with the more
pleasant side. They subject him to discussions of catastro-
phes before he is able to realize that such occurrences are
not daily. They frighten him with gruesome stories of what
happens when certain acts are committed before he is capable of grasping possible consequences in proportion. They
tell him when he is three that the policeman will take him to
jail if he picks up a piece of fruit in the grocery store, and
then wonder why he fears policemen instead of recognizing

them as protectors. In their zeal to teach a child what life is, they plant ideas that will most likely cause a distorted growth. A child cannot grasp certain facts of life until he has a capacity for abstract evaluations that will place those facts in their proper niche in the whole.

On the other hand, some parents overprotect the child from reality. This overprotection can also lead to a variety of repercussions in later development. Reality remains unknown. When ultimately it has to be faced in full force, it can easily be overwhelming. A child who is never scolded for misbehavior at home will find it difficult to adjust to the reprimands inevitable at school! An individual raised on Mackinac Island, where no cars exist, would have a difficult time adjusting to the demands for adaptation if he suddenly had to cross Broadway in New York! The ego needs an opportunity to learn gradually.

The ego may fail to deal constructively with a situation because as a result of either overprotection (or indifference), the child lacks a knowledge that he could have grasped if it had been available to him. The author knew personally of a tragic example of this. A father, in his enthusiasm for what at that time was modern psychology, resolved that his small daughter would grow up without fear. The child was protected from dangers; she was never made aware they existed. When the child was five years old, she climbed to precarious heights on a building under construction. The roof of the building was a partially supported skylight. Fearless because of an unawareness of danger, she walked onto the skylight and fell to her death. This was a failure of the ego not because of its inherent inadequacy, but because of the lack of an opportunity to learn. The ego had failed to govern an internal impulse because of an unawareness of reality.

While this is a dramatically obvious failure of the parents to prepare a child for reality, subtly parallel situations have resulted from some of the modern theories of child care. Because frustration of primitive impulses, when excessive, has proven to have undesirable repercussions on personality development, it has been suggested that all frustration is dangerous. But the child in expanding his world beyond the frame of the family faces situations that are inevitably frustrating, and unmodifiable. If he has not already learned how to deal constructively with frustration, he cannot handle reality any more than could that child who walked onto the skylight.

Similarly, some have felt that because excessive guilt and a too-rigid conscience have resulted in a breakdown of the ego, guilt should be avoided at any price. But the absence of guilt in a child suggests the absence of any conscience to control behavior. Adults *should* feel guilty if they have an impulse to kill someone. Children *should* feel guilty if they violate some requirement of behavior *which they are able to meet.* If a child does not feel guilt he has not only failed to adjust to his world, but has done so because he possesses no internal awareness of what is required for adjustment. He transgresses not through maliciousness, but because no inner voice tells him he shouldn't. He hasn't had the necessary learning experience that would help him adjust to reality. It is only disproportionate guilt and excessive frustration that create later difficulties.

Overprotective parents create another situation crippling to ego growth. Overprotection may imply to the child that reality is so dangerous his parents know he cannot cope with it. If a child, for example, is never left alone, it may indicate that being alone is to face situations that only a powerful adult can handle. The child is too frightened to evaluate what the real dangers are. He only knows they must be there or the parents would not have sheltered him. The extreme protectiveness of the parent results in a distortion of reality in the child's mind. If an adult always protects a child from a dog, the child sees all dogs as dangerous animals. A child can learn, under the guidance of an adult, how to judge and handle dogs—neither always to avoid them any more than to play promiscuously with them. He needs his reality in graduated doses, but he needs the doses. As he assimilates the doses his adaptive capacity expands.

13 : *The child's ego and his parents*

A CHILD DOES NEED TO HAVE REASONABLE PROTECTION PRO-vided by parents, a protection geared to those adjustment tasks the child must handle that are beyond the limits of his own ego, or for which it does not yet have the essential tools. Thus any year-old child on the edge of a skylight might have the impulse to walk across it. He has developed the skill of walking but has not yet the inherent capacity to know that glass is fragile, that it might break and result in a catastrophic fall. The ego would not repress the impulse because the child has not acquired sufficient maturity to comprehend the nature of glass and to grasp the danger involved in stepping upon it. It is time for the parents to act as a substitute for the ego!

The ego gradually gains strength as the need for the strength arises in the life situation. As a child learns to walk, he does not immediately develop a skill that makes it possible for him to walk to town. He toddles around the house, walking outside only with the support and reassurance of an older person. He cannot grasp the danger of crossing a street; but for the most part, he does not have the motor skills or capacity to travel that far. If he does, the external environment protects him by wise supervision or a decoratively placed fence. Without conscious thought, parents often recognize when the child has the tools with which to handle the dangers of the street—when he has the ability to see, the abstract concept of danger, and the judgment to avoid danger as he carries out the impulse to cross the street. Nature in general (but not to be trusted specifically) provides that a skill will not develop until the capacity to handle it also develops. This obviously is true only if one includes in the concept the idea that nature also provides parents who will protect the child until the use of those tools is refined. Some parents unfortunately fail to recognize that they are an integral part of this growth process. They expect the child to show judgment, use memory, and think abstractly, long before those tools have developed.

A child also needs the assurance that adults will carry part of the responsibility for his behavior. Given freedom beyond his ability to govern himself, a child can be very frightened. He may show this insecurity by impulsive, reckless behavior that would seem to indicate fearlessness but that actually is a denial of fear. He may, on the other hand, disclose his insecurity by complete inhibition of his own actions. In each instance his ego is not functioning with its full potential. A brilliant boy very clearly expressed his reaction to a totally permissive environment. He was severely inhibited, as if he feared always that any spontaneous act on his part would prove catastrophic. His parents were convinced members of the cult of unlimited self-expression for children, without any adult direction. The child's therapist, after many unproductive hours with the child, finally commented with non-professional exasperation that the boy's behavior didn't make sense. He could do anything he wanted to, and yet he never let himself do anything. "Can't you see why?" he immediately replied. "Never have my parents said this is the right way, that is the wrong way, this is safe, that is dangerous. I haven't lived long enough to know what is right and what is wrong, what is safe and what is dangerous. I'm afraid of what I might do." An environment that defined wise limits for the child brought about a rapid liberation from his self-imposed imprisonment.

He was right. Children do not have the living experience to know what is dangerous and what is safe. Furthermore, they have many contradictory impulses that they can't reconcile. They need guidance in finding safe satisfactions for internal urges and safe responses to external stimulations. Only after long experience can they even begin to direct their own behavior wisely. If expected to do so too early, they may be in real danger, and may fear other dangers that actually do not exist. A child needs freedom in order to mature healthily. To avoid the dangers of license, he needs that freedom within limits that can be defined only by the sophistication and judgment of adults.

This concept of a framework for children, realistically applied, results in what appears to be a contradiction. As the child develops a capacity to handle his own impulses not only is he given more freedom but greater demands are placed upon him by those around him. Consider the problem of a child who has strong aggressive impulses that he as yet does not know how to handle. At the same time he has poor table manners. Inability to handle aggressive impulses in a socially and personally constructive way can have serious repercussions. Table manners are of secondary importance to this more primary conflict. If the child is frightened by his own impulses, he needs the assurance of wise restriction upon their expression. He may also need guidance in order to channel his aggression constructively. Provided with such a framework, he gains confidence and suitable patterns for expressing his aggressiveness within it. During this period ideally the question of table manners is ignored. Every effort is concentrated on helping him feel more comfortable with his aggressive drives. Prohibitions and permissions are defined and controlled by someone outside of himself. Finally he develops ways of expressing his aggressiveness satisfactory both to himself and to his social world. No longer is he dependent upon the restrictions imposed by others; he has mastered those restrictions himself. At this point he is ready for the struggle to attain table manners.

There are certain fundamental urges that a child first learns to handle. As he struggles to find a pattern for them, adult-imposed limits serve as a guide. When more basic urges are mastered, the child can tackle the finer points of social living. Through the flexibility of the framework established by adults, the more primitive fundamental urges are first directed into constructive outlets; then, and only then, are the secondary aspects of social living brought into the total growth picture. This does not mean, to take table manners as an example, that the child should not be encouraged to use a knife and fork until he has directed his aggressive impulses into adult channels. It means rather that such secondary adjustments are most wisely taught during periods when the child's primary adaptive patterns are adequate to deal with the demands reality places upon him.

As the child becomes familiar with his external world, his adaptation to it will be more adequate if he finds suitable ways of expressing impulses, which, in undirected form, are contradictory or unacceptable. To the extent that he can find gratifying channels of expression for his impulses, the child will be psychologically healthier. He will be freer of anxiety, will have more emotional energy. He will develop more completely his total psychological potential if he does not have to hold in check part of it because in its unmodified form it is destructive rather than constructive.

To translate this concept from theory to actuality, consider the phenomenon of competition in sports. From the struggle for achievement, whether in work or play, comes competition. This urge undoubtedly originates in early childhood, in the child's need to be loved and in his aggressive rivalry with others who seek love from the same sources. This creates conflict. The child may fear the loss of love as a result of his aggressive behavior, a love that he may wish from his rival as well as from the one for whom they are competing. He may divert his aggression toward the one who loves the rival as well as toward the rival, but such an attack would jeopardize his chances of winning the love he wishes most. How he handles this early conflict will determine to a large extent his handling of other competitive situations. It may be reflected later in destructive competitiveness with others, where the desire to be loved is abandoned in order to gratify the desire to attack the rival. It may express itself in fear of any competition with an accompanying resignation to defeat. Neither answer shows optimum ego functioning. Yet a solution can be found in which neither the individual's relationship to the external world is destroyed nor his internal need suppressed.

An example of the many significant competitive situations occurring both in childhood and adulthood is competitive sports, in which the urge to achieve and to express oneself aggressively results in the reward of love and recognition. The reward may come from spectators, if one is actually a participant, or from a sense of oneness with the other loyal spectators, and from an identification with the team. The individual who is able to identify with the goal of a game or with a real achievement shared by others in his field of interest and work has found a channel for expressing competitive urges in a socially desirable way. He has avoided the dangerous choice between being socially destructive or suppressing a normal impulse and thus partially destroying himself. He has found a constructive pattern of adaptation.

Parents have an important role in assisting the child in his slow progress toward directing the expression of his impulses constructively. Helping the child's developing capacity to channelize his impulses is an important aspect of discipline and is discussed in more detail in the chapter on that subject. Suffice it to point out here that the most constructive discipline—though it is not always within human grasp—is that which makes possible the expression of an impulse originally unacceptable but now valued in its sublimated form. The alternative to suppression of an impulse is not necessarily license; it can be wise redirection.

Success is inherently rewarding to many people, but the gratification is enhanced if there is also a sense of appreciation from others, especially from parents. This is equally true of a difficult task of ego integration. When a child successfully masters a struggle between an internal impulse and the demands of reality, he undoubtedly experiences some satisfaction and the ego is strengthened. If, however, in addition to this inherent reward, he gets an appreciative response from those he loves and from whom he wishes love, the success will be much more gratifying. Unintentionally, parents often deprive the child of this stimulus to ego growth. Once a child has mastered a step in development, the parent is apt to behave as if this were unimportant or to be taken for granted. Yet any failure to continue the pattern will result in disapproval and, seemingly, withdrawal of love. One child illustrated this on a superficial level rather interestingly. He had been quite resistant to learning to dress himself, though it was obvious that his motor skills were sufficient. One day in his mother's absence, he rose from his nap and dressed himself, much to the maid's surprise. She praised him for this and commented how pleased his mother would be. His answer was, "Please don't tell her. She'll always make me dress myself then, and I like to have her dress me sometimes." In other words, the achievement would mean that he would be forever deprived of a pleasure. It was safer not to have achieved it.

This situation presents a real dilemma to a parent, a dilemma which they can perhaps answer best by their own intuitive feelings. The child needs praise when he makes a more mature adjustment. He also needs the incentive that comes from the parents' expecting him to continue that maturity. A wise disapproval of failure to maintain gains is an important help in solidifying those that have been made.

Lack of such approval may imply to the child that the parents, though they showed appreciation for the progress, really did not value it particularly because they didn't care when it broke down. On the other hand, disapproval at a time when the child actually is too pressed to maintain the step ahead that he has taken may delay recovery from the ego fatigue he is manifesting.

To say that one should never allow a child to manifest more immature behavior could result in overwhelming burdens for him. To say, on the other hand, that a child should always be allowed to revert to more immature levels would be equally unwise. The intuitive judgment of the parents is often the important basis for handling a particular situation. It will be valid if the parents themselves are mature individuals, capable of parental love for their child. It will also be enriched if a knowledge of signs of ego inadequacy in the child becomes a part of their intuitive response.*

A "CHILD-REARING EGO" FOR PARENTS

It would be reassuring if we had a psychological thermometer to indicate when a child is ready to master more complex steps in development. Then it would be possible to stimulate him with challenges comfortably within his capacity. He would always experience success and thus gain confidence; he would never be defeated and become prey to crippling self-depreciation. In such a Utopia, carefully controlled experience would lead to a realization of his own limits. The impossible would be more tolerable and a sense of failure avoided by not undertaking the task too difficult to complete. Such a dream is at present only imperfectly translatable into real life situations.

It is impossible to maintain a parent-child relationship that can preserve the child's sense of security intact at all times. To begin with, parents are human. Their own prob-

* See Chapter 15.

lems periodically exhaust their emotional energy. Under such circumstances the child is temporarily deserted. He is not secure in his environment. His fear is justified. The child cannot discourse learnedly to himself about the meaning of his parents' ego exhaustion and the fact that it needs only time to convalesce. Lacking this therapeutic capacity, he may react in a way that temporarily provides poor nutrition for his own growing ego. He may return to more immature behavior, or assert his own adequacy. Either way he may adopt methods that break through the parental withdrawal. This reassures him that the parents react to him and can be aware he is present, but it may make him pretty difficult to live with. His ego is getting the only kind of nourishment available.

The child cannot always recognize the parents' justification in making certain demands upon him, demands which he might be able, but does not wish, to meet. A child of nine is obviously capable of brushing his teeth. He doesn't want to. Parents insist. The combination of a toothbrush, parents, and the threatened recourse to the dentist seems too much to bear. It is not surprising if at this point he doubts the love of his parents and is frightened by his doubts as well as his own anger. Even the dentist's dire threats augment his fear. The fact remains that in spite of all the reasons for brushing his teeth *he doesn't want to*. An internal impulse is not in harmony with reality. The outcome of the battle is for a time in doubt. The ego has not yet found the terms of a satisfactory truce. It is uneasy as to whether it should acknowledge defeat or accept the responsibility of victory.

A child who has had implicit faith in the love of his parents may be left unexpectedly by them at a time when the separation proves frightening. The child feels deserted and unprotected. The experience may appear to invalidate all his previous lessons; he feels unloved. Assuring the child of the parents' love will do little to allay the anxiety that has been aroused. He has temporarily lost confidence in those people without whom he cannot feel safe. The parents, on the other hand, may have quite valid reasons for leaving that the child is not able to grasp. Security will return only as repeated experiences reconfirm the parental love he thought had evaporated.

It is impossible to estimate accurately at all times the individual child's readiness to undertake a new level of adaptation. Some children will be sent to nursery school too early, some will be kept from demands they can easily meet. It is not always possible to tell definitely when a child is dealing with a major problem for which he should ideally have available most of his psychic energy. Only in theory can an individual be sure of having only one major demand made upon him at a time. The businessman often does face a problem in his office at a time his wife is ill. The child may be struggling with the problem of toilet training just at the time his mother deserts him to go to the hospital—and on her return she may confront him with the additional problem of a new sibling. If this combination of events is avoided, others more uncontrollable may occur. While the advent of a new baby can be predicted, hospitalization for acute appendicitis cannot.

Even when events are predictable, difficulties arise. Toilet training could be delayed until after the mother comes home, thereby lessening the pressure upon the older child for the time being, but the new baby will continue to create difficulty and the older child has to be toilet trained sometime. Limiting families to one offspring to avoid the problems created by the new arrival is not the answer. Aside from being disastrous to the race, it would be disadvantageous to children. There are real learning experiences inherent in the sibling situation, for both the older and younger child, that are difficult to duplicate elsewhere.

There is a "child-rearing ego" needed also. To be meaningful, theories must be adaptable to reality. One source of confidence is the natural resiliency of the ego structure of the individual. The recuperative ability of children following a damaging emotional experience is extremely reassuring. It is surprising and gratifying to observe the corrective effect of a positive experience occurring after a child has been subjected to repeatedly damaging ones. It is as if the child's ego filters out any nourishment that may be present in a mixture, even one which is, at best, non-nutrient and at worst, poisonous. This explains why severely disturbed children can often be helped toward a healthy adulthood and why basically well-adjusted children recuperate so rapidly.

Ego-resiliency is particularly significant in meeting the day-by-day pressures to which the average child is exposed. The recuperative capacity is determined to a large extent by the nature of the emotional interplay between the child and others in his environment. If the interplay results in basic emotional security, the individual will utilize his inherent capacities with optimum efficiency. It is as if his psychic energy were drawn from the emotional environment. For example, the experience of the small child mastering toilet training at the time he must also meet his mother's temporary desertion and the subsequent arrival of a sibling is not necessarily a catastrophic one. It may be quite the contrary. Though the experience is seemingly shattering, the ego can be reconstructed and in the process actually gain additional strength.* Unable to deal with the problems involved in toilet-training, maternal desertion and the new sibling, the child may revert to more infantile ways; or he may become tense, angry or tearful. If this behavior is met with support from his parents, he will gradually integrate the additional problem into his total adjustment and in addition gain new confidence in his family relationships. He will believe anew that the world is a kindly place and that he can ultimately master its complexity. The advent of a sibling

* Ego failure should not be encouraged with the aim of gaining this additional strength. Certain children are better physically after a tonsillectomy even though the effect of the diseased tonsils had not appeared too marked. This does not suggest, however, that every child should have a tonsillectomy.

is not unnatural. It is a normal life event having many counterparts which will be faced more easily if, given time, the child finds a positive way to deal with a younger (or perchance older) brother or sister.

On occasion, parents have to leave a child without any opportunity to prepare him or themselves for the separation. Such a threat to a child's security cannot always be avoided. But every reasonable effort can be made to minimize the effect. If, for example, a known person with whom the child has had a happy experience is available to substitute for the parents, that person is preferable to a stranger. There is no need to create extra burdens for the child to handle; life itself provides enough. If, however, there is no satisfactory person, a stranger may have to do. Negative repercussions from this episode should be recognized but not given a disproportionate significance. The child who has previously been secure will be so again if subsequent experiences are adequate enough to erase the effect of the damaging one. If those experiences are not provided, the child may persist in clinging to the lesson that one episode appeared to teach.

If a child loses confidence in himself or his emotional environment, he is frightened, thus increasing his problem. His fear can most readily be quieted if someone he can depend on is available. He is not then dependent solely upon himself. If he is basically secure in his interpersonal relationships he will be able to turn to others. Older children (and adults) may turn to other children or adults, who thereby act as symbols of parental support. A younger child will more readily and urgently seek support in actual parent figures.

Every child at times seems to lose the maturity he has obtained, reverting to infantile dependency upon parents or parent symbols. In such an event it can be assumed that something has been too overwhelming for him. What that something is is not always clear. The child himself may not be aware of its nature. His need is apparent—to find safety again in a protective relationship. If he can refurbish himself by a temporary return to the primary source of security, he will with renewed confidence be on his way to maturation again.

A little child often acts out very graphically this impulse to return to the parent. Busy away from the mother, he comes running to her periodically, just to see her, kiss her or make some unimportant comment. He then returns to play. It is as if his own internal security had become depleted, to be replenished by this momentary return to the mother's physical person.

The action of a very small child in seeking contact with parents is often a pleasant experience for the parents. A comparable pattern of behavior in an older child may at times prove quite irritating. The older child may want his father to get his bicycle out of the basement when he can easily do it himself. He may want his mother to abandon her work to help him with some simple task he can handle alone. He may only wish her to look at something he has done in the workshop, asking this favor when she is busily washing dishes or cooking dinner. It is often difficult to evaluate these episodes. Is the child just trying to avoid the expenditure of energy involved in taking out his bicycle, or is he really using these ill-defined ways to get support from his parents? In the latter event he is wisely trying to gain needed nourishment to strengthen an overtaxed ego.

At times theories of child care have seemed to suggest that all children should be reared in an emotional hothouse, protected from the changeable weather, the storms and the calms, of reality. This emotional climate no more prepares the child for real living than a horticultural hothouse prepares a flower for outdoor growth. Some plants in certain geographical areas have to be raised in hothouses because they are being required to survive in an alien environment. Some need only be started in hothouses to become acclimated gradually to the new surroundings. In selected cases such special care may be indicated for a particular child. A mentally retarded child, for example, may require a permanent hothouse environment; or a short period in one with gradual exposure to less protected surroundings. Another, buffeted by unavoidable or avoidable bad weather, may need a period in a "hothouse" to regain his psychological strength. The average child, however, is similar to a plant that can survive occasional adversity. Allowed to avail himself of the protective methods of psychological preservation, he will, like the plant, bow down temporarily, to straighten up again and resume the process of growing. Recuperation is assisted not only if the temporary return to less adequate adjustment mechanisms is tolerated but also if the child is allowed time to recover. One mother, disturbed by her three-year-old child's wish to be held and rocked at the time a new baby arrived, nevertheless agreed to the suggestion, apparently accepting his temporary need, to return to an infantile state. The child obviously enjoyed the experience. But when he asked again, she refused. Her explanation to the pediatrician was that after all the child must have seen how silly it was; that should have cured him. Obviously it only further frustrated him. Having gained the impression that his mother would meet his needs, he then saw that reassurance destroyed.

It often takes considerable time for a child to recover from a disturbance. Not until he shows evidence of improvement should the extra protection be withdrawn. No doctor withdraws the drugs that combat pneumonia just because the patient doesn't recover completely overnight. If there is evidence that the drug is effective, the doctor continues its use until the child is well. Psychological pneumonia needs to be treated with the same consistent long-term view. It may last longer than the physical type. With understanding help from his environment, the child will recover.

The analogy with pneumonia is appropriate in another way. While the doctor will continue the medication *until* the patient is well, he will not continue the medication *after* recovery. Much of the psychiatric knowledge concerning childhood development has been gained through the study of the sick child or sick adult. It is important that the well child not be given the medicine meant for a specific illness. He requires the foods essential for growth, not the drugs effective in illness.

It cannot be reiterated too often that, for psychological growth, certain emotional nutrients are needed. These nutrients are given in different forms as the child matures. Consider another parallel. An infant can utilize liquid foods best; later he benefits from semifluid food, puréed vegetables and meat; finally he needs solid food. In periods of illness, just as he may require specific drugs that are useless and even harmful to a well child, he may also again require fluid nourishment. This does not imply that liquid foods would be better for him when well. So it is with psychological health. When the child is emotionally ill (and most often the illness is just a psychological cold),* he has needs different from those he has when well. A psychologically well child should no more be accorded the treatment due a psychologically sick child than a physically well child should be treated as a sick one. However, no child should be starved for essential psychological nutrition just because he is well. Rather the nutrition should be given in a form compatible both with his health and his level of maturity.

It is not the particular overwhelming experience alone that leaves a serious mark upon the average child's development. The permanent damage is done under two general conditions. First of all, if unfortunate experiences are chronic for the child—if every step in development is not integrated into the child's total adjustment pattern either because it is too great a step and/or if he repeatedly cannot

---

* Often parents can diagnose a cold. Other times parents are uneasy and call in a physician to make the diagnosis and outline the treatment. Professional advice should also be sought when the child's psychological illness does not respond to the treatment effective for the ordinary psychological cold.

find support in meaningful people—a permanent scar is left. Secondly when some particular crisis arises so overwhelming that he cannot effectively make it a part of his total picture, and if there is an absence of emotional support from his environment, the same scarring may occur. Either experience can be permanently destructive.

That demands upon a child that are chronically beyond him may prove permanently crippling to the developing ego is frequently expressed in common parlance. If an adult who has failed to adjust satisfactorily is known to have had a difficult childhood, it will often be said that he did not have a chance considering what he was up against as a small child. The translation into psychological language is that his ego was permanently crippled by excessive demands placed upon him during the formative years. His only pattern for survival then was through tools that reveal his maladjustment to the adult world. Often the significant void in his childhood was one of real emotional deprivation. He did not know the basic security that comes from true parental care in infancy. An adult having had this experience may show it in many ways. He may remain essentially arrested at an infantile level. Superficially he may make a noise like an adult, but underneath lives an ungratified infant striving, many times unpleasantly, to be a dependent child, always anticipating, actually receiving, and often interpreting experiences as rebuffs.* Or he may deny his wish to receive emotionally from others. As a result he loves no one. He lives only to meet his own needs, without guilt over his harmful effect on others. A constructively dynamic adjustment to reality is beyond him. His behavior, his demands and his responses to frustrating situations are not correlated with the long-term actuality.

The childhood history of an adult may reveal that during early infancy he was emotionally secure. Later, as certain problems arose, the quest for support from the parents was

---

* In defense of children, it should be pointed out that they are rarely as unpleasant as a childish, immature adult.

either ignored or more frequently met with hostile refusal. Without such support, his psychological growth was hampered. The immediate effect on the ego structure was paralysis. Certain tools that had formerly handled difficulties effectively became meaningless. The individual could be compared to a carpenter who had, through long years of apprenticeship, learned to handle construction tools and build a house—and who then suffered a progressive neurological disease that ultimately destroyed his ability to use his arms. As a result he cannot use his skills or his tools to build a house. A child may experience a similar ego paralysis.

In an attempt to find some way to survive in spite of his handicap, the child may select a variety of solutions, some of which resemble those used by the individual who never experienced emotional gratification. He may struggle endlessly to attain the security he wants by infantile behavior, trying always to find a support the parents withheld. As an adult his infantile character will persist. He may on the other hand decide that parental relationships have nothing to offer. Struggling with a wish to be loved that cannot be gratified, and unwilling to tolerate the frustration longer, he may abandon the desire and alienate himself from meaningful interpersonal relationships with the family, repressing all emotional response except unmitigated rage. The abandonment of positive relationships and the persistent angry frustration this incurs may characterize his response to people throughout life. His limited adaptation to the external world will be maintained only as long as he can ignore the rights of others. Investing all his energy to gain his own ends, he will run roughshod over all interference and have no feeling for others except hatred.

To avoid the dissatisfactions inherent in these solutions— either remaining infantile or denying the meaning of others —he may, if he has sufficient ego strength, mobilize his defenses, but so intensely and rigidly that flexibility is impossible. Such an adjustment can be maintained only by the expenditure of most of his psychic energy. He adapts to his internal needs and the external reality not by integrating the two but by attempting an ineffectual compromise—a neurosis. Failing even through the neurosis to find a minimum pattern of psychological adaptation, he may give up. A psychotic breakdown occurs. Adaptation to reality has become impossible.

There are two sides to the "ego" of child rearing. Certain disturbing experiences are inevitable for the maturing child. Corrective measures are often required to erase their effect. The child rearing program, vested in parents, needs also to have an adaptive capacity. The child's ego can tolerate inadequacies (within limits) in the parental ego and in the experiences offered by reality. It is equally important that the ego of the parents have an ability to adapt to what are, under the circumstances, the justified demands of the child.

14 : *The ego ideal and the superego*

GRADUALLY, DURING THE FIRST YEARS OF LIFE, THE CHILD HAS formulated a concept of the sort of person he wants to be. This is his *ego ideal*. It will be modified with further experiences, but its nucleus is fairly well established in early life. It starts as an acceptance of the ideals parents show for the child, in their expectations, prohibitions and permissions. These define the type of child to whom parents give the love and security so important to him. Once he learns these parentally-expected standards, the child accepts them as his own. Conscious recall ceases to be necessary—they become in part unconscious and direct behavior automatically. With greater opportunities for activity, with increased parental expectations, prohibitions and permissions, the structure of the ego ideal becomes more comprehensive, progressively evaluating an increasing number of impulses.

At the time of the resolution of the Oedipal conflict, the ego ideal undergoes one of its psychologically most important changes. At that time, even though the process had begun earlier, the ego ideal is sharply defined according to the sex of the child. The little boy forms an image of the kind of man he wants to be. The little girl draws a mental picture of the kind of woman she wants to be. The little boy may say he wants to be Superman, or an engineer on a Diesel train. These are beings that embody all that is masculine, that seem to have all power and courage. They will make it safe to be a man. The little girl may project into the future a plan to be a nurse, a teacher, or a mother. The daughter of a professional woman expressed the wish to be a maid, because maids stayed home with the children! The little girl sees herself most frequently in the role of caring for people, an expression of the feminine propensity to be maternal.

If a child does not live up to a standard of behavior required by the parents, he fears punishment. As has been indicated earlier, the punishment anticipated is not necessarily physical. The greater anxiety is aroused over the loss of the parental love. The child's imagined consequence of a disapproved act may not be the actual parental concept of suitable punishment. The child, using as criterion his own response to the acts of others, assumes the loss of love or a catastrophic attack. He protects himself from such fearful punishment by defining and living up to his ego ideal.

A small child may express his disapproval of himself verbally, and illustrate, in so doing, how parental ideals are becoming his own. About to touch some prohibited object he may comment that "Joey must not touch," an imitation of the parental prohibition now self-imposed because his impulse is not in accordance with the vaguely-forming ego ideal.

Since this identification with the parents insures him of some protection from anxiety, he takes a further step. He incorporates not only the parents' standards of behavior but also their punitive role. He develops a *superego*—in other words, a conscience. Violation of the superego standards brings self-punishment. This self-inflicted punishment and the anxiety over it are fused in the feeling of guilt that results when internalized standards are violated.

The intermediate steps leading to the crystallization of the superego are sometimes clear in actual behavior. A child whose hands have been slapped to prevent him from touching a forbidden object will be seen slapping his own hands to check an impulsive gesture toward the object. A mother

told of finding her three-year-old son, looking very repentant, standing in a corner. This had been one of her favorite
methods of discipline. When she asked the child why he was
standing there he replied that he had been a bad boy, he
had broken a toy. The story was particularly interesting because the child had never been punished for breaking his
toys. The disapproval of the act was self-formulated and the
punishment self-inflicted.

The superego and the ego ideal function to a large extent
unconsciously, but their requirements are readily brought to
awareness when challenged. Failure in achieving behavior
compatible with the ego ideal results in a sense of shame.
Violation of superego standards brings with it guilt. Most
unacceptable behavior in the older child or adult cannot be
categorized as violating one or the other, since the superego's
criteria of behavior are based upon those concepts that make
up the composite picture of the ego ideal. But there are certain areas of the ego ideal that are not normally incorporated
into the superego. An individual, to cite a simple example,
aspires to be president of a bank. That is his ego ideal. He
remains a cashier. He may feel ashamed because he has not
achieved the goal he had outlined for himself. But he will
not feel guilt because he does not see his failure as an act
meriting punishment. It is an indication of his own inadequacy, a blow to his pride, but not a violation of his concept
of proper behavior.

Guilt and shame are important components of a personality. They have positive value in promoting the individual's
automatic adaptation to society and the integration of his
own internal impulses to each other and to reality. On the
other hand, a too rigid superego, a too demanding ego ideal
prevent wise adaptation and full expression of the individual's potential.

Theoretically, shame could be absent from the armor of
the individual without jeopardizing his adjustment either to
his internal impulses or external reality. The child could

structure an ego ideal just at the limits of his capacity. If he received well-timed rewards, he would always strive to attain and never be defeated, though never without challenge. Parents who could instill such an ego ideal and reward progress toward it so wisely would have to have a psychological Geiger counter of extreme sensitivity. Such parents do not exist. Even if a child or an adult can eventually attain a goal he has defined for himself, he will periodically lag in his progress toward it. Feeling shame at not continuing a pace warranted by his ability acts as a stimulus to renewed effort. The reward is the relief from shame and the pleasure resulting from living up to his ideal. If the goal is so easily reached that lagging has no effect on the ultimate outcome, the child may be free of the burden of shame but will not enjoy as rich a life as he could have had. If, on the other hand, the goal is inherently beyond him, his psychological energy may be exhausted by the shame resulting from his failure and he cannot take advantage of the satisfactions available to him. The parental role is, then, to help the child find a reasonably stimulating ego ideal.

The ego ideal is not primarily related to the material aspects of life. It has an equally important function in interpersonal relationships. Impossible goals in this realm are more difficult to define. The child may have had inculcated early the concept that the ideal person is never angry. He therefore feels ashamed if he is ever angry. On the other hand, he may have an ideal for himself that puts no curb on anger and he responds to any situation with uncontrolled wrath. Neither of these ego ideals is serviceable in a social world. The first puts an unnecessary burden on the individual which, if not carried adequately, arouses excessive shame. Actually in this situation the individual's superego would also be punitive and his burden increased by guilt. The second is too destructive to his interpersonal relationships and deprives both his social environment and himself of mutual satisfaction.

As with shame, so theoretically could an individual be reared free of guilt. He could be in an environment which offered no stimulation for other than desirable behavior. The recommendation to parents that they place their Ming statue out of their infant's reach could be carried to the point where every thing or situation beyond the child's comprehension would be out of his conscious orbit. Gradually the equivalents of the Ming statue would be brought to view, as the child could deal with them. Never would he face punishment from parent figures. He would absorb parental standards as a *modus operandi* with no incorporated concept of punishment. In practice it can't be done. It might not work anyway. The superego not only increases the ego's tasks, it also aids the ego by setting up signals warning when previously proven behavior patterns are being violated. The ego does not have to decide every issue on the spot.

Shame and guilt cause destructive strain upon the ego when they are excessive. They may then become the agents of either an overly rigid adaptive pattern or the neuroses and psychoses. On the other hand, if guilt is absent the character disorders manifested are chiefly those of asocial behavior. The absence of shame may be evidenced in either asocial behavior or a failure to strive for a goal that is within the individual's capacity. A desirable and realistic end result of child development is the shaping of an ego ideal and superego flexible enough to permit adaptation to growing capacities and changing environments but with a basic composition clearly outlined and inviolate—the kind of ego ideal and superego that would cause a person to be ashamed and guilty if he stole a diamond ring from a jewelry counter, but that would permit him to pick up an apple under a tree on the roadside without being uncomfortable.

Because the ego ideal and superego are to such a large extent an incorporation of parental ideals, demands and punishments, parents have a crucial role in their ultimate form. If parents demand more than is consistent with the child's maturity, they may encourage the child to adopt standards that are equally beyond his ability. His constant shame at his failure will result in an unhappy loss of confidence in himself. Parents can foster the development of an overly rigid and punitive superego; if they punish excessively any misstep so will the child punish himself excessively as he begins to assume the role of self-disciplinarian. Just as the overly punished child may fear any free activity, so likewise will he unnecessarily curb himself as he becomes his own disciplinarian. The ego ideal and superego form before the child reaches the level of maturity at which he can tell justified from unjustified demands. Consequently, earlier pressure is not easily erased.

A child may react quite differently to excessive parental controls and punishment. He may decide the price he has to pay in terms of the renunciation of his own wishes isn't worth the reward of love. These children do not then adopt the parental concepts into an ego ideal or superego. The only behavior that has meaning is that which gratifies their own impulses. The desire to be loved by others or to love is repressed.

This effect of excessive punishment is seen in stark clarity in the type of delinquent child who appears indifferent to disapproval or punishment. A cursorily obtained history gives the clue. His parents have probably shown little response to him, except that for misbehavior he has received inhuman beatings. Unrewarded by evidence of being loved in any case, he has abandoned his search for what appears unattainable. Beatings, though severe, eventually end, and can, with growing skill, be avoided. Their discomfort does not overbalance the pleasure of carrying out in unmodified form a momentary impulse. Not more punishment but a remobilization of the desire for love will salvage the child for social living. It is a long-term job to undertake, with many disappointments and often only microscopic evidence of success along the way.

In contrast to the problems caused by excessive demands, different ones arise if the parents do not impose justified demands within the child's capacity. The child then has no criterion by which to judge his own behavior and thus no clear ideal for himself. He may flounder about, picking up one idea to abandon it for another, but never finding the answer that is right for him. He may be unable to form either an ego ideal or a superego. Every impulse is acted out irrespective of its effect upon him or others. Or, instead of this freedom from restraint, there may be a quite different development. In spite of the parents' permissiveness, the child inevitably is faced with the clash between his impulses and the repercussions from the world. He may attempt to structure his ego ideal and superego by the categorical black and white, right and wrong, that is so characteristic of the young child. As a result, his ego ideal and superego will take on a rigidity that paralyzes the ego.

The individual's ego ideal and superego are not only the result of standards imposed and rewards and punishments meted out by the parents; they are also the result of imitation of the parents. As the child strives to find behavior that will assist in his adaptation, he incorporates the parents' methods. He imitates them. The parent who says "Do as I say, not as I do" is whistling in the dark. To abide by that admonition requires the child to discard the flesh-and-blood parents for an abstraction. Granted a parent cannot be a saint—can a child be one either? Parents who do not live up to the standards they impose upon the child confuse the youngster. A parent who extolls the virtues of honesty as he flaunts his own dishonesties can expect the child to accept the idea of honesty only at the price of rejecting the parent. Every parent at times confuses the child in this way. Father explains pontifically to his thirteen-year-old (who is small enough to pass for eleven) that though the price of admission to a movie jumps when a person is twelve, he should be honest about his age. At dinner father explains in detail to his wife how, by not clearing up a misunderstanding in a business deal, he made an extra profit. If Honest John, his son, questions whether that was quite fair, father responds, "That's not my problem." A child will eventually clarify the chaos such contradictions create for him. Whether he will clarify it constructively depends in part on how frequently the parents demand standards they refuse for themselves.

When the superego of the parent is seriously inadequate, the child, especially if he has meaningful emotional ties to the parents, is apt to accept what the parent does as his ultimate superego. Incompatibility between what parents say and what they do, as well as apparent or subtle corruptibility on their part, can lead to the development of what is justly termed a "corruptible superego." The individual seems to have desirable standards of behavior but either finds ways to circumvent those standards or to avoid punishment for their violation. For example, there was a girl of ten who stole anything she happened to want. She verbally disapproved of stealing but showed little guilt about her behavior. Why her particular conflicts expressed themselves in an apparent superego defect was explained by a remark of her father's. He stated that when she misbehaved, he would try to correct her but could never carry it out. She would look so cute, so repentant, so helpless, that he just had to hug her. Her superego reacted the same way and was as impotent to control her as her father was. A corrupt superego may say, like parents, "Do as I say, not as I do." The individual may again ignore such feeble hypocrisy.

There is another important way in which the ego ideal incorporates the parental image. The parents' attitude toward themselves will affect the biological role the child defines for himself for the opposite sex, and his idea of the relationship between the two. To explore all of the implications of this would entail a psycho-sociological study of the roles of man and woman in our culture. Certain possibilities can be listed for further speculation.

If the child is fortunate enough to be born into a family in which the mother and father see each other as mutually complementary—each of equal but different importance as separate entities but also half of a total—his acceptance of his own biological place in life will be easier. In the average family many false notes in this ideal composition can occur. Consider some of the situations that perpetuate the confused relationship between men and women.

The father may be an immaturely aggressive person who, ashamed of his dependent relationship on another person, indicates only contempt for the female sex. The son then, in order to win his father's respect, must deny any tender feelings for his mother. He may even outdo his father in his protest against her, simply because his need is greater. On the other hand, his father's definition of a male may be too frightening. The little boy cannot bring himself to discard his mother. He then turns to the mother for solace and ultimately for his model of behavior. The boy becomes effeminate, not because he did not have a masculine picture to emulate but because what he saw seemed unattainable. There is a possibility that he also recognizes the immaturity behind his father's defense and chooses the more effectively mature person, his mother, after whom to pattern himself.

The daughter, in relation to this type of father, may fear him and assume that all men, no matter what their superficial behavior, are like her father. Men have little to offer her and much that frightens her. She will then plan a future free as possible of men. In contrast, she may love this blustering, thoughtless person. The most effective means she can envision to hold his love is submission. Her concept of a gratifying relationship with a man becomes one in which she tolerates his attack for the crumbs of affection he drops. Out of respect for her father's judgment, she may also evaluate women as he does, as a sex for which he has only contempt. To preserve her own self-respect, she may strive to be like her father and be a masculine character in a woman's body. As still another possibility, she may recognize the little child under her father's veneer and look toward a future in which she mothers men, never accepting them as grown individuals.

A passive, submissive, and ineffectual man has an equal effect upon a son or daughter. Both may accept him as a masculine ideal—the son to emulate, the daughter to use as a yardstick for other men. If their mother, as she so often is in such a marriage, is the dominant, controlling person, they may see the feminine role as the more satisfying. Again, the boy may accept the mother as his model; the girl may consider her mother's behavior true femininity. In contrast, both may believe that the domineering wife is responsible for the husband's weakness. Women then become fearful objects to the boy, questionably desirable models for the girl.

If the father is unhappy in his role as a man, if he feels put upon, an overworked slave to his family, friends and his job, he does not offer much incentive for a son to grow up and become a man. The son may wish to cling to childhood, to avoid the catastrophe of growing up. On the other hand, he may decide that his father's adulthood was wasted. Why not grow up and use adulthood as a time in which to do what you want to do? Marriage, work, obligations can all be avoided. Though the father's complaints are taken seriously, his submission is not accepted as the only way out. Finally, the son may conclude that his father's unhappy fate is man's inevitable biological heritage and, preparing himself for the same life, repeat the adjustment pattern of his father.

How does a mother affect a child's ultimate sexual adjustment? As indicated above, the aggressive, domineering woman may suggest to her son that it is better to be a woman than a man. However, he may see woman as destructive to man and someone with whom to avoid a close relationship.

She may appear as the ultimate protector. Fearful of his competence to meet the pressures of the world as a mere man, the son will seek women who can master the world as effectively as his mother apparently had. A daughter may identify with her mother's aggressiveness and the hostile, destructive attitude toward men that often goes with it. She may fear her mother's power and strive to remain a helpless child, as if to indicate to the mother in this way that she, the daughter, is not a worthy person to attack. She may, out of her disapproval or fear, disclaim any regard for women. She doesn't like her sex as she first came to know it through her mother.

The passive, fearful, submissive mother offers as much confusion for her children. From her behavior her son may conclude that all women are so, and pretty dull as such. Actually he may see his father as the brute, who has intimidated the mother; if this is the masculine role, he has little taste for it. He may be fearful of an adult world in which he would have to carry the burden not only of children but of a wife as well. Perpetual childhood or bachelorhood would seem the only desirable alternatives. The little girl may interpret her mother's behavior also as the effect of the aggressive male. Men then become fearful objects. Or, recognizing her own potential aggressiveness, seeing herself more adequate than a woman like her mother and thus more a man, she may disclaim her ultimate feminine adulthood.

Perhaps the most difficult situation for the little girl to cope with is that revealed if her mother does not accept her own femininity gracefully. If the mother is unhappy as a woman, the little girl in identifying with her has either to reconcile herself to perpetual unhappiness or else fight the world her mother blames for that unhappiness. There is much that makes it difficult in this culture to be a woman and at the same time an individual with rights, privileges, and obligations unique to oneself. It is also difficult for a man to achieve that end. Unfortunately, as each sex pities itself, the other is attacked. The battle of the sexes is an attempt to take from each other instead of using the energy to find oneself. Women, unfortunately, have been more verbal in decrying their fate, and in so doing they have bequeathed their own defeat to their daughters, or have driven them to a pseudo-masculine role in life to avoid being women. Women cannot find true fulfillment as pseudo-men any more than men can find fulfillment in being pseudo-women.

Though it is obvious from the above that the parent of the same sex is the more important model, the significance of the parent of the opposite sex cannot be ignored. The little boy not only wants to be like his father but also, if his mother has an acceptable meaning to him, like a man his mother will love, at least asexually. The little girl wishes to meet her father's implied standards of femininity. In this way the child often tries to improve upon the model the parent of the same sex offers.

This attempt is by no means always negative in effect. In spite of their mutual regard, most husbands and wives can see the possibility of some improvement in their mates. It is only when the mother has a confused picture of what desirable masculinity is, or the father as to femininity, that the child's mirrored confusion may have serious consequences in his character structure.

A further complication arises when either or both parents wanted a boy but got a girl, or vice versa. Usually this unfulfilled wish, after the birth of the child, is more or less forgotten. The child is accepted as an individual. In some instances, either or both parents may unconsciously convey the wish to the child, who attempts to comply by behaving like, even though he cannot change to, the opposite sex. Some parents even consciously try to effect a psychological metamorphosis, though a physical one is impossible. The mother of a male child demands that the boy pretend to be a girl; the father of a female child expects her to act like a boy. The resultant confusion and character distortion are then only secondarily the effect of internal conflicts. The primary conflicts lie within the particular parent involved.

Parents not only determine the child's ideal of himself, but his ideal for others. If the mother's relationship to her son has had any real meaning to him, she becomes the criterion by which other women are judged. The father plays the same role for the girl. This is frequently portrayed in later life when the similarity between a man's wife and his mother, a woman's husband and her father, becomes apparent. Often the conscious reasons for choice are quite the contrary, but with time the resemblances become strikingly obvious. It is a platitude that the most successful marriages are those between two mature individuals. It also appears that the individual whose parents were happily mated, who has successfully shifted the sexual aspects of his love for the parent of the opposite sex to a heterosexual love object, and whose chosen partner resembles the parent of the opposite sex, has the greatest likelihood of being successful in marriage.

15 : *Indications of the effect of ego strain*

MANY UNEXPECTED RESPONSES OF A CHILD TO APPARENTLY IN-
nocuous situations are the result of his inability to deal effectively at the time with the significance the situation has to
him. The situation itself may be only the proverbial straw.
Under ordinary conditions it would have been no burden
but the day, the week, or the month, may have produced too
many straws. The child's reaction appears to be caused by
the last straw, but it is actually the result of all of them. He
is like the housewife whose neighbor made a critical remark
at an inopportune moment or the businessman whose secretary snapped her gum.

Failure of the adaptive capacity of the ego to meet the
tasks at hand can result in a wide variety of behavior and
personality problems. Perhaps the one most familiar to parents is the temper tantrum. It is evidence of a temporary
breakdown of the child's adaptation to the multiple problems he is trying to integrate into a functioning whole.* The
child reacts to his helplessness by an outbreak of rage, accompanied often by bodily expression through tension-
discharging movements that have little real direction even
though they have a supposed aim. Frequently the child attempts to hit someone. By preference it is a person most re-

* See page 300 for discussion of the more practical aspects of the temper
tantrum.

lated to the cause of his anger, but, that person being absent, any available person or inanimate object will do. Even with the target at hand, the child's aim may be surprisingly poor. He is in a state in which neither psychologically nor physically can he integrate his impulses effectively toward a chosen goal.

Adults, even though most of them do not go to the extreme of a temper tantrum, have similar responses to unmastered situations. An adult may feel anger when his ordinarily smooth-running adaptive machine is required to modify its functioning because of some new external or internal strain. If with reasonable effort this strain is integrated into his familiar ways of response, the anger subsides. If, however, he is unable to find an answer and remains in a frustratingly tense state of contradictory desires or unattainable goals, he may respond with blind rage or high blood pressure. Having had more experience in draining off the tension created by unsolvable problems, he may relieve it by effective even though irrelevant behavior—throw his pen down, kick the wastebasket or slam a door. He does not always know why this helps. He just knows he feels better.

Some wives find it hard to understand why the tired businessman rests himself by playing eighteen holes of golf. In his defense it must be said that his fatigue stems not from physical but mental activity. It is in a large part the result of trying to reconcile the irreconcilable, to remain alert to unexpected side attacks and to control the anger aroused by the irritatingly petty or terrifyingly large frustrations he constantly faces. The resulting muscular rigidity as well as psychological tension must be relieved in order to reestablish comfortable, constructive functioning.

The golf game permits a discharge of tension through muscular activity. The businessman has more control of his muscles under stress than does the small child in the wild movements of a temper tantrum. Why, asks the reasonable wife, cannot the same relief be obtained by putting up the storm windows instead of playing golf? It doesn't work that way. Perhaps the golf ball itself is of significance. The man meets twenty men in the course of a week that he'd like to knock down but can't. It is fortunate that a golf ball is available on Saturday morning to take the stored up force of those many inhibited impulses to strike out.

A child's temper tantrum is the result of his failure to find a smoothly functioning way to express internal needs through the tools he has available and in the framework of his world. The tantrum both expresses and discharges his frustration. Often the exhaustion that follows is out of proportion to the degree of activity. There is muscular and physical relaxation; the child may fall asleep if the opportunity presents itself. The child during this sequence of events is like a pressure cooker. With the lid on, steam pressure increases until finally it blows off explosively. When the first force of this steam is discharged the cooker, hissing, subsides to its ordinary functioning.

In contrast to the child who handles frustration by explosion, another may be constantly tense. There seems to be a little leak in the lid, not sufficient to drain off all the pressure, but just enough to keep the greater part of the steam just below the explosion point. This child may be chronically irritable, never completely releasing his rage, but neither being completely free of it as long as the frustration continues. He may actually be harder to live with than the child with temper tantrums, with whom at least there may be peace after the storm. With the less explosive child during a period of disturbance, the storm, though never as forceful, never seems to play itself out.

Adaptive failure is not always by any means manifested through anger or irritability. It may well be evidenced only by sudden signs of anxiety.* The child becomes fearful

* See page 292.

of a familiar environment as he can no longer handle impulses or external forces that, unmanaged, will prove dangerous. He may be unable to handle these impulses because the support he depended upon has been, or appears to have been, withdrawn. Or a new task may have been imposed. He cannot divert energy toward its mastery and have sufficient reserve to continue handling the older tasks. His adaptive pattern has been destroyed. He has lost the path through the woods and is frightened.

In some instances the child, instead of exploding or responding with anxiety, walls himself off from the problems pressing upon him. He withdraws into an inner world which he can shape to his own liking. He denies that the external world exists. At such times a child may appear unhappy, as if his solution is only at the price of something he values. At other times he may appear content, finding in his self-created world enough gratification to compensate for what he has given up. In the latter case parents may be pleased to see the child enjoy himself so completely without being dependent upon others. This complacency should not go unchallenged. That child is fortunate who can find satisfaction in internal living when the situation offers no other gratification. However, if satisfaction is found only in this way and if, as a result, the external world is meaningless, an essential psychological component of existence is atrophying. Only on a deserted island can an individual be psychologically a total person if all his gratification in living is experienced in his own internal world.*

Difficulty in school, if not the result of expectations beyond the child's actual ability, may be an indication of excessive strain upon the child's ego. School requires a great deal of adaptation. The child, even in a present-day school, has to curb many of his impulses. Definite rules of conformity are

* See discussion of meaning of fantasy life to the child, page 306.

imposed, justifiedly so, because the average child can profit by an adaptation to them—at least if he has a school faculty that understands children. A particular child may not be able to accept these restrictions because he is dealing with too many other demands for adjustment. He may then be restless in school, unable to focus attention on his work, indulging in impulsive, distracting behavior that is not consistent with his chronological age.

Instead of overtly difficult behavior, the school child may be unable to learn. The inability may concern one subject, most characteristically reading, or it may be reflected in a lack of progress in all academic subjects. Just because a child has difficulty in learning, however, is no justification for assuming the child has emotional problems. A competent psychologist has tests that will determine with relative adequacy whether the difficulty is due to emotional problems or the child's actual mental endowment. It should be borne in mind that only a competently trained and experienced psychologist can evaluate this. The tests given by the classroom teacher, untrained in the finer points of interpreting psychological tests, will only measure the child's functioning at the time of the test. His current functioning may be commensurate with his potential mental ability; it may be influenced by problems extraneous to school; it may be the result of a situation in the classroom environment.

When the strain upon the ego is chronic and diffuse in nature, its effect is often difficult to determine. The development of the ego has many parallels in the physical development of muscles. If a muscle is not used it becomes weak and flabby. While it has potential strength, lack of use prevents its development. Overuse of a muscle, on the other hand, causes a condition recognized as being "muscle-bound." In such an event the individual has large muscles, suggesting real strength, but he does not use them with the skill expected from such seemingly powerful assets. Strong muscles

develop when used wisely. As they become stronger, increased use increases their strength. So too with the ego potential of an individual. If the child is not given opportunities to use the tools of his ego, they become dull and atro-
phied. If he is required to use them in situations for which
they are not ready, they may become inflexible and poorly
functioning. If, however, the demands placed upon the ego
are stimulating and compatible with its strength, the ego
grows.

The "muscle-bound" ego is a rigid ego. It can meet new
situations only as earlier ones were met. It lacks the flexibility to correct responses on the basis of resources that were
not present when the comparable situation first arose. Mrs.
Housewife, in Chapter 9, may have discovered that generally it is wiser to get her dishes done before she talks to her
friend over the telephone. If she refuses to answer the telephone when it rings, simply because her dishes are not done,
she may have many other problems, but one is a muscle-
bound ego.

Instead of rigidity, chronic overstrain upon the ego may
result either in its complete collapse or in an arrest of its
growth. The first is indicated in adulthood by the development of the psychoses. The individual has lost the battle with
reality and has retreated, not in an orderly fashion, but with
his forces relatively disorganized. He remobilizes them on a
level protected as much as possible from the pressures of the
external world.

While a psychosis may also develop in childhood, it is
relatively rare. In a young child, chronic overstrain more
often causes an arrest in ego development. Thus a child
constantly faced with situations with which he cannot deal
may eventually become an adult with the characteristics
classified under the psychopathic, delinquent, or infantile
personality types. There are many factors contributing to
such personality distortions. The failure to develop may not

have come from an inherent ego defect, or from lack of growth-promoting experiences, but rather because too much strain was placed upon the infantile ego, and the battle lost before it had really started. The strain may have been due to excessive external pressures, internal impulses, or the failure of the environment to meet the individual's emotional needs.

A total collapse is not always permanent. The businessman and the housewife, if each has adequate ego strength, will ordinarily recover effectively after a short period of irritation and tension. The developing ego of the child also has recuperative power. It is chronic overstrain that retards the realization of the potential ego strength of the individual.

In the first section of this work, as the psychological development of the child was traced, it became apparent that there are certain major steps in the maturing process. These steps, while stimulating growth in the ego, also place an additional strain upon it. During periods of major psychological pressure, evidences of exhaustion of the ego are inevitable but do not necessarily signal an approaching ego-catastrophe. At such times as well as during difficult external situations, the child needs support. The more his ego can be flexibly strengthened during nonpressing times, the more adequately will he meet unavoidable stress. The more it is wisely supported during periods of ego strain, the more hardily will it weather the experiences.

16 : *Tools of ego*

TO AVOID THE COMPLETE CHAOS THAT WOULD RESULT FROM AN individual's failure to integrate the demands of his internal impulses, the limitations of reality and the requirements of his own conscience, the ego has certain tools. These tools direct thought, feelings and actions in a way which prevents not only disintegration but also painful or anxiety-arousing experiences. They are referred to as "ego defenses."*

The most effective tool is sublimation. Through sublimation, one or multiple forces pressing upon the individual are directed into channels leading to externally and internally acceptable goals.† There are many examples of sublimation. The individual with strong aggressive drives that, expressed in primitive form, might lead to an attack upon his fellow men with the danger of serious retaliation, becomes a surgeon—thus redirecting the drive in a way rewarding both to the individual and to his milieu. Oil painting is a person-

* The following material does not follow entirely the classical delineation of ego defenses, but rather attempts to describe them in more commonplace terms. They can be reshuffled according to psychoanalytic terminology, but there is so much overlapping of defense mechanisms that it is relatively impossible to describe them as unrelated entities.

† There is an academic question involved here—whether sublimation should be considered a "defense." This is a matter of semantics. Sublimation is certainly an ego tool, and one that effectively defends the total personality against psychological dangers. It does not distort the original impulse to the extent other defenses do.

ally and socially gratifying channelization of the more primitive enjoyment of smearing; when the person who adopts this outlet is also gifted, the result may be a work of art. An unmarried woman with a strong desire to be a mother could answer that urge without sublimating it by kidnapping a child. On the other hand, she may constructively sublimate by becoming an effective teacher. In each instance the particular goal will serve not only the one impulse but many others at the same time. Successful artists, surgeons or teachers find expression for many desires in their work. Multiple impulses have become fused toward a common goal.

Sublimation often functions somewhat as a river does. If all the water in the Mississippi River flowed as a sheet over the land, the same amount of water would reach the Ocean. Or if each present tributary followed a separate course, the same amount of water would still reach the Gulf, but without fulfilling the various functions of the giant Mississippi. The Mississippi River is, for the most part, one of nature's successful achievements of sublimation. Similarly, when the ego can integrate the many forces pressing upon it by efficient channelization, the optimum use of psychological energy is achieved. There are certain limitations to sublimation, comparable to those manifested periodically by the Mississippi bed. Sometimes nature turns too much water into the channel of the Mississippi, and the river overflows with disastrous consequences. Human river beds may fail equally. For example, an eagerness to learn may be a sublimation of many impulses that, in unmodified form, were unacceptable to the ego or/and superego. This psychological river bed may be very effective and constructive until an additional strain descends upon the ego. To clarify the concept, consider what may happen when a child, having directed many impulses into learning, wants companionship with his own age group but cannot immediately find a way of gratifying this desire. Consequently, he channels this impulse also into the established river bed of learning. He comes to live with the characters he reads about instead of with real people. The river bed may then inundate its psychological banks, and destroy other possible effective forms of expression for impulses.

Sublimation may prove ultimately ineffectual for the total personality not because of a flood situation, but because too many impulses are chronically directed toward the same outlet. Engineers could probably, if they set their minds to it, remodel the surface of the American continent so that *all* waters of North America flowed into the Mississippi, with serious consequences. The fertile Mississippi Valley would serve only as a river bed, losing its valuable ability to produce food. Areas now watered by other major rivers would become arid. The continental map of transportation would have to be revised to relieve the congestion of production limited to the area watered by the Mississippi. A human being can also direct too many forces into a single channel. He is described as a "one-sided" personality. His productivity is limited to the psychological equivalent of one river on a large continent. It is said that the individual does not have enough other interests; he should have hobbies, or more social life. The result may be a chronic character handicap or a sudden collapse of the adjustment pattern.

The human race is not imaginative enough to find in every instance ways to express internal impulses through external behavior both satisfying to the individual and acceptable to others. Social adjustment and acceptance are important to most individuals. Because other desires may not be acted out without thwarting the wish to be accepted, they may have to be denied release and finally even entry into the awareness of the individual. Also, certain impulses might result, if expressed, in punishment, or the fear of it. Those impulses, drives and needs that threaten to frustrate other more important ones, or that will possibly result in serious repercussions, may be repressed.

Repression rarely solves a problem efficiently. It does not

serve as an integrative tool, but rather as a means of sidestepping the particular impulse so as to clear the way for the integration of other impulses. Repressed feelings, impulses and goals do not evaporate; they are incarcerated by the ego in a jail hidden in the unconscious. They threaten to escape. The ego stands guard to prevent the jail break. While perhaps functioning adequately as a jailer, the ego may have to use most of its energy* in the role. Little psychic energy is left over for more positive uses. Furthermore, unless the effectiveness of the guard is complete, the possibility of a dangerous prison break is always there. The individual himself may experience an ill-defined anxiety related, without his awareness, to the ever-present threat of the break.

Often the prisoner-impulse is not as dangerous as it is assumed to be. Psychoanalysis has demonstrated to many patients that a jailed impulse, allowed freedom, may prove harmless, or at least capable of being modified so as to live in the "society" from which it was withdrawn. Often the impulse was tried, found guilty and sentenced to life imprisonment at a time when the total personality was unable to utilize it constructively. This more commonly occurs in childhood. The adult still endows the impulse with the same disastrously overwhelming destructiveness it had in childhood.

Repression is not completely destructive even though it is perhaps the most taxing and least efficient ego tool. Impulses and feelings are usually repressed only if they can find no satisfactory outlet at the time. Repression decreases tension at the moment, though ultimately producing chronic tension. The immediate effectiveness of repression is somewhat negated by its continued use long after the need is gone. The handling of early sexual impulses, as discussed ear-

---

* Through this material the term "energy" is used, as if it were a measurable force. Since it has so far not been possible to measure this "force," the term is perhaps ill-advised. It has become a familiar word for a characteristic of the psychological structure, and it seems wise to retain it until its nature is clearly enough understood to warrant a change.

lier,* is an example of repression which serves the individual constructively at the time it is instituted but has a potentially unfortunate effect in later life.

Repression is often used transiently as a common everyday tool of the ego. Mr. Businessman is supposed to pick up a
package for his wife at the dress shop next to his office. To do
so means leaving the office a few minutes earlier or else missing his usual train. Five minutes before closing time, he
finds himself reading an important letter that should be sent
in the evening mail. He could easily spend the five minutes
arguing with himself—should he finish the letter, leave it unfinished until tomorrow in order to carry out his wife's request, or finish the letter, get the dress and catch a later
train. If he misses his train, his wife will be irritated. She
will have wasted fifteen minutes at the depot waiting for the
next one, with the potatoes probably scorching on the stove.
Leaving the letter unfinished until tomorrow may also have
serious consequences. And if he chooses consciously to read
the letter rather than carry out his wife's wishes, he will
have to do a great deal of explaining when he gets home. It
is both timesaving and psychologically economical to forget.
He represses his wife's request. With all sincerity he can
apologize; he "just forgot." After all there are limits to a person's anger toward someone who "forgot," since to have forgotten puts fate temporarily beyond conscious control. While
repression does not achieve integration of the particular impulse, it does make possible the integration of other impulses. Were the repressed impulses allowed freedom, they
would delay, cripple or prevent overall integration.

A child (or adult) whose ego is overtaxed by a current
adaptive demand often abandons, at least temporarily, his
attempt to master the problem. Nostalgically remembering
the time when such demands were not imposed upon him,
he wishes to return to such a period of comfortable equi-

* See Oedipal Period, Chapter 6 and Adolescence, Chapter 8.

librium. He "regresses" to a more immature level of behavior. Steps in development that he appeared to have taken successfully are retraced. He wants to be accepted as a more immature person. Thus the wife, tired of being an adult, wishes to nestle in her husband's arms and just have a good cry. The husband, on the other hand, wonders why his wife doesn't remember that he hates casserole dishes for dinner— his mother never forgot! The adolescent transiently is unable to make his own decisions. The grammar-school child runs to mother to be comforted after some seemingly minor hurt. The previously toilet-trained three-year-old soils and wets. The child who has given up the breast or the bottle without protest reverts to sucking his thumb. All have actually regressed to, or have expressed a wish to regress to, a period of life that was less complex.

Regression, like repression, has both positive and negative aspects, and prolonged as well as temporary effects. Since regression occurs when the individual faces a situation he cannot master, he protects himself by reverting to a more immature level of adjustment. At that level he can either handle the situation himself or place responsibility upon another. As an example of the former, a toilet-trained child may be unable to cope with his anger in a way consistent with his stage of development, when his mother introduces a new baby into the family circle. He may then revert to soiling. In such an incident, soiling may represent a hostile attack upon the mother. The same symptom may indicate, not hostility, but that he has abandoned the struggle to maintain self-control, saying in effect to his mother "I can't handle my response to the baby unless I too can be somewhat more helpless than I was. See, I too am little."

Regression may be irreversible unless the individual is given help in dealing with the seemingly insurmountable obstacle that brought it about in the first place. The analysis of adults usually brings out material indicating that certain childhood problems proved beyond the ego's capacity and the child reverted to a more immature level of behavior. A pattern for dealing with problems of that particular nature became permanent in the character; in adult life similar problems are handled in the same manner. In many instances the areas in which regressive patterns are used are relatively small compared to the overall personality of the individual and it is therefore not too serious. Regression becomes of real significance when, in adult life, most tasks of the ego are handled with this particular tool.

Transient regression is, like transient repression, a common mechanism of adults under certain conditions. An ill person who is a "good" patient is often one who has accepted, gracefully and with selective discretion, a return to the dependency of a small baby. He not only allows himself to be administered to, he relaxes and enjoys it. Transient regression in children under overwhelming pressure is frequent. Given adequate help to deal with the overtaxing strain, the child slowly returns to the more mature level. The ego in such instances resembles a man who, fatigued on a long walk, takes a few steps back to sit on a stump he had observed in passing. Rested, he resumes his walk. He may find that the stump was a mirage and, recalling a still earlier one, retrace his steps further until he finally finds a place to rest. If he can't find a satisfactory place or if his fatigue is too great, he may not resume his walk. Furthermore, if he began his retreat not because of normal fatigue but because he found himself face to face with an angry bull, he may have fled in panic and have no desire to resume the walk ahead. He remains "regressed," and will stay so unless he can be assured that the bull is harmless, that it has been removed, or that weapons are available for self-defense. A child sometimes regresses because in his walk toward maturation he comes unexpectedly face to face with an angry bull.

Another ego tool, creating a picture similar to that of regression but based upon a different mechanism, is fixation. The ego defends itself against greater pressure by avoiding the next advance in maturation and continues to battle for integration at the same level. The adult alcoholic is usually a person who remained fixated at (if he hasn't regressed to) an early infantile level. Any stage in development may result in the individual's choosing to stay there permanently. Fixation is a defeat for the inherent impulse to mature; safety, gratification, or rest from further effort appear more assured there than at any place beyond.

Fixation occurs under at least two, and possibly three, conditions. If the child is unsatiated at one level of development he tends to remain there, trying to get relief from his cravings. This is most easily illustrated in those individuals whose dependency longings have never been adequately met. They remain infantile, always seeking but never achieving enough gratification. Later developmental stages may also become the stopping points. The individual continually creates duplicating situations, hoping always to master them and thus obliterate the failure of the past, but always failing to do so.

Fixation may also occur when the step beyond appears too dangerous. As indicated previously, the child whose mother can love only an infant clings to his infancy because to give it up is to precipitate himself into an emotional vacuum. The satisfaction ordinarily found in the maturing process is insufficient if the important component of parental love is deleted.

Some authorities believe that fixation results if the child experiences too complete satisfaction at a given emotional level. Any change is therefore seen as a change for the worse. In my opinion this is a questionable cause for fixation. While superficially certain examples of fixation may suggest this possibility, more intensive study is apt to reveal that actually one of the two other factors is also present and perhaps more significant. It would seem more likely that complete satisfaction would lead to greater ease in taking the step ahead.

The ego has other tools which, in action, are familiar to everyone but which may be manipulated unconsciously and therefore not recognized. Unacceptable impulses may result in overt behavior directly opposite to the original impulse. Fear, for example, of exposing underlying resentment causes the adoption of the opposite attitude. A mother claimed that her older child felt no resentment toward the new baby. In fact, she said, he wanted to hug the baby so hard the parents feared he would inadvertently hurt the infant. Perhaps the child was actually unable to express his love without jeopardizing the baby's safety. It is equally possible that, unknown both to parents and child, the intense love disguised an equally intense resentment. Under the conscious guise of affection there lurked an unconscious wish to destroy.

This cover-up of unacceptable feelings is not intentional dishonesty. It is an attempt to avoid expression of one feeling which would jeopardize either the gratification of another feeling or a reward sought. It is not so different from a conscious technique often used. A husband may be faced with the problem of answering his wife's question as to how he likes a hat which he considers unsuitable. He may deny his feeling toward the hat by convincing himself unconsciously that anything on such a desirable person becomes desirable just by association. He may consciously protect himself by acclaiming the hat's attractiveness instead of risking the firing squad to which disapproval might lead.

It is healthy (and wise) for a husband to consider any item of apparel enhanced once it enshrouds his wife—unless that attitude is only a sample of his inability to handle any justified response conflicting with another's point of view except by denial of his own feelings. There is a difference between the use of any ego defense by a diplomat and by Mr.

Milquetoast. In some instances philanthropic work and so-cial reforms are spearheaded by people who, in their good deeds, are denying both to themselves and others more basic unacceptable impulses. By the use of this defensive tool the individual finds his own identity in his world and avoids the discomfort from external punishment or his own guilt if the original impulse were expressed. Society also benefits from this ego defense.

The fable of the fox and the unattainable grapes is an ex-ample of another protective device of the ego. Children often use this mechanism to lessen internal tension. It also serves the purpose of exasperating parents! Deprived of something as punishment for a misdemeanor, the child claims he doesn't care, he didn't want it anyway. By this response he can perhaps allay some of his own frustration by half-con-vincing himself he didn't want it. At least he can try to match his frustration with the one he creates for the par-ent! Eventually, faced with comparable frustration, he may really believe that he doesn't want what is unattainable. It is healthy for a person to be able to renounce a goal that he realistically cannot achieve rather than constantly to frus-trate himself by striving for it and thus perhaps lose the prize that *is* within his power. A "sour grapes" attitude is un-healthy only when an individual fails to strive for some-thing he wants and that he can get.

At times an individual avoids the consequences of an un-desirable act by placing the blame upon others. The shoe clerk, unable to sell many shoes from the new stock, blames the shoe department buyer. He may be correct; on the other hand, he may have neglected to use all of his salesmanship upon his customers. Uncomfortable in the vague awareness of his own part in his failure, he explains the difficulty by "projection," placing the responsibility upon others. Emo-tional responses are similarly projected. Many times when a person feels disliked, he is actually projecting his own dislike. Not comfortable with his feeling of antagonism toward another, he says in effect that it really is not he that is irritated by the other person, thus justifying his avoidance of that individual without facing his own involvement.

This protective device is frequently observed in children. One child blames another for an act which they both shared. In many instances this is a deliberate distortion to avoid punishment and thus is a conscious ego defense. In other subtle situations it may not be deliberate. The child believes what he says, thus relieving his own feeling of guilt as well as avoiding punishment from others. Having taken cookies at the forbidden pre-dinner hour, he claims he didn't want to do it but his friend urged him to. In this evaluation of the situation, his friend, not he, is to blame.

A child blames his teacher for his poor school work; she does not know how to teach. He blames his mother when he is late to school; she doesn't get him up in time. (She probably tried!) He blames his sister for not putting away the game they were playing. In each instance he is protecting himself from the consequences of his own behavior by placing the responsibility upon someone else. He would not have to do this if his ego could tolerate the possible repercussions of acknowledging his own responsibility.*

An interesting use of this defensive technique occurs in the play of some imaginative youngsters. The child blames an imaginary companion for his behavior, particularly if that behavior is not permitted. In such instances the child rarely has any illusions that the parents will be swayed from their knowledge of the true culprit. He has rather externalized a part of himself. Unconsciously he separates his "good" self from his "bad" self, the latter the imaginary companion. Joyce's mother gave an interesting description of this device. Joyce was able, at the age of two and a half, to play many hours by herself, accompanied by an imaginary playmate,

* See Chapter 22, Lying.

Quicky. Quicky was sometimes a boy, sometimes a girl, but usually had many more characteristics of the neuter gender. At the onset of the play period Joyce would announce that Quicky was at the door, could he come in and play? The mother would agree if Quicky would promise to be good. If Joyce felt that Quicky would not promise, her mother knew it was time to stop her own work and play with Joyce, or else have a cross and whiny child on her hands. If Quicky's response was an assurance of good behavior, her mother knew that peace would reign for some time. However, if she took too great an advantage of Joyce's imagination and left her alone too long, Joyce would become angry and quarrel with Quicky. She would ask her mother to send Quicky home. Quicky always carried the blame when Joyce was troublesome; when Joyce was at peace with herself, Quicky was a part of her happy state. Ultimately the "Quicky" part of the young child is taken back into the self to be integrated into the total personality.

Fantasy life is another device for relieving periodic strain on the ego. The automobile mechanic dreams of owning a garage, the bank clerk of being a bank president. The use of fantasy as an escape from reality can reach abnormal limits in which the dreamer comes to consider the fantasy real, ignoring evidence to the contrary. In contrast to this destructive aspect of fantasy, it can be extremely useful; it is closely interwoven with ambition. The clerk may become so intrigued by his fantasy of being a bank president that, by many years of hard work, he finally brings his dream into reality. Many great works, of art as well as science, have their origin in the fantasies of one or more people.

Children often use fantasy to deny the painful aspects of reality. A little boy, feeling pretty unsure of himself, imagines he is Superman or the Lone Ranger. The fantasy gives momentary relief to his painful awareness of his own inadequacy. The stronger he grows, the more confident he feels that there is a place for him as he really is in the world, the closer he relates his fantasy to reality. He then dreams, perhaps, first of playing baseball like a professional, next as well as his own coach, finally as the star of the team or an important member of it. With developing skills his fantasy comes closer to reality and is used not to escape but to point the way to an ultimate goal for himself.

A common way of relieving the ego strain that results from having acted out unacceptable impulses is rationalization. Having, on impulse, acted in a certain way, the individual repents at leisure. He trys to defend himself from the effects of his behavior by explaining it rationally. The motives behind many acts are clearer in hindsight rather than in foresight. Rationalization is a good example of how a defense against anxiety may become a constructive ego tool for integrating the internal impulses, reality and the conscience. A philosophy of life often has its roots in the combined rationalizations of many impulsive acts which, woven together, result in a point of view toward the self, other people and the non-human aspects of reality. When the point of view becomes effective in directing future impulses, the individual has a philosophy by which he lives. The more encompassing and effective it is, the more predictable will behavior be and the less psychic energy will he have to use in consciously determining action.

These defenses of the ego, and many others, are used in the everyday living of individuals. The study of disturbances reveals how destructive any ego defense can be. Yet it is not the particular tool that is most significant in the disturbed personality—it is the intensity and inappropriateness with which the defense is used, the amount of psychic energy unnecessarily sapped to maintain it, and its degree of ineffectualness that result in psychological upheaval.

There is a fallacy popular at the present time as a result

of the exploration of unconscious ego defenses. It is too often assumed that if an individual shows tender love he is really hostile; if he is angry he is denying love; if he is scrupulously honest he is driven by desires to steal. In certain cases these conclusions are valid. Most frequently however, both contradictory drives exist but the one shown is the stronger, either because of direct or associated rewards. If a person shows love, then his love is stronger than his hostility; if he is hostile, then he finds hostility safer than love would be. He may have an impulse to be dishonest, but honesty offers greater gratification. Just because a child expresses affection for a sibling he also resents does not inevitably lead to psychic exhaustion or personality distortion. It is only when he can tolerate no hostile feelings toward the other child—if because of fancied or real deprivations to himself, his hostility is excessive, or if he so fears the consequences from legitimate hostility that he has to deny his anger and proclaim a nonexistent love—that his defenses are being used in a way precarious to the total personality structure. When a child reminds his mother that he loves her, he isn't necessarily defending himself and her against his anger. When he says he hates her, he is not necessarily trying to escape from loving her. He may both love and hate her, but at the moment one or the other emotion is dominant.

Even when a real emotion *is* denied by proclaiming a false one, it is not always necessary to denude the child (or adult) of his temporary defense in order to avoid a neurosis. All individuals, including children, have a right to their defenses until more adequate techniques for handling situations are available. Mrs. Housewife will gain nothing by clarifying for her husband the implications of his "forgetting" her dress unless she is able to accept the demands of his work and let him assume it is safe to return home either without the dress, or on a later train. Until she herself has reached that point of ego adaptation, she would probably construe his repression quite incorrectly. She could interpret it as an uncon-

neurosis: functional disorder of mind or emotions
psyche: spirit, soul, mind

sciously hostile attack upon her, when actually all he wanted
was as pleasant an evening as possible. No one should psy-
choanalyze the unconscious of his family or friends. Parents,
in their eagerness to have their child comfortable with his
hostility toward a sibling or themselves, sometimes press too
hard to have the child reveal his feeling. In this way they
fight against the child's attempt to adjust to the situation.
Fighting his adaptive attempts can be as destructive to the
child as over-acceptance can be, or the expectation that he
will continue a particular pattern of defense too rigidly. Providing acceptance of mixed feelings, support in situations
which the child cannot handle alone, and gratifications in
certain aspects of living to make up for frustration in others
—these will tend to keep the defenses utilized optimally.
Only when the defenses are crippling or distorting to the
self or reality do they need to be exposed to conscious inspection. Again the question of how to know demands an answer.
Empathy with the child and faith in intuitive responses are
the first resorts. If they prove ineffective, the objective point
of view of a trained person is needed.*

* See Chapter 30, When and Where to Seek Help.

PART IV

EMOTIONAL MATURITY

17 : *Emotional maturity*

WHAT IS EMOTIONAL MATURITY? MANY ATTEMPTS HAVE BEEN
made to define it, but a complete description is very elusive.
Perhaps one reason is that the definition, if comprehensive,
must of necessity be theoretical, since no one becomes, in all
facets of the personality, emotionally mature. To a certain
extent defenses established in childhood remain unmodified
by subsequent changes. To a certain extent behavior remains overly determined by parental attitudes valid in
childhood but invalid in adult life. To a certain extent everyone deals with reality as if it were an echo of childhood
rather than a new experience.

If the attempt to define maturity is less ambitiously pursued, and a lesser goal of a partial and pragmatic definition
is accepted, the task is less baffling. From all the material
discussed in this book come the criteria for recognizing maturity: 1) how successfully have the characteristic emotional
responses of the different phases of psychological development
reached adult levels; 2) what direction is given to the instinctual drives; 3) how great is the capacity to integrate the internal urges, reality, and the demands of the superego.

It is perhaps valid now to recapitulate some of the points
brought out in the previous chapters. Describing psychological
growth by periods does not mean that the characteristic response of each period becomes obsolete once the child masters
the inherent conflicts. Mastery leads to maturation, not disap-

pearance, of the response. This culture values a man who pulls himself up by his own bootstraps. He is considered the truly independent man. This attitude distorts the concept of maturity for it would imply that to be mature, a person must be completely independent. Obviously no one living effectively with others is totally independent. If a writer had to manufacture his own pencil and paper, a bricklayer his brick, a musician his piano, they would have little time for other goals. It is not only in these mechanical aspects of living that people are mutually interdependent—they are equally, or more, so emotionally. A person cannot give unless there is someone to receive. He cannot be really meaningful to others unless he can love others and accept their love in return. But, the protest arises, that is not dependency! Isn't it? Dependency has come to have a connotation relating only to the infantile state. The adjectives "dependent" and "infantile" have come, unfortunately, to be synonymous.

During infancy a child longs to be, and is, dependent. But if he were completely so, he would have to be fed with a stomach tube! He does his independent share within his capacity—he sucks. The sense of security created by the intake of food has an element of his own contribution, his sucking. There is an interaction between himself and the source of his nutrition. As he develops more ability to gain his own food, the interrelationship with others becomes less physical and more emotional until gradually a capacity for mature interdependency evolves. The mature individual is able to accept dependency, and gratify it in others, in accordance with the reality of the adult world. The child who clings to his mother's skirts when faced with an unknown person is a dependent child. An adult who turns to a dictionary when faced with an unknown word is a dependent adult. A child who, when unhappy, curls up in his mother's lap for comforting is a dependent child. The man who turns to his wife, friends or trusted business associates to discuss current problems is a maturely dependent man. Unfortunately, in contrast to the child who accepts his need for comforting, the man may be ashamed of the emotional meaning of his goal. He tries to disguise his legitimate emotional need for support—he wants, he says, an objective opinion. The individual who prides himself upon his independence and the absence of any emotional dependency upon others is immature. He can conceive of his dependent needs being adequately gratified only as a child's dependent needs are gratified and respect for himself is threatened by his lack of emotional maturity in this particular area. To defend himself against this self-revelation he denies the existence of his desire. A mature individual accepts an emotionally dependent relationship with meaningful people in his life, but accepts it as an adult, not as a child.

The overevaluation of emotional independence is revealed more sharply in those dramatic situations in which the person's ego is overstrained. As the chapters on the ego have shown, one of the aids in remobilizing ego strength during childhood is the support others give the child when he is unable to deal effectively with a situation himself. An adult may consider any acceptance of support from others, at times of excessive ego strain, a sign of weakness—but the same person having broken a bone in his leg will not protest against a cast and insist upon walking on the fractured bone to show how strong he is! He recognizes that the leg will not mend satisfactorily unless the bone is kept in a proper position. He will "regress" in the use of his leg to a point which will allow healing—perhaps he will have to be at bed rest with traction; perhaps he will need a walking cast; perhaps he will only need a cane, or under certain circumstances to walk carefully for awhile. He accepts the support for the leg determined by the actual condition of the bone without feeling that he has returned to neuro-muscular infancy.

Egos also "fracture." Everyone at times has experiences demanding an emotional adjustment that overtaxes the ego. Avoiding emotional dependency upon others at such times can lead to as catastrophic results as the refusal to treat a compound fracture of the leg.

The individual's degree of emotional maturity can be evaluated by seeing whether his infantile dependent needs have grown with the growth of his total person so that he is capable and willing to be dependent upon others according to adult patterns. Complete emotional independence is not only impossible; its attainment would be evidence of failure in the maturation of an inherent human characteristic. A capacity for mutual dependency is a crucial component of social living. To accept or desire it is not a sign of weakness. It is the way the dependency is expressed that indicates the emotional maturity or immaturity of the individual.

There is another aspect of maturity involved in the way a person responds to the dependent needs of others. The donor of support should also be able to recognize the maturity shown by an adult who can reveal such desires. A wife who meets her husband's dependent needs *as if* he were a child is belittling him if he is mature, or embarrassing or crippling him if he is really immature. The husband who meets his wife's craving to be dependent by "fathering" is doing the same. Some men and women are really immature and are seeking actual parental figures instead of someone who symbolizes on an adult level that which parents give a child. On the other hand, the emotions of motherliness and fatherliness need not only be expressed to those who are chronologically or emotionally childlike. The mature individual is able to express such feelings toward other mature adults without evaluating the latter as children. Many people avoid any emotionally dependent relationship, not because they cannot accept their wish for it, but because they cannot find the type of support they seek. What they have received has been given as if to a child.

A child is aided in this area as his parents are sensitive to the form of dependency he is seeking. If parents offer only gratification of infantile dependent longings, or if they consider independence the sole criterion of maturation, the child must either remain a dependent infant or suppress his inherent urge to establish interdependent relationships with others. In the latter event he will strive to become the completely independent individual, who is really only half a person.

Just as infantile dependency evolves into adult form, the ambivalent responses of the anal period change into adult patterns if the conflicts are handled adequately. As indicated in the chapter on the anal period of development, the child recognizes his growing ability to master the world through his own resources. This is a happy feeling. But in attempting mastery he meets the frustrations of reality. This angers him, and since the parents are most often the agents of this frustration, he is angry at them. But he is frightened because their love, which he wishes, may be withdrawn if he expresses his anger. This period of development is thus characterized by ambivalence. As shown earlier, the problems are resolved as a child learns to gratify his own impulses in ways that are compatible with the demands of reality. He does not have to choose between defiance and submission and therefore his frustration and thus his anger decrease. With a decrease in his anger, his ambivalence toward his parents, the dichotomy of loving and hating at the same time, becomes less sharply marked. He can accept contradictory feelings toward the same person. He can also recognize that he does not lose parental love completely if they disapprove of a particular act but he concludes that the gratification from certain acts is not sufficient to counterbalance the disapproval. This adaptation does not mean that the characteristics of the period are forever gone. In the mature individual the responses are different, the psychological roots remain the same.

The manner in which an individual deals with frustration shows how extensive the maturing process in this area has been. The mature individual does not meet frustration with a temper tantrum, as a small child does. On the other hand he doesn't inevitably submit to the frustration—he attempts to overcome it. Because his capacity is greater than the child's, he has more resources for constructively overcoming the difficulty. When a direct way is barred he seeks another route to the same goal. Only if there is no acceptable way does he have to decide whether the goal is worth the price he would pay for it. He makes a decision without vacillating between answers.

A mature individual does not conclude that because parents love him in spite of his behavior all the world will do likewise. In maturing he has put his parents and others who are most emotionally meaningful to him into a separate category, but he continues to react to the rest of the world as he reacted to his parents in childhood. He curbs certain behavior in order to be loved and accepted by others, but he no longer fears their rejection or retaliation as strongly as he feared parental rejection and retaliation. He calmly circumvents that which before he anxiously avoided.

A mature adult is not free of ambivalence toward important love objects, but his ambivalent feelings live together comfortably instead of trying to push one another out of the house. If love is stronger than dislike it governs most of his behavior, but the dislike is allowed to be present. If hostility is stronger, it dominates the relationship, tempered by the soothing presence of affection. A friend may have a characteristic that arouses resentment. The friendship is worthwhile in spite of the resentment. On the other hand, an individual may be an undesirable person, but as a human being he can be treated decently even if not taken to one's bosom. In both instances, ambivalence exists but does not lead to complete confusion. That person would be quite unique who loved everyone unambivalently and believed, with good reason, that he was loved by everyone!

Still another area of adulthood reflects the growth from childhood ambivalence. An individual who remains immature

in the sense that he cannot handle ambivalent feelings can
never make up his mind. The woman shopper who, liking
many dresses, always finds a "but" about them is indicating an
immature ambivalence. The businessman who has difficulty
in weighing opposing arguments reveals the same immaturity.
On the other hand, the woman who never sees a "but"
about a dress not only usually dresses in poor taste but is
also unable to handle ambivalent feelings and thus represses
one side of her response. The businessman who fails to see
the pros and cons may have no difficulty in making a decision but may have trouble as he tries to carry out that decision. The woman shopper and the businessman, in spite of
their ability to make quick decisions, have not attained maturity. The mature individual faced with a choice to make
quickly recapitulates the infantile conflict but with adult
tools. He sees and weighs opposing sides equally. As a result
of exploration he finds the most constructive solution and
makes a decision. Here again, maturity is not characterized
by freedom from ambivalence, but rather by a capacity to
resolve each ambivalent response as it arises and in accordance with present demands rather than those of an infantile
situation. A child will be helped to mature in this area if
he is assisted in weighing the multiple sides of a question—
within his ability to grasp them—and then is helped to interpret his reading of the scale. Too many parents say to the
child "make up your mind" without giving him enough help
to do so.*

The mature expression of the Oedipal period has been
touched upon before. Its contribution to the adult personality is quite apparent. An adult is able to love heterosexually
because his earlier feelings toward the parent of the opposite
sex have matured. The rivalry with the parent of the same
sex may be expressed during courtship in sexual rivalry with

---

*A warning—this does not mean to imply that parents should spend hours
pointing out many confusing sides of a question to a child. What cannot be
done briefly and clearly usually shouldn't be done at all.

others for the same love object. Cyrano de Bergerac, who won his beloved for another man, may be a touchingly romantic figure to read about but he is scarcely the personification of a mature man! Maturity does not only involve the ability to bring sexual feeling to orgastic culmination—the Don Juans of the world are not sexually mature people. Sexual maturity means the fusion of direct sexual responses with those aspects of love that involve tenderness, protectiveness and companionship.

Latency again is not a time that is passed through and left behind forever. Since it is a period during which the greatest advance is made toward socialization, the patterns established then continue. The latency child is beginning to learn how to live in the world he will inhabit as an adult.

Adolescence is the age span in which the most dramatic realignment of the emotional forces occurs, bringing about the shift in interpersonal relationships, the change in the image of oneself and in the internal drives. It is the bridge between childhood and adulthood. The dreams and ideals of the adolescent are not lost in the mature individual—they are simply seasoned by reality and become a part of the life philosophy.

Thus we never completely discard any part of our emotional past. The stages of development are the cornerstones upon which we build the structure that is our adult personality.

The maturation of the instinctual drives offers another criterion by which to judge maturity. There are two general categories of the instinctual drives, one encompassing the desires to be loved and to love, the other concerning the impulses to strike out aggressively against unpleasant situations. Maturation brings about their fusion—while in their immature form they are usually at odds. A small child acts out his aggressive drive irrespective of parental attitudes. He also expresses it in his hostility toward those who will not permit the fulfillment of some impulse he has. He curbs his aggressive drive at times because he fears its expression will deprive him of the love he seeks. Gradually the child learns to express aggressive impulses in forms acceptable to himself and others. He comes to evaluate when the desire to be loved is very important and when it can be sacrificed for the fulfillment of other aims. He is able to tolerate not being loved by everyone but to value the love of those who have a meaning to him. His aggressive impulses, expressed in a desirable form, win him love instead of depriving him of it. The fusion is so complete that he finds himself expressing his love to others through an increased aggressiveness toward a chosen goal.

With maturity, love and aggression become focused not only upon gratification for the self and for those who are especially meaningful; they are also directed toward ever-wider spheres. A mature individual loves himself, his immediate family, but also friends, countrymen and the human race. He is capable not only of aggressively and constructively attacking situations unsatisfactory to him and his family, but also those that are undesirable for the anonymous masses of the world. He is also able to hate without fear of his own disapproval or the attack of others, because he has constructive control of the modes by which he will express his hatred.

Maturation is indicated in the changes that have occurred in the ego ideal and superego from childhood to adulthood. The ego ideal modifies so that the fantasies of childhood are converted to the real possibilities of adult living, and the child who dreamt of being a lion tamer becomes a veterinarian. The superego of childhood creates perhaps the greatest difficulty in the maturation process. The standards and punitive attitudes that make it up became a part of the personality structure before reality could be evaluated with sufficient accuracy. The readiness of the superego to discipline for any infringement reinforces the individual's anxiety and thus his submission to archaic demands. The superego of the mature individual has modified its infantile standards as a consequence of the differences between what is expected of a child and what is expected of an adult. Distortions that occurred because of the child's limited ability to grasp parental attitudes clearly have disappeared. The mature superego is effective in its control but flexible as it reconciles its demands with reality.

A final criterion of maturity is the capacity the individual has developed to find expression for internal impulses and gratification for internal needs within the framework of reality. This adaptation does not imply passive compliance but rather a pattern of response that has as its aim a constructive modification of the undesirable without destroying the desirable components of reality. The mature housewife would throw out a rotten apple, keeping those that were not spoiled. The immature housewife would throw out a bag of apples because a glance in the bag revealed a spoiled one. Perhaps a mature race of people would deal with all problems that arise by evolutionary rather than revolutionary methods!

Throughout this book much stress is placed upon the importance of security to the child, with the implication that the needed security is emotional rather than physical. An ideal childhood would bring the individual to adulthood basically secure in his world, whatever the reality. He would not suffer from anxiety. He would fear only those situations that warrant fear and would be unafraid once he saw a way to defend himself.* It is true that people, no matter how mature, would always function better if they did not fear starvation, and if they were assured of an income adequate to meet their basic needs for health, nutrition and shelter.

---

* An arbitrary distinction is made in this book between the terms "anxiety" and "fear." Anxiety is a response to a threat to the emotional life of the individual. It is irrational even though rationalizable; it may be aroused by a real situation but it is out of proportion or has a broader symbolic meaning. Any defense against it is apt to be neurotically patterned. Fear is a response to a real situation and mobilizes constructive defenses that have a realistic goal of either protecting the individual from the danger or helping him escape it.

However the cultural goal to have everyone secure in every
way is perhaps a dangerous one, for cultural growth occurs
in part in an attempt to eradicate insecurity! Insecurity dynamically utilized is a stimulus to learn more, to formulate
wiser laws, wiser philosophy and wiser interpersonal relationships. Overall security, physical plus emotional, is possible only within four walls too strong to be invaded. To live
within those four walls is to be imprisoned even though secure.

A mature individual believes in himself and those that
love him and whom he loves. He has a capacity to deal with
those who hate him and whom he hates. He approaches a
disturbing situation with confidence that he can either modify it or adjust to it, knowing that he will not lose his own
identity in the latter event because his own identity is so
strongly established within himself. He is not anxious in a
reality situation in which he is insecure. It is a challenge to
him. He is not imprisoned and safe, but free and safe, or
able to tolerate the lack of safety. Emotional security in
childhood is important in part because it makes the adult
strong enough to deal constructively with his besetting in-
securities.

PART V

THE PERSISTENT PROBLEMS

There is no theoretically correct way to rear a child. One child's need is another child's poison. In the following chapters there is a discussion of some of the more common difficulties that arise and some of the possible answers to questions often raised by parents. The answers should not be considered definitive but, rather, provocative in helping the reader to achieve fuller understanding of the child.

18 : *Discipline*

THE TERM "DISCIPLINE," AS COMMONLY USED, IS A MUCH MA-
ligned word. Its origin is significant: it is derived from the
Latin *disciplina,* meaning "instruction and training." Unfortunately, however, it has come to have the connotation of
"punishment," as if learning could be achieved only by such
means. Punishment does have a place in discipline, but it is
only a small part of valid disciplinary methods.

Discipline is important for everyone. It is an external
manifestation as well as an internal way of maintaining or
developing the integrative capacity of the ego. Discipline
from without teaches the demands of reality and how they
can most constructively be met. For example, the law that a
driver may not go through a red light was established to facilitate survival of as many drivers as possible; the violator is
subject to punishment. Thus, punishment properly has just
as much significance of protection for the culprit as it does
for the potential victim.

An infant does not know what the requirements of reality
are. He does not know wherein lies danger to himself. He
does not know the behavior that will cause him to be loved
and accepted by others. Nor does he know how to find gratification for his impulses without jeopardizing his acceptability. He does not know what, according to the patterns of his
culture, is right and what is wrong. His parents are his first
and most important teachers. They are constantly teaching

him, and whatever form their teaching takes, it is—in its best sense—discipline.

The most constructive discipline is that which helps the child to redirect an unacceptable impulse into a channel that adequately meets the goal of the impulse and into a form compatible with the reality and the cultural concepts of proper behavior. When a two-year-old child wants to bang two pieces of fine china together and, as this act is prohibited, is offered a substitute of two kitchen pans, the child has had a valuable learning experience. The prohibition concerning fine china is important; the substitution of the pans is an equally valuable lesson, for the impulse to make noise has been satisfied by a permissible substitute. While parents have to gauge the learning experience by the response of the child, constantly isolating a child from untouchables is not as instructive as helping the child to rechannel an impulse stimulated by a forbidden object toward a suitable substitute.* As has been pointed out earlier, much of the process of maturation is the discovery of ways to express impulses through channelization leading to a goal compatible with reality and acceptable to one's own standards and those of others.

The belief that a child will interpret parental disapproval as withdrawal of love has made many parents hesitant to express disapproval. It certainly is not wise to confirm a child's fear by threatening to withdraw affection. Ultimately he needs to distinguish between loss of parental love and mere disapproval. On the other hand, certain behavior will in the long run deprive him of love, the love of those who are not his parents. As he becomes aware that his parents love him though they may not like his behavior, he also learns to separate his parents from other people. Other people will not love him if his behavior is unacceptable. The lesson he

---

* The author apologizes for the example of fine china and does not recommend utilizing it for the education of the child. The lesson might not be learned quite quickly enough to preserve the china!

should learn during the anal period of uneasy relationship to his parents is that his parents are different from other people in their capacity to love regardless of his misbehavior. This does not have to be spelled out completely for him. He usually identifies the uniqueness of parental love after a few disappointing experiences with other people. The greatest shock comes to the child who, never having encountered disapproval in the secure framework of parental love, is suddenly confronted with disapproval by others.

Punishment is a valid disciplinary tool if used with discrimination. The most effective form of punishment is that which is the logical consequence of an act. If a child does not complete his bedtime routine promptly enough to allow time for reading, deprivation of a story is a logical punishment. Parents often, because they love their child, weaken when given such an opportunity for teaching cause and effect. A touch of weakness is an extremely desirable component of parental love, but parents should not be weak every time a punishment can fit a crime. Children need to learn the causal relationship between misbehavior and punishment within the sheltering environment of loving and loved parents.

Sometimes a logical punishment cannot always follow a bit of misbehavior which for important reasons must be curbed. For example, a small child who is too young to judge danger runs out into the street. The incredibly logical punishment would be to have the child safely but emphatically hit by a car. No parents would plot such a punishment. If no other technique works, it is preferable that the parent rather than the car hit the child, thus establishing a conditioned reflex against running out in the street, even though the punishment is *non sequitur*.

While no sane parents would condone having a car hit a child to teach him a lesson, it is not an uncommon practice to teach simpler lessons of danger by comparable methods. If the child tends to grab hot pans, the parent may illustrate the danger by forcing the child to touch something warm enough to burn him but not as seriously as a hotter object might. This method has doubtful merit as discipline. The chosen object may not burn enough to demonstrate the real danger; as a result the prohibition seems illogical to the child—just another example of the frustrating idiosyncrasies of his parents. If the object is hot enough to be painful, the child may interpret it as cruelty rather than education. This can be more destructive in terms of the child's concept of his parents than constructive as a learning experience. A conditioned reflex is a much more desirable psychological technique—and it can frequently be established with surprising ease. A sharp expression of disapproval has considerable effectiveness, even though it may have to be repeated on several occasions before the inhibition is firmly established. If that does not prove effective, an accompanying slap may be influential enough.

The pros and cons of spanking have probably been argued since the days of Adam and Eve. The motto "spare the rod and spoil the child" has alternated periodically with "let the rod spoil and spare the child." Each motto has its validity and its fallaciousness. Certainly there is no justification whatever for merciless beating of a child. Other methods of control should be attempted before spanking is resorted to. There is an implication of failure when parents can gain obedience only by physically hurting the child. It is often pointed out that spanking is more important as a release for the parent than as a learning experience for the child. That is probably true at times. But if parents can handle unpleasant child behavior at all times only by hitting, it is hard for the child to see why that is not an equally effective way for him to handle unpleasant parents, teachers and playmates.

There are times when only spanking works. This may occur particularly with a child too young to grasp the significance of other disciplinary methods but who must be taught to check certain behavior. In other words, while spanking a child is not the preferred method of discipline, it may for some parents with some children be—if wisely used—a successful approach to a specific disciplinary problem.

Punishment can mean love to a child. This is not as distorted an evaluation as it may seem at first glance. A child is often fearful of his own impulses. He feels more secure if he can trust adults to carry out part of the responsibility for directing those impulses. By punishing him the parents indicate their willingness to meet this desire; the punishment becomes evidence of their love. If punishment is wisely administered, this paradoxical interpretation is valid and counteracts the child's opposite deduction that the parents do not love because they punish. The latter interpretation of punishment is frequently charged by the child, the former usually kept as his secret!

A child who has had little response from parents except punishment may prefer to be punished rather than ignored. The child may invite punishment in order to believe himself loved or in order to be noticed at least. A child who had been reared until the age of nine in an orphanage where the adults had little meaning except as agents of punishment verbalized this rather clearly. She had been placed in a home with foster parents who had a genuine love for children. Their tolerance for her provocative behavior was remarkable, yet the child, instead of becoming easier to handle, became more and more difficult. Finally a psychiatrist was consulted. The child, a bright youngster, explained the problem very clearly. In the orphanage they cared about her; when she was bad they spanked her. Her foster parents didn't like her; she could do anything she wanted to and they never bothered to punish her.

Punishment may be invited by a child because of unbearable guilt over some act he has committed. Punishment relieves the guilt, is less painful than his own self-torture. The wisest way to handle this pattern cannot be defined so as to have universal application. There are various implications to this behavior. The significance of the behavior of a particular child must be evaluated in the context of that child's total personality. As indicated previously, reasonable guilt serves an important function in establishing good ego control. Some children may find external punishment always preferable to self-imposed punishment, but the complete responsibility should not always rest on external control. On the other hand, a child's concept of punishment may be a barbaric one, established when he had little capacity to evaluate fine points of difference. His guilt may be excessive, and so he is wise to delegate the punitive role to someone else until his own internally directed punishment takes on a more reasonable pattern.

Under other circumstances the child may be seeking punishment for a lesser crime, hoping thereby to alleviate his guilt for what to him is a more serious offense. He may, for example, have strongly hostile feelings towards a younger child in the family. These feelings he considers bad and relegates them to an unconscious sanctuary. Though unaware of these feelings he strives to relieve his ill-defined guilt. He misbehaves, bringing upon himself parental wrath. In so doing, he, transiently at least, relieves his guilt over the unknown misbehavior. No matter how self-punitive he may be, he may regard his self-inflicted punishment as inadequate. He therefore augments the retribution he pays by bringing additional punishment upon himself.

Finally, punishment may be a pleasurable experience. Fear of punishment creates tension. Tension is relieved when the punishment is inflicted. Anticipatory tension and fulfillment of that which is anticipated is a common source of pleasure. Some children find pleasure in the superficially unpleasant situation of being punished.

Other factors may enter into the child's pattern of provoking punishment. Perhaps the above indications of possible aspects to the picture are sufficient to suggest that parents should not too quickly say that their child was asking for punishment all day, so they finally administered it and the child (and often the parents too) seemed to feel better. Children should sometimes be given what they want, other times not.

This generation of parents is recovering slowly from the era in which "reasoning with the child" was advocated. The assumption was, in those families in which the principle was carried out *ad absurdum,* that a child has the reasoning ability and the objectivity of a justice of the Supreme Court. All that parents had to do was explain to the child why he should or should not do something, and the child would be convinced by parental logic. The child would not commit an unreasonable act. The child who answered "but I want to" or "I don't want to" was only revealing the inadequacy of parental reasoning. No child would think of doing an undesirable act or refuse to do a desirable one if he really understood clearly the reasons why it should or should not be done. Only adults are that recalcitrant!

A corollary of this philosophy was the assumption of the child's mature judgment. Accordingly the parent's wishes would never be imposed upon the child. The child should always want to do what the parents wanted. A parent did not say under this regime, "Johnny, it's time to go to bed." Parents who respected the individuality of the child's wishes said, "Johnny, don't you think it's time to go to bed?" Most Johnnies were not as naïve as parents assumed. They faced the fact that the question was purely rhetorical, to which the only astute answer was "yes." Some Johnnies were not so malleable to the unspoken word. They took what was said at face value. Having been asked their opinion, they gave it and it was "no." Then came the strain on the parent's reasonableness, the involved discussions pro and con, finally ending as the parent originally intended: Johnny was told to go to bed. At this point Johnny was often in tears and the parents usually in the clamp of exasperation. To the parents Johnny was an unreasonable child. To Johnny, the parents offered a choice which they didn't mean at all.

As it became obvious that a child could not always understand the reason for a prohibition—or accept those reasons as more important than his own desires—modifications of this educational philosophy occurred. The first change was the suggestion that, since the child could not grasp the reason for a prohibition, the behavior should not be prohibited. This removed the stigma of stupidity from parents but it permitted the child to avoid all self-restraint. It exposed him either to real dangers or the imprisoning vigilance of parents. If, for example, a child was too young to understand that the danger of crossing the street should outweigh the desire to be on the other side, the parents faced the alternative of having the child hit by a car or of never allowing him outside without close, alert surveillance.

Finally parents, educators and psychiatrists recognized that they could not always wait until the child readily understood to impose essential restrictions. In desperation they decided that if they talked long enough the reason would be absorbed by the child even though he was not mature enough to comprehend it. As a result they lectured and lectured. The child developed a deaf ear to these incomprehensible lectures. When the child was old enough to understand, selective deafness persisted and the parents were defeated. The child often summarized his immunity very succinctly by saying that he didn't listen to his parents, they talked too much.

Wise disciplinary methods give a child a choice when a choice is acceptable. It is an extremely valuable experience for a child to choose between alternative answers and bear the burden of his choice, if the decision depends on pros and cons he can readily weigh and if the consequences of a wrong choice will be bearable. If the choice has more implications than the child can comprehend, or if parents will accept only one answer, the child should not be given a choice. This does not justify parents who assume the prerogatives of a dictator. When the child can grasp the reason for behavior being for bidden or accepted, he should know the reason. If it is too subtle for him to understand, parents can still impose their requirement without being tyrannical. Gates down at a railroad crossing are not tyrannical, but they must be obeyed. A guard standing there threatening to shoot anyone crossing the track as a train approaches might be considered a tyrant.

Parents often make tyrannical noises because they have such a poor concept of their own strength. They assert themselves as if certain that they will not only be opposed but probably defeated. They gird to fight windmills. Hiding behind the windmills is the surprised child. The battle is then on, anger-arousing for the parents and often frightening to the child. Both want to win. The parents fear they won't. The child may be terrified because he doesn't know what he would do with victory. Many times when a child forces the parent into battle he does so with the hope that finally the parents will win, because their victory, not his, gives him security.

Parents forget that they are in control. Unsure of themselves, when confronted with obstacles created by the child, they fear they have met the proverbially immovable object. Unless parents give away their secret, the child evaluates the situation quite differently. To him parents are the irresistible force to which he will finally have to bow. Though the parents may be weak, to the child they are very big and very strong. Confident parents will achieve their goal. They are not wishy-washy in their discipline. They are reasonable in a request, certain that it will be carried out, and tolerant of an understandable delay.

What is expected of a child—and the results of conformity or non-conformity to those expectations—must be within the child's capacity to comprehend and achieve. A child of six can understand that unless he goes to bed promptly he cannot have a story read. A two-year-old can neither grasp this complexity of cause and effect nor be expected to retain the lesson until the next night. There is no simple, universal chart that would indicate at what age a child should grasp and respond to parental requirements. Parents must map their own chart for each child.

Some parents are ineffectual in their discipline because the child's particular behavior is in an unconscious way vicariously gratifying to them. When parents gleefully tell of some mischievous misbehavior of their child, they are obviously enjoying it. Such a sense of humor and pleasure in indirectly experiencing a less stodgy life than that which most parents impose upon themselves is one reward of parenthood and offers leavening to what might otherwise be an overly solemn and overly heavy hand of discipline. As in so many aspects of the relationship between the child and the parents, a little is good, too much unfortunate. If the parent unconsciously gains gratification out of serious violations by the child, or out of every successful evasion of parental or other authority, unfortunate consequences may result. Studies have indicated that many delinquent children are acting out the unconscious wishes of the parent.

The child not only learns through wise parental discipline about the demands of the external world and how to find gratification for his own wishes in the resources provided by the world; he also feels freer within the limits established by the parents. Unable to judge the safety and danger of expressing his own impulses or the consequences of exposing himself to the world beyond, the child is reassured when others more competent clarify for him the point beyond which he cannot go. An adult would be foolhardy, if, unable to swim, he went wading some pitch dark night in a pond in which dangerously deep holes with precipitous sides were known to exist. If, however, an area in which no holes exist were fenced off for bathing, he would be free to enjoy himself in the confines of the demarcated area. A child without guidance may feel as frightened as the bather without safety zones. The child may respond as the foolhardy bather would, plunging into the danger zones because no barrier has been provided. With a wise guard against the dangers beyond, the child can be safely free.

Even the wisest parents make mistakes. Parents are not, as the result of a magical power vested in them as parents, always right. In the past this was denied; parents were always right, regardless. Life was much simpler when parents could say with conviction that something was right because they said so. With an awareness of their fallibility, parents face the problem of dealing with their own mistakes. There is no reason why parents should not acknowledge their errors. If parents have said "no" to their child, when "yes" was just as valid and more satisfactory to the child, they should say so and gracefully reverse their stand. This reversal is sound, however, only when the implications of reversal are sound. Many parents say "no" spontaneously because it is easier to deny than to evaluate the effects of permission. They are impervious to the sound arguments of the child that would justify a reversal of position. Finally, the child, exasperated by the parents' blindness, gets angry. This awakens the parents to all the good arguments the child has presented. Belatedly they agree, not as the result of the child's convincing arguments, but as a reward for a temper tantrum. The child is not impressed then by the parents' honesty, but rather by the power of his anger! Rarely should a temper tantrum be so rewarded.

Some parents consider it important to indicate to the child how fallible they are. Every time they get angry at the child they apologize. Actually, maybe, they were justified in their anger. If they reach a decision the child does not like, they change it. Maybe their first decision was correct. They justify this by saying they want the child to realize parents too can make mistakes. That is a lesson a child learns easily; he does not have to be reminded of it constantly. Others explain their behavior as a means of teaching democracy: the child will learn to tolerate different points of view in this way. This method doesn't teach democracy; it teaches the child he is a tyrant!

Parents do make mistakes, and, when they do, other considerations being equal, they should acknowledge that they have. If they make mistakes repeatedly, it is time for them to discover why. They are expected to have better judgment than a child. Why aren't they using it? If they have slipped into the habit of saying "no" without evaluating the question, it is perhaps time to say "yes" indiscriminately until the result convinces them that neither a "yes" or a "no" should be said without thinking. With the average child, the parent should have more "yeses" than "noes" on the daily scoreboard. The child will accept necessary "noes" more willingly if arbitrary, senseless ones are not imposed.

In every discussion of discipline the value of consistency is always stressed. There is no doubt that a child feels more secure if the demands made and privileges offered are predictable. It would be difficult to drive in a large city if one day red meant stop, green go and the next day the reverse were true. It would be practically impossible if a driver never knew whether green meant stop or go until he had driven through it, to be reprimanded or allowed to go on according to the whim of the traffic policeman. Many parents, regardless of their theoretical beliefs, handle their child just as whimsically. An act is condoned or forbidden not because of its inherent nature, but because of its effects for good or bad upon the parents.

Since one of the major resources the child has for learning the details of his cultural heritage is through the definition parents give of that heritage as they forbid and permit various acts and responses, the inconsistent parent gives the child a very confused picture of acceptable behavior. When he is beyond the realm of the parents, he is really at sea. Close to the parents, he often utilizes a talent for evaluating parental mood, guiding his behavior not so much by what is considered permissible and what is not, but rather by the evidence he has of the parental threshold of tolerance at the time. Away from the parents, he faces a situation in which certain behavior is expected of him with no temperamental variables to be taken into consideration. His yardstick is gone.

The superego of the individual reared by inconsistent parents is typically inadequate to govern behavior wisely. The superego tends to take shape from those requirements consistently imposed by parents. A parental attitude expressed one day and negated the next is typically left out of the superego structure. Some people have a superego that directly reflects the parental inconsistency. Superficially the individual appears to have a minimumly structured superego, but its ineffectiveness may be due to inconsistency in demands by the parents.

It is not always possible to maintain discipline that is perfectly consistent. Parents, in spite of themselves, will react when they are tired, worried, or irritated quite contrary to their usual mode of response. Sometimes they "give in" just to have peace for a while. Many times they are not quite sure about the stand they should take and vacillate from day to day until some thought or experience clarifies their point of view. This type of inconsistency rarely has significant consequences. It is the consistent inconsistency that confuses the child. Sometimes parents, in their eagerness to be consistent, make a caricature of the concept. They ignore extenuating circumstances or the existence of factors that invalidate their usual stand. If a child is supposed to be in bed at nine o'clock, and if a history assignment is to describe the signing of an important treaty which will be shown over TV from 9:00 to 9:30, the parents' insistence upon the usual bedtime is not consistency; it is senseless rigidity.

Discipline is a broad term covering much of the interplay between parents and child. It sets limits, gives permission, translates the standards of society into a language comprehensible to the child, directs the child's impulses into acceptable modes of expression, and becomes an important part of the child's superego. The most successful discipline is probably never recognized when it occurs. When a mother says to her son that she doesn't think he should play in the snow today because of his cold, why don't they join in a game of monopoly instead, when the child agrees that would be fun and the game occupies an otherwise dull hour before dinner, wise discipline—in its most skillful form—has been imposed.

19 : *Eating*

MRS. P. ARRIVES AT THE PEDIATRICIAN'S OFFICE OBVIOUSLY
worried. She is concerned over Johnny's poor appetite. He,
who during infancy ate so well, now eats nothing, "literally
nothing." A little questioning discloses that "nothing" is not
so literal. He does eat something but not as he used to. The
doctor weighs Johnny and finds his weight average for his
size. Mrs. P. and the doctor don't often understand each
other from that point on.

There are two potential areas of misunderstanding in this
situation. First of all, Mrs. P. may not remember or know
that the food requirements of a child change during the
growth period. Growth during early infancy is much more
rapid in comparison to body size than it is later. As the child
gets older, less food is needed to maintain physical growth.
A year-old baby has at least tripled his body size since birth.
If a five-year-old triples his body size in a year, it would be
cause for alarm. Knowing this fact might help Mrs. P. lose
her concern about Johnny's eating.

Secondly, Mrs. P.'s own emotional problems may be involved in her anxiety. The child's first experience with love
is with the food the mother gives the infant. As the infant
matures and he interprets other experiences as expressions
of maternal love, food should lose a great part of its significance as love. Paralleling this, a mother's first tangible expression of giving love to a child is in giving food. Mothers un-

dergo a change in their ways of expressing love just as children undergo a change in their interpretation of receiving food. Some mothers, finding this shift difficult, cling to food as a symbol of their maternal love, partly because it is a familiar symbol and sometimes because unconsciously they feel unable to give love in any other way. The decrease in the child's appetite suggests to such a mother that her love is being rejected. Her conscious concern is about nutrition, but her anxiety is rooted in the threat to her own image of herself as a mother. If the child does not accept her love as expressed in food, can she give it in any other form? The doctor's assurance that the child is getting adequate nutrition may only confuse her, for her deeper concern is over an ill-defined anxiety that other needs of the child are not being adequately met.

It is interesting to observe how frequently this concern over giving, through food, to the child is present in a mother with her first child and absent in her response to subsequent children. The experience with the first child has undoubtedly convinced her of the healthy nature of a decreased appetite. It is possible also that, having found that her capacity to be a mother developed from the giving of love through food to new patterns and as the child's acceptance of the new patterns reassured her of her capacity to give emotionally, she became confident that she could give love fully enough to her other children.

It has been experimentally demonstrated that children allowed free choice of food will eat a balanced diet, over a period of time choosing foods that have particular nutritional validity during the growth period. As a result not only will the caloric intake be sufficient but the protein, fat, carbohydrate, mineral and vitamin composition of the diet will be in accordance with bodily needs. This is directly translatable into daily living of the small child only if food has no other meaning to the child than nutrition! Rarely does food remain that limited in significance. As a result many factors may lead to disturbances in appetite.

Forced feeding by anxious parents results in food being unpleasantly associated with anger, unreasonable demands and tension. It is not surprising that, if continued, such feeding experiences lead to distaste for food. Children sometimes are hungry when the household schedule provides food. Other times they are not. Insisting upon the consumption of a certain amount of food even though it is not desired creates a resistance to food. Some foods are distasteful to some children. Adults have food idiosyncrasies too, and the child actually often picks up the food dislikes of his parents. Noble parents, in their attempt to convince the child, may set a good example by eating food they dislike. The child has difficulty grasping the sense of that. When a father says to his son that he doesn't like spinach either but he eats it, a more rational answer from the child's standpoint would be for mother not to cook spinach! Even if father pretends to like spinach, he often is not too convincing. If there are only a few foods that are disliked, it is better to omit them from the menu. Granted it may be embarrassing to take a child out to dinner and have spinach served by the hostess, but hostesses should have some tolerance for the idiosyncrasies of a guest even though the guest is a child. Remember, children cannot use the defense that adults use: that they are allergic to the particular food.* Children will tend to have fewer food dislikes if their eating preferences are accepted with little comment one way or another and if the adults at the table accept their food as a pleasant necessity without too much discussion of likes and dislikes.

Refusal to eat may also be an effective means for the child to gain attention when all other attempts fail. Some children prolong their eating, fuss about the food, demand substitutes and eat inadequate quantities because this has proved to be one way to keep one or both parents concentrating upon

* While this defense is not always valid, an allergic child actually does at times have an aversion to a food he proves on test to be allergic to. This may, of course, be a somatic response to a psychological problem but the allergy nonetheless exists.

him. The type of attention he gains may be pleasant or unpleasant but at least the child is not ignored. The answer is not to ignore the child's feeding difficulty also! It is rather first to find other ways—healthier ones—to satisfy the child's wish for attention. Once that is achieved, attention to his eating can be withdrawn.

A child rejects eating at times not because he dislikes the food itself but because his association with food is unpleasant. This occurs under conditions of forced feeding and endless nagging about the amount or type of food consumption. It may occur without reference to the food itself. Overstress on table manners, constant reprimands at the table, tense meals as a result of tension between the adults (as well as in the parent-child relationship) create feeding problems. The child can hardly be expected to enjoy being at such a table. Eating should be a pleasant experience if food is to be enjoyed!

At times a child's eating peculiarities are determined by an association to particular foods. If the rejected foods are few in number, unless other signs of disturbance are also evident, there is no reason to explore the nature of the conflict aroused by particular dishes. One child, for example, developed an aversion to chicken after seeing her father kill her pet chicken for the family dinner. Her response undoubtedly was indicative of a problem greater than her disturbance over the destruction of the pet. Other pets had been killed before. Her horror at seeing her father the instrument of the destruction was not compatible with her life situation since as a farm child she had seen him kill chickens weekly. It undoubtedly had some new implication at that time, confirming her belief that her father was a dangerous person. The chicken was an example of—not the cause of—her concept of her father's dangerousness. She could survive without liking chicken, but how was she to handle her fear of her father? If she couldn't handle that, she needed help, not so she could eat chicken but in order to feel safe with her father and men in general. It is again the total picture, not a fragment of it, that indicates how seriously the fragment should be taken.

Eating habits can be affected by the use parents make of food. Depriving a child of food as punishment can result in the child overvaluing food as a symbol of acceptance by the parents. Such an approach can lead instead to rejection of food because, if a child convinces himself he does not like food, it is no punishment to be deprived of it. It is admirable foresight that enables the child to diminish the effect of punishment by learning to depreciate that which is used as punishment. There is also a physiological reason for not using denial of food to punish a child. The value of punishment is to indicate to the child that certain behavior is unacceptable. Out of this it is hoped will come an ability to find a way, not deserving of punishment, to reach the goal the child sought through his undesirable behavior. Hunger is physically debilitating and reduces the amount of energy available for adaptation. In this way to withhold food as punishment is to lessen the ability of the child to deal with the struggle for adaptation with which he is faced.

There is another questionable practice common among parents. They use certain foods as a reward. This is particularly true in regard to sweets. If the child behaves, if he does this or doesn't do that, he can have some cookies, a piece of candy or a dish of ice cream. Then the parents are surprised that the child prefers sweet foods to others! Gold is no more beautiful in itself than cheaper metals. Its appraisal as beautiful is in part the result of its rarity. If tin were as rare, its lustre, softness and its rich gray color would probably be valued as much as gold. It is a characteristic of human nature that that which is rare and given as a reward has a value over and above its intrinsic worth. If candy is given as a reward for service beyond the call of duty, is it surprising that it is valued for reasons beyond its inherent quality? Most dentists believe that excessive intake of sweets increases dental caries.

If so, sweets should never be a reward. Casually given, they will have less significance to the child. "If you don't eat your dinner, you can't have any dessert." "If you are good you can have a cookie." "If you don't cry at the doctor's office, I'll give you an ice cream cone." "You know if you are good the dentist will give you a lollipop." What better way than these to enhance the value of sweets? Parents in these remarks indicate there is nothing like sweets, even though scarce or forbidden. A change in approach to sweets will not in all instances relieve the problem. Some children have a compulsive need to eat sweet foods. This may be related to the early nursing period with the high sugar content of feeding formulas. This does not mean the sugar content of formulas should be decreased. It is rather that the child attempts to relive the infancy feeding experiences. In such instances the child is expressing a much broader problem than simply a compulsive interest in candy.

Overeating is as difficult a problem to solve as is really inadequate or erratic eating. All the problems that create a resistance to food may also result in excessive intake of food. Overeating that results in great obesity is difficult to correct. It has become a proverb that an individual who overeats indicates his need to be loved, a need that is not being adequately met. Overeating is more complex than this simple saying implies. Unique individual factors play a part and can be evaluated only by an understanding gained from a study of the particular person. As a few examples but not as a comprehensive list: obesity may be unconsciously valued as evidence of being big; as a protection against the pain of attack, the fat serving as padding; as a symbol of being good-natured, therefore harmless, therefore not one to attack; as an unconscious equivalent of being pregnant; as a representation of being maternal; as a means of protecting oneself from a favorable response from the opposite sex; or as an excuse for being disliked since the real reason would be too painful, etc.

Obesity at times is related also to endocrine imbalance. Endocrinologists, having discovered some of the glandular causes for obesity, should not rest upon their laurels and place the responsibility for correcting all other forms of obesity upon the shoulders of the psychiatrists. There may be other physical imbalances as yet not determined that contribute to obesity, even in those people whose obesity is related to a psychological difficulty. Obesity in some instances may be a psychosomatic disease rather than solely psychological or physical.

The fantasy of a happy home often includes the dream of a delightful meal together. As a result, mealtime becomes important. Because typically a father is away from home so many hours of the day and the bedtime hour is so close to the end of dinner, the dinner hour in many homes is one of the few times parents can share experiences with the child. From this standpoint it is preferable to have the child eat with his parents. In actuality it is not always wise to strive for this goal. The dinner hour may be so late that the child is overly hungry. A hungry child is rarely a delightful child and rarely finds parents delightful. The child should eat earlier.

Parents vary widely in their motivations for teaching table manners and their tolerance for the clumsiness of a small child in manipulating table utensils. Some parents need to face their own inability to accept the normal messiness of a small child's eating patterns. If a father can tolerate eating with the child only if the latter doesn't smear his food, or only if the adult can "hold himself in," the atmosphere at the table will hardly be conducive to an enjoyable experience. Under such circumstances it is preferable for the child to eat earlier, even though such a program creates extra work. It is usually less exhausting for a mother to cook an extra meal than to bear the tension that would arise were the hapless child to smear creamed spinach over his hands, face and the tablecloth. A slice of bread and butter may give the child a sense of sharing the meal with father, without father being quite so disturbed. Eating together is not the *sine qua non* of family life. It is only one of the opportunities available for consolidating positive inter-relationships—if it is effective. If it isn't, it had better be avoided.

Table manners can be taught if they are not pressed upon the child before his muscular control is adequate or during a period when other more important stresses are utilizing most of the child's adaptive energy. Just because they are learned at an appropriate time does not indicate that they will be used at home! Only the neighbors may be aware of how properly a child eats! A child gradually absorbs table manners from adults. He wants to be comfortable in a new and strange situation and so he (sometimes) calls upon his ability to imitate adults when he dines in other homes. Frequently he sees little point in making the same effort at home.

The more relaxed and pleasant the eating experience is, the more readily the child will probably use his skills. No dinner table experience can be expected to compete with a ball game about to start on the playground or with an essential TV program. Under such circumstances a child will gulp his food down as fast as possible. Parents need not remain silent and suffer. They can protest occasionally without ruining either their child's eating habits or their relationship with him. It is the constant unpleasantnesses, not the occasional ones, that are disrupting.

At times the problem of table manners extends beyond the manipulation of utensils. The child will not remain at the table. He jumps up to get something; he runs around to hit his brother who is annoying him; he suddenly goes to find the dog. It is a rare family that can always avoid such interruptions. It is difficult for a small energy-laden child to remain still at the table as long as most adults can. When a brother kicks under the table, the victim naturally wishes to remove the shield the distance across the table provides. Pets are potential diversions at any time. Some adults still believe that children should be seen and not heard. Adults talk of their interests and expect the child to sit in respectful boredom. They never seem to recognize that they justify their conversation by indicating either that they would be bored listening only to the child, or that they haven't seen each other all day so they want to exchange experiences. Should a child really be expected to have more tolerance for boredom and for being left out of a conversation than his parents? Extreme restlessness during a meal may indicate that the general dinner atmosphere is not gratifying to the child. It may also, of course, be a reflection of general restlessness, which should be evaluated not in terms of table manners, but in the light of the overall problem reflected in the behavior.

Good table manners are a relatively essential social pattern of adaptation. They are the frosting on a cake. Frosting is added to cake to enhance it; it is not used to cover a cake-shaped piece of wood if the creation is to have other than decorative merit. Good manners, whether at the table or elsewhere, can deceptively cover a personality structure that is as unsatisfactory as a wooden cake. Added to a healthy basic personality, they are a rich embellishment and a sign of well-being.

20 : *Fears*

EVERY ADULT SUFFERS FROM CERTAIN FEARS, SOME OF WHICH
are universal, some of which are unique. Everyone fears a destructive force—wars, fires, floods, earthquakes or the reckless careenings of a drunken driver arouse fear if their appearance is imminent or possible. The farmer fears drought
or unusually wet weather; the businessman fears a recession
or a depression; the laborer fears unemployment. Everyone
living in a reality world has certain fears that are based upon
dangers that actually exist in that world.

Fear in itself is not always an unfortunate emotional experience. It simply represents an awareness of danger for
which the individual should take precautionary measures if
possible. The businessman, laborer, or the farmer, if they
did not fear reverses, would not save money for the lean
years. If people did not fear war they would not encourage
diplomacy as a substitute nor would they prepare defenses
against those that threaten war. The emotional response of
fear is a warning signal to the individual who experiences it.
Its function is to mobilize the defenses against that which is
feared, enabling the individual, when possible, to prepare to
defend himself or to flee. If the ego can integrate it into the
total pattern of behavior at the time it is experienced, fear is
the force that stimulates an evaluation of reality and, on the
basis of reality, leads to a plan to ignore or deal with danger.

If a person smells the smoke of burning wood, he is not showing supreme wisdom by trying to analyze what childhood experience caused him to fear fire; he should find out from where the odor comes. He can be expected to fear that his house is on fire until he determines that it is not and that the odor is from his neighbor's newly constructed barbecue pit. If his house is on fire, fear of destruction will lead him to put the fire out, call the fire department, attempt to save some valuables or, if the conflagration is great, flee from the house.

Many fears manifested by children are just as justified, within the limits of their experience, as are the rational adult fears. Many small children fear the dark. They fear the dark because within their ability to comprehend it, the dark is void of familiar people and objects since nothing can be seen. Darkness represents aloneness and desertion. The child calls to his parents as a way of investigating the validity of his fears. Their voice reassures him but often not for long. When darkness descends again the same danger may exist. Only fatigue in some instances overcomes the fear. Sometimes when a child fears the dark he is reassured if the light is left burning. In those cases in which darkness means absence, the light helps the child to see that objects at least are not absent. This reassurance places him back in a familiar world which he then assumes is complete. Incorporated into this completeness is the availability of his parents even if they are not visible. He no longer feels deserted.

In the somewhat older child, fear of the dark is of somewhat different significance. The dark becomes peopled with dangerous persons of the child's fantasy. As such it creates fear not because of the darkness itself but because of what can be present and not seen. These fantasy people often represent the punishing or revengeful parents, separated off from the reality parents of daytime who are kind and protecting as well as punishing.

An adult patient revealed an interesting picture of the

meaning of her fear of the dark which dominated a great part of her childhood. In this instance the fear was of the loved parent. It was the loved parent who lurked in the dark. She feared that she would be kidnapped. This fear occurred only when it was dark and when she was alone. The kidnapper was always a man. She recalled that at first she would feel some pleasurable anticipation but immediately fear would erase the pleasant aspect. She then fantasied a conversation with her kidnapper. She would explain to him that she wasn't pretty and couldn't sing well. A little girl down the street was both beautiful and talented; he should kidnap that girl instead. Then she believed the kidnapper would release her. She visualized running home fast to the embrace of her mother. She recalled that her parents often commented that in reality she never wanted to go any place alone with her father though "he adored her and she him." Her parents always cited this as an example of how important they both were, that she was not happy unless they shared the same pleasure. The kidnapper represented her father! She was fearful that his adoration of her and hers of him would alienate her mother—in effect, kidnap her from the mother. The fear aroused could be resolved only by denying her own attractiveness and returning to a more infantile relationship to her mother.

Fear of the dark finally becomes colored by a realistic evaluation. Darkness does hide dangers that may be lurking near and thus requires a generalized mobilization to be prepared for attack upon any or all sides. Gradually, with increased experience and more ability to clarify reality, fear of the dark subsides. Many adults retain to a larger or smaller degree remnants of this childhood fear. The fear was a logical fear in childhood, in the light of the child's concept of reality and only later became an invalid fear because it no longer was based upon the individual's comprehension of reality, but rather upon the retention of a childhood response. But if a person is out alone on a dark night and hears stealthy footsteps behind him, footsteps with a rhythm and sound a casual pedestrian would not make, he is not being childish when he experiences fear and, accepting his feeling, maps out a plan of self-defense!

While fear of the dark is only one of many fears a child may have, it is probably the most common. When the factors causing it are considered, the way to meet it and help the child through the discomfort becomes more apparent. The child who fears the dark is not helped by punishment, ridicule, torture by exposure to it or anxious solicitude. He needs calm reassurance that parents are available, that they have not deserted him. He will also handle his fear better if his parents are themselves not fearful in the dark! Part of his learning about reality will come from actual experience, but part of his evaluation of that reality will be colored by his parents' evaluation of it.

Childhood nightmares are closely related in origin to fear of the dark. The nightmares of young children fall into three general categories. The psychologically more immature nightmare involves dreams of being lost. For some reason the child fears his dependent security has evaporated. The more mature nightmare is the fear of attack by wild animals or bizarre people. This, as indicated in the chapter on the oedipal period, is often related to the parent most feared in the triangular struggle. In a third general category of nightmares are those expressing the child's fear of the consequences of his own unacceptable impulses. A child patient once told of a "bad" dream from which he had awakened terrified. Before telling the dream he made it clear that the "bad" part of the dream was that it represented something naughty but he did not know why. In the dream he and his little sister were watching a parade of soldiers; suddenly his sister dashed out into the midst of the parade and was trampled to death. He awoke at that point in uncontrollable panic. The "naughty" part of the dream was actually the wish that motivated the dream. Part of him wished his sister dead, a wish he could not tolerate consciously. It was unbearable to a small extent because he also enjoyed his sister. More importantly his parents tolerated no expression of resentment towards the sister. His resentment was not consciously withheld—it was repressed, to be revealed only in the "naughty" dream.

Occasional nightmares are almost universal during childhood. Their significance does not have to be analyzed. The child only requires immediate comforting and reassurance from the parents until, the anxiety allayed, the child falls back to sleep. Repeated nightmares indicate the child is struggling with a problem he cannot handle and professional help should be sought.

Parents often become distressed when a small child is hesitant, say, to go into the water for the first time or down a slide in the park. They know it is not dangerous. They expect the child to either evaluate the situation with the same acumen or at least accept their word for it. Some children can evaluate the situation accurately or can totally accept the opinion of the parents. In some instances those children present an excessive freedom from fear. They not only go down the slide or enter the water without concern, but are also "fearless" in really dangerous situations. Their judgment is no sounder than the more reticent child; its limitations are only revealed at the opposite end of the spectrum of danger. A new situation is always a potentially dangerous one until its nature is known. The fear a new situation stimulates is frequently, especially in adults, so transient it is not recognized. It offers a stimulation for intellectual evaluation of the nature of the new, mobilizes memories of past experiences with which to compare the present and thus is a starting point for the final conclusion that something new can be accepted, rejected, attacked or fled from. Fear does not cripple unless it reaches such an intensity that it is not a *part* of the response but becomes the *whole* response. In children more frequently than in adults, fear takes over. When this occurs the role of the adult is to provide the other parts that in the child have become submerged. Again this is not done by ridicule, punishment or angrily verbalized reasoning. It is done most effectively when the adult can quietly encourage and reassure without making a tremendous issue of protecting the child from the thing he fears or exposing him to it.

Consider the example of the child who doesn't want to go down the slide in the park. It is not disastrous as far as his future life is concerned whether he goes down the slide or not. If parents insist that he do so, a successful and safe experience may overcome the fear. Then he can slide fearlessly the rest of his life. In some cases of this nature a side action occurs that is not always obvious. The parental insistence that he overcome his fear may intensify the fear. A successful slide may eradicate his fear of sliding, but a new situation arousing fear may reactivate the intensity of fear that was associated with that moment just before the slide was achieved. Any fear may then become panic without necessarily the feared object or experience being dealt with, as his parents forced him to deal with the slide. If given time, the child will eventually experiment with the dangers he thinks exist in the slide. If he doesn't, he can still survive in this world of playgrounds without sliding.

Rational fear is not the fear that cripples most seriously. The crippling anxiety is that which comes with an unconscious distortion of reality. The distortion results because the actual situation is equated with an anxiety-charged previous experience, the exact meaning of which is usually repressed. These are the neurotic anxieties of which everyone partakes and which, when too intense or activated by too many reality situations, becomes so limiting for the individual. Often their origin can be traced to an actual episode. It is the symbolic meaning of that actual episode—or the later symbolism attached to it—that determines whether the frightening event aroused legitimate fear to be erased by later corrective experiences or whether it will become the nucleus of neurotic anxiety. A frequent example of this is seen in the apprehension some adults experience in the presence of dogs. They attribute the anxiety to an early childhood experience when a dog jumped on them, perhaps knocked them over, stole a mitten or growled at them. They continued to be uneasy about dogs from that time on in spite of having many opportunities to find that a dog does not always attack. If this fear of dogs can be rationally explained upon this one episode, why then does not every person fear every other human being since everyone at some time or other has been attacked by another human being? Many people have had an unfortunate experience with a dog and yet like dogs, evaluate accurately the reliability of any individual dog and approach or avoid him according to that evaluation. When an individual fears a species of animal or type of event because of a previously unfortunate experience and in spite of later corrective experiences, continues to respond in the same way, what is feared has usually come to have some meaning over and above its reality. Undoubtedly one of the values in driving a car shortly after having been in an accident, remounting immediately after being thrown by a horse, or any other attempt to provide a corrective experience after a frightening one, is to keep the episode in the framework of a reality experience before it becomes serviceable as a symbolic representation of a hidden anxiety.

Anxiety may also be displaced upon a coincidental event. This was interestingly demonstrated in a child of three who feared running water. The day her little sister was born she had been taken for a picnic. The picnic site was by a waterfall. She had shown some concern over her mother leaving for the hospital, but this seemed quickly erased by her enjoyment of the picnic and the waterfall. Suddenly she became panicky and insisted upon being taken home. From that time on any water coming from a faucet brought on an attack of panic. Actually the noise of the water was associated with her uneasiness over her mother's sudden desertion of her. The mother's return from the hospital did not clear up the panic response to running water because the running water was always associated with the anxiety experienced at the time her mother did leave.

An adult patient described a feeling of uneasy sadness whenever she ate fish salad. It evolved that during her childhood her parents for some reason limited most of their evening social activities to Friday nights. Being Catholic, fish was served on Friday. The evening meal was usually fish salad because it was easy to prepare. The patient had never felt really secure when cared for by a sitter. Fish salad still brought the earlier emotional experience back even though the actual events were long past and no longer recalled except as a result of efforts to associate the feeling of uneasy sadness with past experiences.

No child or adult should be completely fearless. Unnecessary fears resulting from lack of familiarity with the safety of a venture will gradually disappear with encouragement, familiarity and increasing ability to judge its nature. Anxiety that persists in spite of adequate time and experience to invalidate the fear does so because of some symbolic significance attached to what is feared. If the anxiety does continue and cripples the child's overall activity, it is not for his parents to diagnose and treat. It is time for an expert.

21 : *Temper tantrums*

A PSYCHOLOGICALLY HEALTHY PERSON BECOMES ANGRY UNDER certain conditions. Some of those conditions are generally anger-arousing for most people, while others may cause anger in one person and not another. Mature individuals usually handle their anger in one of several ways. They may recognize the cause and attempt to correct or avoid the situation. They may be angered by one particular aspect of a situation, but after weighing it against other—more gratifying —features they may decide the latter has greater importance, whereupon the anger disappears. They may discharge some of the tension with a game of handball. Others may escape into fantasy when action can't be taken, imagining all the things they would do "if." They may repress their anger and develop high blood pressure. Or, instead of repressing their anger, they may express it in a "blind rage" and still have high blood pressure. The difference between "blind rage" and a temper tantrum is defined, as a matter of courtesy, by the chronological age of the individual. An adult has a "blind rage"—the child has a "temper tantrum." They are the same.

A temper tantrum occurs when a child is unable, because of his own stage of development, to integrate his internal impulses and the demands of reality. The child responds to the frustration irrationally because he has found no rational way to relieve it. The strength of the internal impulse is of such intensity it cannot be repressed and reality, defined either by the actual situation or the limits imposed by the parents, does not permit expression. When no substitute solution is effective or available a temper tantrum results.

Internal impulses cannot always be mastered by subterfuge. Take the case of Teddy, whose domestic problems centered around his ten-year-old sister. Frequently angry at her he would attack her with animal-like intensity. His teacher, completely sympathetic with Teddy and aware of the sister's irritatingly provocative personality, suggested that he relieve some of the tenseness accompanying his rage by smashing boxes in the basement. By pretending the boxes were his sister, he could carry out the homicidal impulses his parents' censorship and his sister's strength forced him to curb. Also, he could thus avoid the severe remorse that always followed a rage attack. Teddy thought this an excellent idea, but it failed when he tried it. He explained that it didn't work because when he tried to pretend the boxes were his sister he was too mad to pretend. Then he got angry at the boxes because they weren't his sister, angry at his parents that they wouldn't let him do to his sister what he could do to the boxes, angry at his sister that she made him so furious. He couldn't pretend. He concluded the interview with the comment that nothing works, and that he would just have to get to the point that he could say to himself that his sister was a pain in the neck and so what.

Other modes of defense fail the child also. The child often cannot avoid the anger-arousing situation as readily as an adult can. Parents, particularly, are difficult people to escape. The child also has less capacity to weigh the pros and cons of an overall picture. His anger is more sharply delineated from his other responses. He can repress the anger. If he does it too often not immediate hypertension but a personality disturbance results. A child sometimes strives to solve his anger by fantasy. He mutters to himself all the things he would like to do. Parents often destroy even that tentative solution by threatening the child with punishment or actually punishing him for attempting to solve his problem in this way. He is only behaving like the adult who imagines what he would do "if."

Parents often prevent the child from mobilizing defenses against irreconcilable forces. To telescope a hypothetical situation, parents may follow somewhat this procedure. Freddy wants a cookie, parents say no; the insolvable conflict comes into existence. Freddy (not sweetly to be sure) says he didn't want one anyway. Mother (not sweetly to be sure) says he should not be impudent. Freddy kicks the kitchen chair, displacing his anger from the mother to the chair. Mother slaps him. Freddy mutters inarticulately but audibly enough to suggest a fantasy that would, if carried out, bode poorly for mother. Mother slaps him again, accuses him of impudence, forbids him to talk that way. Finally, Freddy's ego gives up. He has a tempter tantrum. Mother might have been wiser to ignore and thereby allow the original defense by denial. She had won her point; Freddy wasn't getting the cookie. Why should parents always try to conquer beyond their original goal? When the child's anger cannot be released constructively, the resulting tension is expressed in the futile moments of attack on anybody or anything, and in verbalizations, both movements and words constituting the temper tantrums.

A temper tantrum is difficult to handle. Parents and parental possessions may be in a dangerous spot. Parents have a right to protect themselves and their possessions from destruction. This frequently can be done only by restraining the child. Restraining him often increases the temper tantrum because it prohibits the one outlet he has found. For this reason a child in a temper tantrum should not be held unless there is risk of real injury to himself, to his own valued possessions or to the person or possessions of others. When real injury or destruction may occur, even though restraining the child may lead to increased anger, it has a preventive value over and above that bearing upon the welfare of others. It is also of value to the child. If a child is not prevented from injuring valued possessions of his own, other people or their possessions, once his rage passes he may be overwhelmed by his own guilt for what he did in irrational anger. This guilt only adds another burden to his already strained ego. He will have sufficient, if not excessive, guilt over his malignant rage anyway. There is no need to increase it.

It is sometimes recommended that a child be isolated from others during a temper tantrum. The wisdom of total isolation is questionable. Some children calm down more readily if the provocateur is not present. This calming effect of total isolation may be because the child feels he is deserted and unloved because of his behavior. He calms down then because of panic, not because his problem is solved.* On the other hand, a child will usually solve the immediate tension if he can be removed from its immediate cause and from the environs of all but one person. It is important that this one person not be struggling with his own "blind rage." The person should be objective enough about the situation to recognize that the goal of immediate treatment is to restore the child's shattered ego—not to discipline the child for ego failure. Time, patience, calmness and warmth on the part of the adult is thus the immediate therapeutic agent.

In providing this therapy parents should avoid forcing the medicine upon the child. Trying to pet the child, reassure him or comfort him may only increase the rage. When the time arrives, the child will ask for comfort. Often he will not ask for it verbally but by bodily language. The sobbing changes tone. His vituperative attack loses force. His body rigidity lessens. Then is the time to take the child in the parental lap, suggest something to eat or a quiet game. The aim is not to achieve the fulfillment of the suggestion but rather the re-establishment of a mode of communication between the child and the adult.

---

*The sharp slap or the dash of cold water may be as efficacious immediately but may have the same questionable implications for the future.

If the temper tantrum was precipitated by the refusal of a request of the child, the reward for the temper tantrum should not be a reversal of the parental point of view. If it is the reward, the child soon discovers he can get what he wants by having a temper tantrum. That, in the author's opinion, is a minor disadvantage compared to a more subtle side-effect of the parents' reversal. By such behavior the parents become unpredictable. Faced with a demand or a refusal by his parents the child does not know what to expect sequentially. The resultant temper tantrum is then not only a technique for gaining his end, but also indicative of an uncertainty that has resulted from parental vacillations of the past. In such instances the child does not even have the bedrock of parental consistency upon which to build his world. Past experiences with this inconsistency make it more difficult for him to integrate opposing forces or to defend himself against ego disintegration as a result of the irreconcilability of those forces.

After the storm has subsided, the fewer comments the better. If parents can say casually and reassuringly that they can understand the rage and know it's hard when something just can't be done, it may have some effect in reassuring the child. A long lecture on the subject, a sanctimonious exposition on the futility of a temper outbreak, or an oration dedicated to the theme of parental love does little except to re-arouse irritation or create unnecessary shame or guilt for the child. His ego needs a rest, not further needling.

Sometimes a child isolates himself as he feels his anger mount. He wishes to remove himself from the situation until he establishes some mastery of it. This behavior is quite different from the removal insisted upon by the parents after the storm has broken. Some parents who intuitively time reactions well can help the child by suggesting he isolate himself until he can manage. This suggestion, if given wisely, is not punishment but rather support. If withdrawal relieves the acuteness of the pressure, it is an effective temporary measure. The child should not be left to his own discretion to terminate his withdrawal unless he shows wisdom in when he does so. If, for example, a child withdraws to his room and is not heard from for an hour or so, parents should investigate. If he is playing happily the withdrawal is over and all is well. If still emotionally upset, either still angry or now depressed, it is time for parental intervention by suggesting a pleasant activity, entering into a casual conversation or becoming involved in some planning with the child—the aim again to establish an emotionally pleasant communication.

A child who always handles a difficult situation by withdrawal will eventually need help in facing his difficulties more directly. If over a period of time every frustration is met in that way, if there is no evidence of progressing ability to deal with situations more directly, the reasons should be evaluated. If on the other hand there is evidence that the less intense conflicts are being mastered, the withdrawal occurring only when the conflicts are of major nature—and if many of the major conflicts are becoming minor, to be handled directly—the child is wisely dosing his own therapy.

Occasional temper tantrums of greater or lesser intensity are common in childhood and are indicative of a transiently overwhelmed ego. If they are frequent they are evidence that the balance between demands upon the ego and the capacity of the ego is disturbed. If parents cannot determine why this is true, professional help is needed.

22 : *Lying*

MOST PARENTS CONSIDER IT IMPORTANT THAT A CHILD BE TRUTH-ful. Truthfulness involves many considerations that are not always as clearcut as slight inspection would indicate. When and what is truth? It has a reciprocal relationship to the age of the individual, his awareness of reality and the legitimacy of the goal he is seeking.

Adults may consider a child's story untruthful because their point of reference is different from his. The small child comes home with a tale of having been chased by a bear. The parent knows there are no bears in the neighborhood so the adult interprets the child's story as lying. The child who tells of being pursued by a bear is trying to find comprehensible words to express his own emotional experience. Perhaps he was frightened by his jaunt home. He could explain the intensity of his anxiety only by the fantasy of a bear. Perhaps he was feeling very adequate as his own sole protector and could convey this feeling only in the symbolism his fantasy created. In such situations the child is not lying. The adult and the child simply have a different point of reference.

Sometimes a child falsifies only to add zest to life through his fantasy. He becomes so engrossed in his fantasy that it becomes reality. Endowed with a rich imagination, the sterility of his particular environment can be counteracted by his fantasy living. When he tells of his fantasy life he is not lying. That is the life he is really living. A falsification would be to tell the objective truth about the reality in which he is not really participating.

The displacement of fact by fantasy is typical of the very small child. Gradually the child finds that reality offers sufficient satisfaction so that fantasy does not play so significant a role. He does not verbalize his fantasy then to describe what appears a distortion of reality. An older child who continues to confuse reality and fantasy is not "lying" but is indicating that for some reason he must live in fantasy as if it were reality rather than place fantasy and reality in their proper roles.

At times a child distorts reality not because he really believes his distortion but because the distortion alleviates the strain truth would create. One child at the age of nine indicated that long after she knew there wasn't a Santa Claus she clung to the fable as truth. If she didn't pretend to believe he brought the Christmas presents, she would have to be grateful to her parents for their gifts. Because she was angry at them she would feel uncomfortable accepting from them, particularly if her parents knew her realistic knowledge. Thus she accepted the statement of her parents about Santa Claus. Who was lying?

Children (and adults) often falsify reality in order to achieve some end they cannot achieve otherwise. They indicate painful or glorifying experiences they have had because they hope thus to inspire the sympathy or respect which they crave and which they cannot win by a revelation of reality. A child tells of brutal treatment, exciting exploits, terrifying challenges he has met. He does so because he is emotionally hungry for some response he is not obtaining in any other way. Such falsification of reality is not an indication for punishment but rather for an evaluation of what the child is seeking, why he cannot obtain it in the normal course of events, and why he needs it.

Usually none of these forms of falsification really concern parents. Unless the child is beyond the age in which fantasy and reality are relatively interchangeable, they just pass off the falsification of reality by recognition that the child is young. The type of lying the parents object to is lying which often has a logical basis. A parent asked the child if he took fifty cents from the household purse and the child says "no" when the truthful answer would be "yes." Why does the child lie? Perhaps the more rational question should be why wouldn't he lie? A child in lying often shows what is from his vantage point good judgment. It is the most practical way to gamble on avoiding disapproval or punishment. He responds to an implied threat by defending himself with a lie. What better tool has he? Consider the following two dialogues.

Dialogue 1:

MOTHER: Johnny, did you take fifty cents out of my purse this morning?

JOHNNY: (*Aside*) Why is she asking me? Does she want information about the fifty cents or about me? Maybe she wants to know if her mathematical skills are poor. I'll risk that. (*To mother*) Yes. I needed it for some paper at school.

MOTHER: Oh good, I wondered if I'd lost it. Next time you take money out of my purse, let me know.

Dialogue 2:

MOTHER: Johnny, did you take fifty cents out of my purse this morning?

JOHNNY: (*Aside*) Why is she asking me? Does she want information about the fifty cents or about me? There is something about her tone of voice that implies she is angry that I took it. (*To mother*) No.

MOTHER: Johnny, tell me the truth. Did you take it?

JOHNNY: No.

MOTHER: Johnny, if you tell me the truth, I won't punish you. Did you take the fifty cents?

JOHNNY: (*To himself*) If I say yes now, I'll be caught be-

cause I told a lie before. Better try to bluff this
one out. (*To mother*) No.

MOTHER: Johnny, I happen to know you are not telling
me the truth. I know you took the fifty cents. I'm
going to spank you to teach you not to lie to me.

JOHNNY: (*To himself*) Who lied first? By asking me she
implied she didn't know who took it, but she
did. How was I to know I wouldn't be spanked
if I said yes the first time? The lie might have
worked.

Children take naturally to the Fifth Amendment. They believe they have a right not to testify against themselves and
thus avoid the sin of lying. The average child does not deny
an act unless he fears his confession will result in punishment. Lying is a conscious defense against repercussions
from his environment. It is much more logical than most
defenses.

The logic of the defense does not necessarily mean that lying should be condoned. But its validity from the child's
standpoint should be recognized. Any child will occasionally
deny an act in order to avoid the consequences. A child who
always tells the truth when the truth will only bring him disapproval is either showing poor judgment or gratification in
being punished. Also the child who always can avoid punishment by acknowledging he did something could use truthfulness as a way to avoid consequences that are deserved. He
is not learning to curb his behavior, he is only learning to
avoid the merited discomfort from it. As the growing child
becomes less fearful of disapproval, more assured others will
understand an impulsive act, more confident of his own control of seriously disadvantageous acts, he will have less need
to deny his behavior.

There are two practical implications in this consideration
of lying. If parents know a child did a forbidden or disapproved act, they should not ask. This only tempts a child to

compound the felony. If they ask, they should ask in good faith because they really want to know. If the child clarifies their doubts and acknowledges he did it, the child then deserves to feel his parents will explain why the act is unacceptable. If, however, the child uses confession to avoid consequences, it is time for the parent not to ask but state a fact known to them and discipline the child for his unacceptable behavior rather than trying to force a confession out of him. The problem is most difficult to handle when the parents really don't know the child has misbehaved. This creates a real dilemma. If the parents ignore the possibility they are not offering guidance to the child. If they accuse unjustly they are not giving the child the support he deserves. If they defend him by claiming he did not commit the act when he did, they may increase the child's guilt beyond a bearable level or imply to him that he can successfully get by with anything. Sometimes under such circumstances parents just have to wait for clarification of the situation; sometimes they can discuss the possibility that if the child committed the offense it is to be disapproved of for such-and-such reasons; sometimes they need to do some detective work before they do anything else. They need to know the truth to avoid acting in ignorance. A man, particularly skilled in working with delinquents, many times stated that he would rather falsely believe a person nine times to find out the tenth time that his faith was misplaced than once falsely to accuse a delinquent who trusted him. He was not advocating blind belief maintained until the facts hit him unexpectedly, but rather that the child not be accused by those he trusts until the truth is known. Even in our courts, a man is innocent until proven guilty. Should not children have the same privilege with the additional help of adults trying to find out the truth?

There are other reasons that will cause a child to falsify a situation. He may falsify not to avoid punishment for himself, but to bring it upon others. How often a child will mildly distort his picture of the behavior of a sibling who he feels is a parental favorite, in order to place himself in a favorable light and his sibling in a punishment-deserving one. He may falsify a situation in order to place the blame he merits upon someone else. As a simple illustration, he claims his teacher did not assign homework (which she did), a distortion of fact because he does not want to do homework (which if he had confessed, would be the truth but perhaps a dangerous truth to reveal). He may distort a report of a situation in order to preserve his own self-respect. Adults indulge in the latter fabrication. Mr. Jones at the close of a day of irritation resulting from an irascible boss, dreams on his way home of what he would like to have said to that dictator, instead of the meek "yes" he did express. By the time he tells his wife about the episode he implies quite falsely that in saying the "yes" he conveyed his anger, contempt and superiority. A child may report a similar episode with less éclat but with a similar motive, namely, to save face with those he cares for. The falsification is more pleasant than the truth.

There are many reasons why an individual, whatever his age, does not tell the truth. Falsification is a symptom of some adjustment problem. The important questions are what need the falsification serves and why that need cannot be served except in that way. This does not imply that a child should not be encouraged to value the truth and experience disapproval if he falsifies. It only implies that further steps should be taken in order to understand and correct, if necessary, the causative factors.

Many parents in their legitimate appreciation of the truth become concerned about their own falsifications. These they consider justified because of their desire to live in a social world. They are concerned about the effect of their white lies upon their child. If as an illustration, they are invited, in the presence of their child, to spend an evening that would inevitably be boring, they avoid the boredom by replying that they will be busy. The child discovers later that the only activity that occupies their evening is television. Obviously this confuses the child. He lies, the parents disapprove. They lie, and they explain it as different. It is. Parents have no reason to be angry when the child challenges their veracity. The difference between a social grace and an unacceptable fabrication is a fine ethical point. Only time and maturity will make the line of demarcation clear. If parents use fabrication ethically and accept the same kind of choice by their child, the difference between unethical and ethical falsification will finally become clear. The confusion leads to unfortunate consequences when parents deny obvious falsehoods and attack the child for ethical falsehoods.

23 : *Stealing*

ONE OF THE MOST DIFFICULT DEMANDS OF SOCIAL LIVING WITH which to comply is the prohibition against stealing. In facing the prohibition, two diametrically opposed impulses join battle. One strives by the most direct methods available to attain what is badly wanted. Often the most direct method is simply to take it. This brings the individual into conflict with the person who has the object, values it and does not wish to give it up. If it is taken from him he will be annoyed and resentful. The wish to have something and therefore to take it clashes directly with the wish to be loved by others, not to be punished by others and to feel one's own possessions are secure.

Very young children take from each other with no awareness of any significance to their act other than an expression of their wish to have the object. Fortunately most parents and other adults recognize this as immaturity rather than stealing. They tend to place their emphasis on the capacity of the child to identify, and thus sympathize, with the owner (which probably does not have too much meaning to the child at the time) rather than upon the crime. The prohibition of the act, implied in parental disapproval, without the reasons being too clearly defined, is probably the first significant learning experience in regard to coveting that which others have. Parental prohibitions are finally incorporated into the superego. The impulse to take from another is curbed without rational reasons playing too important a part. The child usually respects the possessions of others before he could be expected to grasp the philosophical verities of why the rights of others should be considered.

As indicated in the chapter concerning the development of the superego, the child utilizes his ability to incorporate parental standards into internalized control established by the superego for two important reasons. He wishes to be loved, and behaving automatically—by self determination and self control—as the parents wish will assure him, he hopes, of the love he seeks. He also wishes to avoid punishment, a punishment which may be expressed by the withdrawal of love or by more direct punitive responses. The superego, by controlling the impulse to take from another, assures the individual of the love of others and the avoidance of punishment. The child can accept the rationale of this because he can recognize that if he were the victim of stealing he would withdraw his love and inflict punishment. The acceptance of the prohibition against taking what another has begins as the result of parental or other adult disapproval. It is strengthened as the child comes to value acceptance by his own age group. The first identification with a sufferer is identification with the anger of the victim. Fear of the consequences of that anger results. Identification with the pain another experiences in losing a valued object probably is a later development in most individuals. Thus, when parents ask a two-year-old how he would feel if his favorite toy were taken from him by another child, it is a harmless question but probably not too effective. A somewhat more mature child would be apt to answer that he would be mad. Only later is he really apt to feel that he doesn't want to make another unhappy. Obviously there will be some individual variations to this.

An older child who has an ineffectual superego may steal. Typically with these children, love itself has no particular value; it has proved to be an ephemeral experience at best.

Punishment alone has some meaning, for fear of punishment may inhibit behavior. It may, on the other hand, offer a stimulus to develop greater skills in avoiding punishment. Growing skill in avoiding detection for an act justifies gambling that the act will not be discovered, so punishment can be avoided. If detection should result, the punishment is endured, and the act is then repeated with more precautions against discovery. Delinquents of this type often show no guilt over their behavior, only self-depreciation because they were detected. The crime to them was not the act but the fact that they were caught. It is their own love for themselves that is jeopardized; that the love others have for them is withdrawn is meaningless to them. In such cases the problem is not to devise effective punishment since no punishment in a civilized country can be severe enough to overcome the gambling spirit but rather to reactivate, if possible, the individual's dormant desire to find that acceptance by others is sufficiently rewarding. This kind of individual, so often met in the courtroom, is the most difficult to handle; other people mean so little to them.

Some children and some adults steal because of the symbolic meaning of the object they steal. This motivation for stealing is a complex one and can be evaluated only by a study of the individual. To give a few examples but by no means a complete list: Stealing may represent stealing love of which the child feels deprived; a little girl may steal from a boy as a symbolic representation of stealing his penis; a little boy may steal from his mother because the stealing means depriving her of her power over him or perhaps of the baby he fears will grow inside of her to replace him. Such symbolic factors in stealing obviously are neurotically determined and can be dealt with only by a person trained to explore such behavior.

An individual may behave in such a way as to bring punishment upon himself because of the meaning punishment may have. Stealing may be the way he invites this punishment. Again, this is most clearly demonstrated with the delinquent child, although more subtle examples can be found in the less asocial youngster. People working closely with both delinquent children and adults are often struck by the way the individual carries out a crime. He makes obvious mistakes, is careless in his planning. In such cases it can usually be assumed that the mistakes are the result of an unconscious desire to be caught. For this reason it is sometimes said that the most valued ally of the detective is the criminal himself.

This pattern is often seen in the average child. The child whose face is smeared with jam after he has invaded the forbidden jam pot is the archetype. Why didn't he wash his face before his parents caught him? Many times the child takes something or behaves in some other disapproved manner so as to determine parental response and gain parental support for that side of himself that disapproves of his act. He may take money from his mother's purse when he knows she is aware of how much money she has. He may make purchases his parents know exceed in value the amount of his allowance. He wishes to be punished in order to strengthen his own internal disapproval. This pattern of behavior typically is a transient one. If it persists the underlying problems are more significant than they appeared at first.

There is a period in the lives of many children when stealing is an adventure. Farm children may steal watermelons from the neighbor's field or apples from the neighbor's orchard. Urban children do not have an opportunity for such adventure without it having more serious implications. The urban child picks up things from the ten-cent store, the hardware store, the grocery store, the knicknack shop. Often they take objects that are wanted; so in rural areas the stolen watermelons may be eaten. They may take trinkets that are not wanted, the adventure being gratifying in itself. So too with the watermelons. This type of stealing is often either done in groups or its excitement relived in telling about it to the group. Obviously this behavior should be controlled and not condoned. Its seriousness, however, should not be overrated! Parents become frightened when this "delinquent" pattern appears. They react in a way that may be most conducive to perpetuating it. The child often sees the act in better perpective than his parents do. The parents' evaluation and their disturbed response to it angers the child. He may as an expression of that anger, convert a game into a serious project. He may only practice it more diligently so the parents are less apt to know about his behavior.

It is often difficult to handle the situation with real wisdom and no two children can be handled wisely the same way. The aim of whatever is done, without question, is to give the child a clearer evaluation of what he is doing, to give him a way of finding adventure with wiser goals, and to stop his behavior before it shifts from adventure to delinquency.

Some parents hope to correct stealing by shaming the child. They insist that the stolen object be returned to the owner in the parent's presence. This often works. It is a humiliating experience for the child and it is questionable whether it is necessary to make the child that uncomfortable in order to stop his misbehavior. It should be born in mind also that some people respond to humiliation with anger and defiance—a response the child may not dare show but which he may allow to smolder until it breaks out finally in another area. With the same goal in mind the parents may insist that the child work to pay for the stolen object and confess his act to the storekeeper. Again the goal is to teach him through humiliation. Or, instead of exposing him to humiliation beyond the intimacy of the family, they may limit it to the family circle, treating him as an outcast. They may even discuss his crime before friends, spreading the word that he has leprosy of the soul and is to be avoided.

All of these methods may work and may be necessary with some children. But they are better reserved for extreme situations when more commensurate measures have failed. It is certainly important that the child not "get away with" his misbehavior. It is important that he be aware of parental disapproval and know why an act mischievously committed may have ramifications beyond the child's immediate awareness. All this can be done without humiliating the child and causing what is a molehill to the child to be magnified by the lens of parental eyes into a mountain.

Stealing, instigated chiefly for adventure, tends to lose its exciting value as other possibilities for stimulating pleasure become available. This raises the question of whether, rather than concentrating all attention upon the act, there should not be an exploration of what other possibilities are available to the child. Sometimes children become involved in unacceptable behavior because without that their life would be pretty dull. If the child is motivated chiefly through a desire for adventure the time will come when his group will say "that is child's play." The activity will then lose its appeal.

Stealing, as with every other aspect of child behavior, cannot be dealt with by the absolute scale of good or bad, black or white. Its meaning can be discerned only by the perspective gained through an understanding of the total child and the home of which he is a part. Some parents do not expect the child to refrain from taking money from their purse; they wish the child to know that when money is required he can get it for himself out of the family purse. In another home this "open-purse policy" may not be maintained; the parents feel that the child steals when he takes the money. Parents in the first home are shocked by this attitude; they wouldn't consider it stealing; their child always takes money from the family purse when he needs it. Actually the parents of the second home are correct in their evaluation, for their child has ignored a prohibition they have imposed; he has violated a cultural pattern of his home. The cultural pattern of another home is of no significance in estimating the meaning of his behavior.

MOST CHILDREN AND MOST ADULTS AT ONE TIME OR ANOTHER
fantasy running away. Adults have an advantage over children. Adults can easily carry out their fantasy in a socially
commendable way. The tired businessman goes fishing. He
may go with a group of his fishing cronies, running away
from his wife, his secretary and women in general, into a
man's world. Adults can run away from the pressures of day-
by-day living, taking their family with them, to the wilds of
the North Woods for peaceful isolation. Or they can go to a
resort hotel to play bridge in the card room, away from the
grinding monotony of their daily work. In each instance
they are running away, but their act is called a vacation. When
life gets too complicated, one wise solution is to run away—
and call it a vacation.

A child may run away for the same reason. Trying to live
with parents, a toothbrush, a washrag and a clock is just too
much. A courageous child dares to escape all that and to
attempt survival on his own. This courage would be more
effective if all he leaves is the predictable availability of food
and warmth. Those he hopes to obtain by other means. The
child who runs away from parental love and the security
such love provides rarely has the courage to maintain his
vacation from home routines. He returns home because the
absence of the parents proves more painful than the toothbrush, washrag and clock. Even a fantasy of running away

does not give him much pleasure for long. Depriving himself, if only in fantasy, of parental love, is too painful to be counteracted by the pleasant aspects of the fantasy.

Sometimes a child's wandering away is misinterpreted. This is particularly true of the small child. He is not running away but is led on by the tempting unknown and the few steps ahead. The child goes exploring for a time, oblivious to what he is leaving behind. His eagerness to see more overcomes the tie to what he has. Fatigued, he stops and suddenly finds himself longing for what he had left and not knowing how to regain it. He is lost. He did not run away *from* something—he ran *to* something, forgetting that what he valued was not following close behind. An older child similarly motivated cannot understand parental concern when he, having left on Saturday morning on his bicyle to go over to a friend's house for a few minutes does not return until late Saturday night, excitedly telling of a long bicycle ride into the country. He always intended to return; he can't understand why his parents didn't know that. It may take some parental firmness before he understands their point of view and conforms to their restrictions.

Children run away for more complex and more emotionally charged reasons. A child may run away because he is so unhappy at home that he feels any other situation would be preferable. It is easy to understand when a child runs away from really brutal parents—in fact, it is hard to understand why he doesn't! But a child may be unhappy at home not because of brutality but because of subtler unhappiness. Perhaps parental control thwarts his every desire; running away offers the only possibility of freedom.

A child may run away to relieve a tension he experiences at home. He wants to be loved but doesn't feel his parents love him. By running away he hopes to escape the desire to be loved that is aroused by their presence. If he doesn't see them maybe he will be free of the desire to be loved by them.

Unwisely gratified earlier longings as well as a residue of the oedipal conflict can play a part in the child's impulse to run away. If parents smother their child with love in a way that cripples his maturation, the child may run away to avoid the type of love his parents give. He may try to escape from a bear that hugs with such force it crushes. A boy may run away because his mother's intense love offers him gratification that if accepted would expose him, he believes, to his father's destructive wrath. A girl may run away because her tie to her father is so intense that she must either escape from the temptation it offers or endure the imagined wrath of her mother.

A child may run away not from an emotionally charged situation, but instead to one that in a fantasy is emotionally gratifying. A pathetic example of this is the adopted child who in moments of unhappiness runs away, unconsciously or at times consciously seeking his natural parents. A child of divorced parents may also thus run away seeking the absent parent. Or a child may be running to fantasied substitute parents because his own parents do not meet his qualifications as well as fantasied substitute parents would. In the latter instance the behavior has the same meaning as the idea children frequently have that they are adopted.

A child may run to his fantasy world and away from reality. As he runs away from the familiar environment, his surroundings become instruments of his fantasy rather than expressions of reality. The child that runs away to ride back and forth on the streetcar, to spend an entire day and evening in the same movie house, or to wander aimlessly down one street and up another is often running from reality to fantasy. Obviously this is unhealthy. Such an evaluation, however, is not for the parents to make but rather for an expert.

A child may run away from home in order to test parental love. In doing so he usually remains close to his home to spy on the parental response. If his parents are upset and eager to find him it implies to him that his parents care. The wave of running away so often observed following a much publicized episode of another child is often related to this. This parental concern, revealed by the publicity, for the notorious runaway suggests to the child that he can test his parents' love in the same way. When this is recognized as the motivation, the first response of parents and their advisors is often to argue the importance of defeating the child. The parents decide or the advisor recommends that it is better not to show concern. Why should the child be deprived of that very evidence of their love he is asking for if it is really available? Certainly he should learn of their love under wiser circumstances; that is parental, not his, responsibility. In the meantime, if he can find no other way to assure himself, he should at least be assured by their concern about his absence.

Publicity about children who run away may lead to an epidemic of running away for another reason. The child might see running away as a means of punishing the parents. This punishment can take one or both of two forms. His parents will suffer and worry. The child's theme song is "you'll be sorry when—." They will also suffer from social condemnation, for the newspapers quote authorities who say that parents are to blame for delinquency. The tables are finally turned: the child can now expose the parents to punishment. A child who finds his parents relatively satisfying loves them sufficiently so that he does not want to punish them so severely. If he does want to punish them severely and frequently, it is time to find out why.

Children are truant from school for the same reason that they run away from home. School may offer too few gratifications and too many unsatisfactory situations. The logical answer is to get away from it by playing hookey. School may expose the child to emotionally charged situations he cannot handle. It may represent reality when fantasy is more satisfying. To some children, school offers a happier life than home, or at least a way to escape from home. Under such circumstances the child wins social approval and society is unaware that the child actually runs away from home under the guise of enjoying school. Also children can be truant from school in a more subtle way. They daydream through the school hours. By this method they can be corporeally present but away in spirit. Truancy from school, whenever it is manifested by persistent prolonged daydreaming, indicates a serious incompatibility between the child and the real world. Short periods of daydreaming are harmless means of enriching reality. Prolonged, consistent retreat into daydreaming is serious, and, when this occurs, it is again time to find out why.

25 : The "spoilt" child

A "SPOILT" CHILD HAS BY NO MEANS A PLEASANT PERSONALITY.
He objects to practically everything. If he wants something,
he whines until he gets it. If whining doesn't work, he has a
temper tantrum until he gets what he wants. He wants to
have attention directed entirely to himself. If he does not
get it by fair means, he uses foul. Neighbors and friends
comment that the child is "spoilt" because he gets anything
he wants.

To prove the child is "spoilt" the same neighbors and
friends describe the great love that is lavished upon the
child. The parents are always hugging and kissing him, they
are always asking him if he wants something before he has
even thought of it. He has every toy in the toy shop the parents can possibly afford—usually a supply out of all proportion to the family income. Everything in the home appears
to center about the child. The parents scarcely dare breathe
unless the child gives a nod of approval. The child, to the
neighbors and friends, is over-indulged and over-loved.

It is the belief of some psychologists and psychiatrists that
some, although not all, of these children are fixated at an
infantile level as a result of over-indulgence. "Spoilt" behavior, in other children, is the consequence of too little
satisfaction at the infantile level and the later demand for
indulgence is meaningless except as the mask of a fundamental emotional vacuum. The author has never seen a
"spoilt" child to whom the first category applies, although

many have been seen whom neighbors and friends describe as over-indulged and over-loved. In the author's experience the "spoilt" children are those who are frenzied because of an unsatisfied hunger, the hunger being the result of emotional starvation that usually begins at a very early age and grows in magnitude with the years. The following discussion must therefore be viewed in the light of the author's experience in this particular area of child behavior.

The "spoilt" child has a characteristic history. Often he is described as having been fussy from birth. If not from birth, a specific time can be established at which his fussiness started. This would suggest that (1) the infant-mother relationship was strained and continued to remain so, (2) some change in the environment occurred as a result of the child's psychological growth, creating a situation with which neither the child nor the parents could cope, or (3) some change in the actual, physical environment occurred.

When the fussiness dates not from birth but later, careful exploration of the time of its onset will usually indicate what it was that the parents, the child, or both could not handle. In many cases the parents will reveal that they were not ready for a family when the child was born. While they had always planned to have children (or else had planned not to) this pregnancy occurred at a time when it was most inconvenient. Parents often express guilt about their rejection of the embryo, marveling that they could have rejected the future child when they love him so in the present. This attitude seems to give one clue to the picture. The parental guilt over this early rejection can be handled by them only by an overt over-expression of love, effecting a denial of the fact that they really did not want the child. Their own ambivalent feelings are intolerable. The "spoilt" child thus becomes a victim of his parents' inability to tolerate conscious ambivalence because their defense against ambivalence is to deny the rejection and over-compensate by an exaggerated expression of love.

The child and his parents unconsciously know this protestation of love does not ring true. The "spoilt" child's craving is for the kind of love sought in early infancy, a warm symbiotic relationship that either never existed for him or was disrupted too early. Its absence created emotional hunger. The seeming affection the parents offer is non-nutrient even though it looks good. The child experiences what a starving person would if presented with what looks like a well-broiled steak. As he eats it, he finds the steak, in spite of its realistic appearance, to be made of sawdust and therefore without nutrient value. It would not be surprising in such an event if the starving person believed his illusory notion of the steak and ate more and more of it, hoping to relieve his hunger. The manifest affection offered by parents to the "spoilt" child is also made of sawdust and therefore does not relieve the emotional hunger from which the child is suffering.

Both child and parents have a sense of frenzy about this hunger. Because of their inability to give real love, the parents are unable to get the emotional nutrition obtained in the early symbiotic relationship between parents and child. Thus a vicious circle starts. The parents deny their own deprivation; they also feed upon the sawdust steak the child offers. This is frequently observable when the "spoilt" child demands attention because his mother is, for example, talking to a friend. Any small child may object to this diversion of the mother's interest. They can often be comforted by some small gesture of contact, such as quietly playing with the child's hands or making occasional playful gestures. There is then a natural flow between mother and child that continues in spite of the mother's major attention being directed elsewhere. If this does not appease the child the mother can comment casually (because she herself is relaxed) that the child is tired, hungry or bored and she had better be on her way. Not so the mother of the "spoilt" child. She plays tensely with her child, diverts her attention to the child completely (with some panic frequently quite evident) and with exasperation or martyrdom hurries away from the disturbing situation. When the mother is casual the child feels relaxed. When the mother is frenzied, the child is not satisfied by the mother's concession to him. He responds primarily to the frenzy and feels panicky himself. Quieted by a removal from that which seemed to arouse the panic, he is relieved temporarily, but a repetition of the situation (if he has too many experiences of this nature) will reactivate his feeling of frenzy and he becomes a "spoilt" child. His behavior is not the result of his mother's giving in to his fussiness but the *way* in which she gives in.

All parents give some love to their child that could more wisely be directed elsewhere. Within limits this has no unfortunate effect and in small doses, because it gives satisfaction to the parents, enables them to be more gratified by the child, with a resultant enrichment of the emotional nutrition the child receives. As an example, a mother may love those characteristics in her son that are like her husband, her favorite brother or her father. Since this similarity stimulates her love, she will be freer to love the child. The response is unfortunate when the child is not a person in his own right but is *only a symbol* of the person with whom he shares certain characteristics. This latter response creates various complications in a child-parent relationship. In some instances the child and the parents unconsciously respond to the failure of the child to be an individual in his own right. The child is not loved as a person but only as a substitute for a loved person he resembles. He is a picture, not a person. As a result no matter how much love is shown to him, he receives it only as a proxy. His own needs are unmet.

This type of constellation in which the child serves only as a proxy is occasionally observed when parents, having lost a child, have another child to replace the one that is dead. It appears to the outside world that the parents are overly attached because of their fear of losing another child. More deeply significant is the attempt upon the parents' part to bring the dead child back to their emotional life through their relationship with the new child. They are frustrated because the new child is not the other child. Instead of accepting the new child as a person, they eat more and more sawdust steak, always remaining hungry. The child senses that he is but a substitute, playing only a proxy role, which does not satisfy his desire to be a person.

May, at the age of four, illustrated a conscious response to having been given life as a substitute for a dead sister. She was preoccupied with what an individual might experience before birth and after death. Her fantasy was finally revealed: she believed she was the same person as the baby who had died before her birth. She was concerned about the time between her supposed death and her return to life. She tried to recall her experiences during the two years between the death of the baby and her own birth. No fantasy was enough to satisfy her fully. Her mother had been quite open in explaining to everyone that May would never have been born had not the other child died. May could not, therefore, feel really loved as a person unless she convinced herself that she was the original little girl in the family. Little wonder that the child was seriously withdrawn into a fantasy world.

A parent may create a difficult situation for the child when the child serves as an outlet for feelings that should be directed to the marital partner. The child then not only finds such love non-nutritious but dangerous. This is clearly discernible when the mother turns the love that should be directed towards her husband to her son. Her son may not only be deprived of a needed child-mother relationship; he may have imposed upon him a role he is not mature enough to fulfill. He may be frightened by the stimulation that results. His behavior, if characteristic of a "spoilt" child, may then be multiply determined. Starved and trying to gain what is never available, he may regress to an infantile pattern of behavior because to respond at his own level of development, particularly if he has attained the Oedipal phase, is too frightening. This type of situation arises when the marital relationship is unsatisfactory or, at times, in the absence of one parent as a result of death or other separation. It is certainly not an inevitable result of these conditions. It occurs only when a parent, unable to obtain gratification from other adults, contaminates parental love with love that belongs elsewhere.

The material generosity of parents of the "spoilt" child is often a substitute for love—not a symbol of it. The child remains unsatisfied. The parents give more and more materially because they cannot give the love that is really asked for. Blaming the giving for the creation of the "spoilt" child is to put the cart before the horse. Parents can give endlessly of material objects without ill-effect if the giving is an expression of their love rather than a substitute for it. They can also refuse to give things when there is a reason without being worried about the effect of their refusal. Confident in the love they give, they do not have to express it through material objects. Of course the child may resent the withholding. Every child at times considers his parents unreasonable. The loved child can tolerate his own anger and his parents' refusal because his wish involves only the object itself and not the substitute meaning of that object. The object *per se* is not overwhelmingly important. Just because a child gets angry when he cannot buy a toy does not mean he considers himself permanently unloved. At the peak of anger he may feel unloved and say so. His immediate response means only that he wants the toy badly. He is within his rights to be angry; his parents are within their rights to refuse. Once the storm is over, he evaluates the situation more accurately. A loved child and loving parents do not live in continual peace. All are human beings and have the privilege of behaving in accordance with human reactions. The anger of the child does not necessarily indicate that the child is "spoilt" or that the parents are unloving. Again, it is not the isolated experience but the chronicity of the reaction that is significant.

Parents become concerned over a particularly common reaction of children. The father, for example, if frequently away from the home, returns with gifts for his child (even sometimes for his wife). Finally the time comes when the child greets him at the door with "What did you bring me?" Has the child come to value the gift more than his father? To understand the child's response, it is perhaps worthwhile to consider the wife's reaction. She too, without verbalizing it, probably has the same question in mind as the child has. Her reason for the question will vary according to the nature of her relationship with her husband. If the primary value of the relationship rests in the material things her husband brings, she will be glad to have him go away to return with a gift. She may see the gift as an expression of his guilt: he enjoyed being away from her. Her enjoyment of the gift may then have hostile implications suggesting that she too was glad to be free of him. If her relationship with him is more emotionally sound, his gift will have a double value: she will like it for itself, and it will indicate that he thought of her in his absence.

Likewise, when a child asks "What did you bring me?" he may be indicating an interest solely in a new toy if his father has no pleasant meaning to him as a person. If his basic relationship with his father is a happy one, however, he will want the gift both because it is fun to get presents and because it also indicates that his father continued to think of him and love him as he does at home. In the latter event the gift is enhanced in value because it is a symbol of, not a substitute for, his father's love. What he is expressing when he says "What did you bring me?" can be determined only by a frank evaluation of the underlying response between the parents and the child.

The emotional response of parents of the "spoilt" child

has another characteristic. It is unpredictable. These parents frequently give to the child, both of affection and materially, as it suits them. They withhold when it does not suit them to give. Such parents are typically emotionally immature people; their love is not a continual response but is impulsive. When they have an impulse to give to the child they do so. When they do not, they withhold. Because of their immaturity their impulses come and go dependent on what other gratifications are available. To these parents, parental responses are at times fun, at other times inconvenient. The situation is difficult to correct because people cannot really act maturely unless they are mature. Mature parents give consistently, not because they control their impulses but because, within reasonable limits, they always have a parental feeling for their child. Maturity that results in a capacity to be wise parents cannot be imitated or pretended satisfactorily. On the other hand, if parental feelings are not inherent in the person, it is better to imitate them than to excuse the failure and indulge in immaturity. Sawdust does not offer nutrition, but it at least provides bulk that decreases hunger pains. Imitation of parental love may have a characteristic sawdust does not: in time the imitation may develop into the real thing—and thus have nutritional value!

26 : Siblings

THE FAMILY IS MORE COMPLETE IF IT IS NOT COMPOSED SOLELY of a mother, a father and a child. The emotional interrelationship in the family is enriched when there is more than one child. To use the concept of the family triangle, each child becomes an angle of such a triangle. The several triangles that develop in a family in which there is more than one child are not lined up in series, with only the mother and father as the common points. In a good family structure, triangles form a three-dimensional pattern with many interlacing currents of relationship. That these currents are alternating currents, both negative and positive, does not decrease the efficiency of the system. The only child has difficulty in developing as complete an emotional interrelationship because this interlacing does not occur.

The problems of the only child are familiar to everyone. He has many difficulties that persist during a good part of latency, problems that could have been ironed out in the family were other children members of it. He tends to cling longer to his concept of being the center of the family and later of the world beyond his family. As he discovers that he is not the center, he is frightened; he attempts to make himself a focal point since this is the only way he is convinced of his security. It is more difficult for him to learn the give-and-take of social living with other children because this experience is first met in the impersonal environment of the nursery school, the playground or a neighbor's home. In none of these places does he have parent figures who love him and provide him with security at the same time that they do so for the other children. Any attempt to duplicate the family picture is valid but inevitably less effective. A nursery teacher, for example, may love, and be loved by, all the children. That love is a weak concoction compared to the deep love of parents for each child in the family and the child's love for his parents.

The family offers another setting that is difficult to create elsewhere. Children in the family are of different ages. While this limits their companionship it makes a more significant contribution to the child's learning. It gradually clarifies for the child why one individual is given certain opportunities, protection and restriction while others are not, even though each is fully and equally loved. In the family also the child learns that others can be loved without diminishing the love he himself receives. In short, he learns to share. The learning experience has deeper implications than this socially polite evaluation suggests. Sharing in the home is not a social gesture with a mild emotional implication, as it may be so easily on the playground. It is a sharing that is at first charged with strong feelings of love, resentment, jealousy and rivalry, feelings that finally fuse into a comfortable sharing that is emotionally rich. The struggle that is finally resolved gives depth to the experience of sharing and shows up the shallowness of polite social sharing. A person may share because he is obedient, because he is afraid of rejection, or because he will be rewarded by others sharing with him. All these considerations play a part in learning the give-and-take of social living. But mature generosity involves the more fundamental satisfaction that is derived from an emotionally meaningful living with others.

The end-result of growing up with brothers and sisters is not always evident during childhood. The interplay between the children is more often manifested in resentment rather than in the pleasure of family unity. This overt disharmony begins with the birth of the second child. Parents always have an ideal in mind before the second child is born. They expect to so conduct themselves towards the first child that he will feel no jealousy towards the second. This is easily fantasied by the parents until the second child is actually in the home. No matter how much the parents may desire a second child, the first child is the only child until the second child actually arrives. They may love the fantasied second child before he is born. They cannot love him as a person because as a person he does not exist. The first child does. Many parents are convinced they can avoid jealousy in the first born when the second arrives because they often unconsciously see no real reason for jealousy. The parents without realizing it do not love the future second child as they love the first who is real. This validates their conviction that the first child will have no reason to be jealous.

It is almost inevitable that the first child will be jealous of the second. He has had all the parental attention; now he must share it. He considers parental love a measurable quantity, which must now be divided in half. Gradually he will learn that parental love is not a quantity but a quality and that the new child does not take the love he himself previously enjoyed. But this is a difficult lesson to learn and often is not mastered until late in childhood. More characteristically the child considers himself a favorite or at least an equal when his immediate family experience is pleasant; he considers himself the deprived one when he is the center of a family storm.

Even with the realization that parents can love each child, the rivalry does not necessarily disappear. Parents cannot always give equal attention to each child. The newborn makes demands upon a mother's time to an extent that necessitates the older child relinquishing some. When the older child wants the mother's attention, how complete is the solace offered in the awareness that his mother loves him just as much? He cannot always time his wishes to fit into infant feeding schedules or infant colic, nor can he time them so as to avoid their coinciding with maternal fatigue. The older child is naturally jealous and resentful of the younger. Even if his parents love them both, the way he wishes that love expressed at times will not be fulfilled because of the reality demands of the other child.

Other factors enter into the older child's attitude towards the younger. The younger child is always enjoying that which the older child has relinquished. The two-year-old child sees the baby held in the mother's arms and fed, while he, criticized for his clumsiness, has to feed himself. The younger child stays at home with mother while the older child is sent to nursery school or sent out to play. The younger child later enjoys the play at kindergarten while the older child has to learn arithmetic. The older child has the skill to mow the lawn and run errands while the younger child is deprived of such questionable privileges because he is not old enough!

The older child, because of his greater skills and more mature intellectual endowment, certainly has advantages over the younger. These he recognizes. He really wants both the advantages of being older and the privileges of being younger. He resembles the adult who praises primitive society because primitive life is so simple but dreams of enjoying it with the advantages of modern sanitation, motorized transportation and a tribal membership in a country club. Even though it is gratifying to have the advantages of maturity, there is a nostalgia for the pleasures of the more immature life. Even though a child enjoys the skill of feeding himself, the baby's contentment while nursing has an appeal. The argument that the older child has many more opportunities, resources and equipment than the younger child rarely is impressive. The older child wants both.

No matter when the second child arrives in the life of the first, the older one can be expected to have some difficulty in accepting the new family member. If the children are close together in age, the older child may feel deprived of his dependent gratification before he is ready to renounce it. If the new child arrives during the toilet-training period, the older may resist giving up the self-indulgence the baby is allowed. If the baby arrives during the Oedipal period a new problem is added, for the child resents the parent of the same sex as a cause of the arrival of this interloper and the parent of the opposite sex for his or her disloyalty. During latency the new baby may be primarily a plain nuisance, interfering with noisy play and destroying elaborate constructions and prized equipment. During adolescence the new baby in the family may be very embarrassing. It, among other aspects, disproves the asexual nature of the parents. Except at adolescence it is often the next child in sequence who is most difficult for the older child to accept. Having adjusted to the advent of one, the resentment can remain focused there and interest (or disinterest) can be directed at the next in line.

It is not only the older child who faces problems in a family of more than one child. The younger child envies the older for his skills and his greater freedom. He strives to emulate the older child, and is defeated. He too may be resentful and jealous. The middle child, caught between an older and younger child, has an even more complicated situation. He envies the older child for his freedom and skills, the younger for the indulgences granted him. The baby always stimulates "ohs" and "ahs." The oldest child is praised for his achievements. The middle child cannot compete with either.

Parents who wish to avoid the pains of childhood for the young members of the family had best cover the living-room shelves with statues of children and avoid live ones. If they reject this solution, they must take a long-term view of the average child's joys and pains, realizing that out of all the ups-and-downs there ultimately develops an adult more prepared for social living because he has known the security of love as well as the resentments in the family.

It is impossible to avoid all tense situations, all frustration and all resentment. The child should not be protected within the family walls from the impact of reality. The value of the family lies in the atmosphere it creates by which the child is helped during childhood to develop constructive ways to deal with those problems. Practically every situation of childhood has its counterpart in adult life, and the child in a sound home environment acquires skill in handling the problems of adulthood constructively.

There are no perfect techniques to assist the older child in adapting to the arrival of the baby. Some methods work with some children and fail dismally with others. Parents sometimes stress that the new baby is the older child's baby. This is not true, and if believed, at least during the Oedipal period, might be quite disturbing. The new baby is the older child's brother or sister, not his baby. If the older child really believed this fantasy that the baby was his own he probably would throw it away in time! Some little girls are able to identify with their mother and give to a doll that which the mother gives to the newborn. This undoubtedly, when effective, softens the impact of painful reality and strengthens her feminine identification with her mother. It is more difficult to foster the boy's identification with the father. Certainly he should not be invited to identify with the mother by being the mother of a doll! When a child chooses a solution of regression to the point of competing and identifying with the newborn, it is probably wisest to allow the regression for a time, making certain that more mature behavior has worthwhile rewards.

Parents at times unwittingly increase the difficulty of an older child. When the toddler gets into the six-year-old's room and takes or breaks a toy, parents criticize the older child for his protests, insisting the younger child doesn't know any better. Since the younger child doesn't know any better, the parents should! The older child should have the same privilege of defending his toys from the destructiveness and covetousness of the younger as the parents have of protecting their own valued knick-knacks. Parents often urge brothers or sisters to play together, have friends in common and share activities. Actually each child should have the privilege of being away from brothers and sisters as well as being with them. A child frequently enjoys other people's children more than he enjoys the children of his parents, and it is as important for him to have social experiences away from the family as within it. Brothers and sisters who have lived chiefly with each other may cling in their adult life to patterns still centered upon each other. The child who never enjoys playing with other children as much as he enjoys playing with his siblings may well become a spinster or bachelor as an adult, too crippled emotionally to achieve mature heterosexuality. Experiences with brothers and sisters should facilitate a child's social adjustment outside the family, not make it unnecessary.

A child may have a particularly difficult time with his siblings during adolescence, especially if their ages are close to his and if they are of the opposite sex. A boy, for example, may be extremely critical of his sister. She doesn't act right with boys, she doesn't dress right, she doesn't study right, she is too fat or too thin, too tall or too short, too smart or too dumb. This verbalization of criticism of her may be a way of disguising a conflict he has that is similar to that centered about his relationship to his mother. He is confused in his feeling towards a girl, with whom he has lived closely for most or all of his life, who is now developing into a woman. He must deny her attractiveness by dissertating on her limitations. This depreciation of her keeps him free of any awareness that he might find her attractive since she is just as is the mother, a forbidden sexual object. This depreciation may be very threatening to his sister. If her brother sees nothing charming in her, she has little confidence that other boys will either. She often needs a great deal of subtle support to maintain her own self-confidence against the brother's barrage. On the other hand, she is also reassured by his rejection because her brother is, for her, a forbidden sexual object. Of course, his criticism may in part be valid. He can teach her, even though his methods may at times be cruel, how to get along with the opposite sex. Both the brother and sister will be more confident of meeting the expectations of the opposite sex because they have learned of the acceptable patterns of behavior from each other.

Sometimes brothers and sisters get on surprisingly well without damage to their emotional development. Sometimes the resentment and jealousy of each other is of such intensity it in itself becomes the source of personality distortion. The smoothly established or stormy sibling relationships can be evaluated only as they are seen as a *part* of the total picture, not as a total picture. No child lives only with his siblings, be he happy or unhappy with them. Their significance to him are best seen as it is reflected in his total adaptive pattern, especially in those areas of living not directly shared by his siblings or parents.

Siblings frequently have quite different personalities. This is not surprising. Their life experiences are quite different. The first child has parents and an infancy very different from that of the second child. This modification in the family environment continues with each subsequent child. Furthermore, a child often develops patterns of response in order to be different from his brothers and sisters, thereby establishing himself as an individual in his own concept of himself as well as in the minds of others. One child in the family may be quickly obedient and compliant. The other may be mischievous and defiant. Parents may attribute this difference to "heredity." John, who is gentle and compliant, is like Uncle Robert, who became a college professor. Joe is just like his Uncle Bill, who was Peck's Bad Boy in childhood and now owns a large distributing business. Certainly, the parents of Joe and John will state, both boys were brought up in the same environment, treated the same, loved the same. But were they? Probably, whether determined by heredity or other factors, John and Joe were different from birth. The inherent difference was perhaps minor compared to the difference in the environment in which they were reared. John, the first child was a much-wanted child, born to his parents when they were in their early twenties and one year after their marriage. His father was extremely proud of his ability to encompass his new responsibilities. He worked long hours to prove he could be successful and as a result saw little of the infant John. John's mother loved babies but was frightened in her new role. Her anxiety was expressed by solicitous care of the child, protecting him from all discomforts and all dangers. John snuggled into the protective nest her anxiety built, avoiding any aggressive attempt to go beyond it because, if he did tentatively go a step beyond the nest, his mother's heightened anxiety was quickly transmitted to him. He was a treasure to her because he was a good quiet child. When Joe was born, his parents were much less starry-eyed about the miracle of parenthood and more realistically pleased with the addition to the family. His mother no longer responded to her baby as perishable in an adverse wind. His father felt less impressed by his own ability to meet his responsibilities because he was adequately successful in his work. He had time to play with Joe as he never had with John. Joe responded to the less anxious environment by having less fear of stepping out of parent-created limits. As a result he was frequently the focus of his parents' attention. They either diverted him into safer activities or punished him for misbehavior. This behavior on Joe's part had an effect upon John. The difficulties Joe found himself in and his punishments alarmed John and made it even more important to John that he behave circumspectly to avoid that to which Joe exposed himself. John, not daring to seek attention as Joe did, could best preserve his own niche in the family by being the good child. The problems John had with the birth of Joe were handled also with the safe-non-aggressive behavior that gave him security. Joe, as he grew older, resented John's apparent preferred place as the good child of the family, but instead of imitating John to win the same approval, defied the temptation in order to preserve his feeling of being a total person. Thus, John and Joe were really reared in entirely different environments from birth on. Because of this early difference they developed differently; as a result their environments contrasted more and more, thus increasing the personality contrasts in them. Neither child was doomed to an unhappy adulthood, unless the parents assumed one type of personality was desirable and the other unfortunate or unless the parents failed to recognize that John and Joe were quite different people and therefore needed different environmental experiences.

The interaction between siblings and between siblings and parents is an invaluable learning experience for each child. If it is a constructively meaningful learning experience each child will use the lessons he learns within the context of his other experiences, his own talents, drives and overall personality. The lessons can be learned more readily when the family responds to its members as individuals who together compose the group, for difference in the individuals is not a defect. Nothing could be more destructive to the individual and to our society than an insistence upon blindly rigid uniformity.

27 : Sexual attitudes and sex education

ON A STRICTLY INTELLECTUAL PLANE, IN THE PAST FIFTY YEARS the approach toward sexual behavior and toward dissemination of sexual information has been sharply changed. How much this has affected the deeper attitudes of many individuals is uncertain. Many parents, consciously convinced that sexuality is a normal component of life, find themselves inarticulate (or, in a compensatory way, overly articulate), self-conscious, and surprisingly uninformed when confronted with the sexual behavior or questions of their child. This conflict between intellectual beliefs and the inability to apply them comfortably is determined to a large extent by the parents' own childhood experiences and inhibitions. If this difficulty is the result of a social heritage entirely, a race of people free of sexual conflict will finally evolve after enough generations have experiences with the more diluted inhibitions of the previous generations.

Since most cultures, however, have some defined customs governing sexual behavior, it may be that some type of sexual inhibition is essential to the structuring of a society. This suggests that, because there is an inherent human need to exist in a social structure, the biologically determined sexual drive cannot be integrated into the pattern of living without, at some points in development, some repressive restrictions.

No glib procedure can be offered that helps the child grow

into a sexually conflict-free adult. Much more needs to be learned about the sexual drive, its flexibility in permitting sublimation and direct expression under socially acceptable circumstances, and the most effective way to facilitate its maturation. The immediate problem in our society is the severity of the inhibition, the strength of the internal repressive force, and the confusion between unconscious attitudes and conscious intellectual formulations that results in an inconsistent approach to the entire question. The contradictions and confusions are often more obvious than the progress being made. Yet, advances have been made in the integration of the inherent sexual impulses and their goals into the social mores.

Parental attitudes towards masturbation is one of the areas in which confusion is apparent. Children are curious about their bodies—curious enough to explore. And from this exploration comes the discovery of the pleasurable sensation resulting from tactile stimulation of the genitalia. Out of this comes self-masturbation, and later, as relationships with others develop, mutual masturbation.

Masturbation is a difficult form of behavior for parents to accept. To some it recalls the prohibitions of their own childhood and the continued feeling that it is "bad." Intellectual disavowal of this attitude does not readily dissolve a concept that had, in the course of childhood, become a part of the superego structure. Parents often *know* masturbation isn't "bad," but they *feel* it is. Those parents who were threatened in their own childhood with dire consequences of their masturbatory behavior or desire often have residual anxiety. In them the fear arises that the authorities of today may be wrong. To cite an example, they may have been told in their childhood that masturbation causes insanity. Even though now assured that this is not so, they have in the face of convincing evidence a remnant of concern that maybe the present authorities are wrong. The idea that masturbation was related to insanity was originally conceived because the history of insane people usually revealed childhood masturbation. A false cause and effect was thus established because the histories of non-insane people were not studied as carefully. Actually, such unsound thinking might have led to an infinitely more striking conclusion: that, since all mentally ill people drank milk in infancy, milk is a cause of insanity! It is true that mentally ill people often masturbate frequently and openly, but the explanation is that mental illness destroys mature adaptation and consequently victims return to an infantile pattern in which masturbation is one aspect.

More commonly in our sophisticated age parents are vague about their reaction to seeing a child masturbate. It makes them uncomfortable. It arouses either feelings long repressed by their own self-restriction on masturbation or guilt over their own occasional indulgence in the same act. They even mobilize the familiar defense of avoidance by strengthening the opposite reaction. Just as a revulsion to soiling may be an unconscious defense against a more primitive desire to soil, so revulsion to masturbation may be an unconscious defense against the wish to do it. This response makes it difficult for such parents to take masturbation casually, for their heart, or more accurately their unconscious, is not in it.

Masturbation is probably a universal experience of young children. It becomes prominent behavior during three different periods of development. The small infant exploring his body discovers the genitalia as well as other parts. This exploration is done more through feeling than seeing. Touching the genitalia creates a pleasant sensation . . . a repetition is invited. This very early masturbation is frequently limited to those moments when the infant is undressed; it is not too apparent because other parts of the body also invite exploration. The masturbation of this period tends to be abandoned as wider horizons—created by toys, by expanding visual range, and by increased mobility beyond just lying or sitting in a crib or play pen—are opened. A child whose interest in the genitalia does not diminish for a brief period when other interests become available probably utilizes masturbation as another might utilize thumb-sucking: as a way of creating pleasant internal feelings when the external world is too lonesome or too ungratifying.

Masturbation becomes inviting again during the Oedipal period of development. The explanation for this rests in some of the unanswered questions as to why the Oedipal period occurs at all. More sensitive tests may indicate a glandular change at this time. More detailed studies of the nervous system may reveal a significant neurological development. Whatever the explanation, increased masturbation is a frequent component of the overall picture of the Oedipal period, with the physical sensation of masturbation incorporated into the emotional experience of the developmental phase.

Much of our knowledge about the fantasy life of the Oedipal period as it is stimulated by or stimulates masturbation is gathered from children who have required intensive psychiatric treatment. These fantasies reveal all the various ramifications, comforts, drives and anxieties characteristic of the Oedipal period. Some adults whose sexual adjustment is adequate can recall fantasies associated with childhood masturbation. Others may either have repressed the fantasies or actually never indulged in conscious awareness of the problems of the period, and thus did not fantasy much, that period having been quickly relegated to the unconscious. So-called "normal" children will at times verbalize a fantasy accompanying masturbation that utilizes the Oedipal longings present at the time; others do not do so. While, within the limits of our present knowledge, it is probably justified to assume that masturbation during the Oedipal period is accompanied by fantasies, it is the privilege of a child to have privacy enshroud *his fantasies* if he wishes it so, unless the fantasies must be known by a therapist in order to understand a conflict that is crippling psychological growth.

As a child finds some solution to the Oedipal conflict and directs his interest to the world beyond the family constellation, masturbation either disappears entirely, or, more frequently, becomes a secret and occasional activity. It is during this period most commonly that, if it is indulged in, it may become a social experience. Mutual stimulation between two children of the opposite or the same sex occurs. This is undoubtedly in part a reflection of the socializing process during latency. Most activities at this age are more fun if shared with others.

During adolescence the urge to masturbate again becomes strong. Fantasy life is an important part of adolescent masturbation. To enrich the fantasies in which he seeks a gratifying answer to his increased sexual feelings, the adolescent creates an accompanying physical response. Some adolescents experience this physical response as a result of the intensity of their fantasies alone; others enhance the fantasies by physical masturbation. Masturbation is thus utilized to experience the fulfillment of sexual urges and to release sexual tension. The fantasies often reveal the nature of the child's sexual confusion and the answers with which he is experimenting. As with the small child, however, the adolescent has a right to keep his fantasies secret unless—only unless— he *wishes* to reveal them or a therapist *needs* to explore them.

With the attainment of heterosexual development *and* heterosexual gratification, masturbation becomes unsatisfactory and is abandoned. If, however, heterosexual maturity is not attained or a heterosexual outlet is not available, and if the sexual urge is not completely gratified through constructive defenses or completely controlled by destructive defenses, masturbation either continues or at times is resorted to in adult life. Even though second best and therefore not completely satisfactory, the individual prefers it to the persistence of unreleased sexual tension.

Masturbation may play a role in the ultimate attainment of heterosexual expression. It facilitates the fusion of normal psychological components of sexuality with the normal physical aspects. It focuses sexual desire upon the physical organ normal for the expression of that desire. Unfortunately, it can also have the opposite effect. This is demonstrated in some instances of adult sexual inhibition. Some people are unable to separate masturbation (which they consider bad, dangerous or forbidden) from adult heterosexual experiences. The similarity in sensation inhibits them. Undoubtedly in such cases there are many ramifications of the masturbatory inhibitions. But in most people, unshackled by those ramifications, the masturbatory prohibition as compared to the force of the drive towards a heterosexual goal is weak and ineffectual.

Masturbation is not the only universal experience of childhood. So is curiosity about the body structure of others. The small child wishes to see if his friend's toys are like his, if his book is similar, or if his friend lives as he does. He also wants to see if his friend's body is like his. He therefore does a little research. If the question is primarily prompted by curiosity rather than by anxiety, it is soon satisfied and the child's efforts are directed toward other questions.

The child not only wants to confirm that some people are similar in body structure; he also wants to see those that are different. If a child does not know the exact nature of the difference between boys and girls, he still knows they are somehow different. If no one will tell him the difference he has to learn for himself. More disconcerting to parents is the child who has been told and who still wants to look. Parents will comment that they cannot understand why their boy wants to see how the hidden area of his female companion is constructed since they have clearly told him the difference between boys and girls. Is that so surprising? The boy's interest was already present; the description merely satisfied part of it. How perfectly natural that he should want to see for himself!

Parents are often confused as to how to evaluate and deal with their child's sexual play. Certainly it is very unwise to threaten a child with illness, castration, or insanity as the result of masturbation. It is equally unwise to suggest to the child that the genitalia should not be touched because they are "dirty." If the child is severely condemned for his sexual play an additional barrier may be built against ultimate heterosexuality.

Punishment is not the answer. A child who is masturbating excessively at an age when there is usually a decrease in masturbation does not need punishment but rather an awareness that he is struggling with some problems he cannot handle constructively. He needs help with the underlying difficulty, not with the outer symptoms. Masturbation itself does not injure the child; it is not the primary threat to his ultimate maturation. The threat lies in the same area as does the cause of his excessive masturbation.

The child who has discovered masturbation should have an opportunity to discover other pleasures too. To the average child during periods of development in which masturbation occurs the sole role of the parent is to make available to the child other inviting experiences in the external world. This should not be done in a panicky way to interrupt the masturbatory activity. Parents who suddenly suggest a brilliant idea of other activity only when the child is masturbating convey to the child their disapproval of masturbation just as effectively as though they slapped him.

When the Oedipal period of development is mastered, masturbation—at least in our culture—tends to become secretive. This secretiveness itself is evidence of the child's adaptation to the culture. The meaning of crassly open masturbation during latency or adolescence should be explored. It should be borne in mind, however, that fatigue, quiet reading, or casual inactivity may be accompanied by half-hearted masturbatory movements. Before becoming concerned, parents should evaluate the overall picture of the child and his total activity rather than seeing him only as the incarnation of masturbation. Under rare conditions parents can skillfully acquaint the child with the social taboo against open masturbation. But generally that suggestion comes more effectively from someone less emotionally involved with the child.

There is nothing necessarily wrong with the child who never in his life has been known to masturbate. There are several possible explanations for this. There is a remote possibility that the child actually never has masturbated. The more likely explanation rests in the ignorance of the parents and the repression of memory by the child. A child may masturbate in a way the parents do not recognize. That is a privilege of the child. A child may prefer to masturbate privately, perhaps because he senses the prohibitions which the parents try to hide or deny. Perhaps it is just more fun when other stimulation does not interfere. This latter possibility is not meant to suggest that such a child should have long periods by himself in order to have an opportunity to masturbate. He'll find more than enough time to be alone in normal living!

Parents need not constitute themselves as detectives in order to discover if their child, who is psychologically healthy in every other discernible way, is masturbating, in order to complete their belief in his normalcy or to be prepared to give an adequate history later to a professional person. Psychiatrists can understand if parents say they never were aware of their child's masturbation. Parents can be good parents by living with the obvious life of their child. They need not relieve their own curiosity concerning the hidden in order to be adequate parents.

Mutual masturbation between children presents some additional considerations. It too is not wisely handled by punishment. In some instances parents too quickly blame the other child in cases of mutual sexual play. The child who is exonerated by his parents indicating that the child's partner in the act is "bad" or "dirty" is presented with a real dilemma. Unless he denies to himself his own role and his own pleasure in the act, he also is bad or dirty. If he can successfully deny his own part and his own response he may in adult life have some difficulty in accepting sexual behavior in another or in himself without regarding the behavior as "bad" or "dirty." If a neighbor's child is known to be preoccupied with sexual play to the exclusion of other activities, it is well to supervise the play when he visits in order to provide other activities. Sometimes a child needs more direct and verbalized support in order to abandon a playmate who, because of his own problems, is preoccupied with sexual play. This is wise only when the child, wishing to enjoy other types of fun but unable to interest his playmate in them, needs some encouragement in giving up a companionship and a game that are unsatisfactory to him. If he finds little enjoyment outside of this particular activity, he also has a problem. A child with access to other friends and other activities will usually lose interest in activities dominated by sexual play if he himself is not struggling with some unmasterable conflict at that time.

The gratification of curiosity about others is least disturbing to the child when he is somewhat prepared for what he will see or has available a person who knows enough to explain it. A little boy, totally ignorant of the bodily configuration of the female, may become quite disturbed on discovering at the age of nine what the difference actually is. Such a boy might interpret the female genitalia as support for his fear that he might lose his penis. The little girl, thinking she originally was molded from the same form as the boy, may see herself as having lost something valuable.

Obviously every little boy and every little girl does not come to this conclusion, but there is no reason why a child should not know the similarity and dissimilarity between himself and his friends. When the opportunity is available, the child's first awareness of bodily differences comes most easily in observation of a small baby. The naturalness of the mother and the baby in accepting infant nudity creates a casualness to the experience that facilitates the child's looking at and absorbing what he sees. This same casualness persists when the children are of the same general age up until roughly the onset of the Oedipal phase. After that, looking becomes stimulating and it is well that the knowledge of bodily differences be established before that time. Steps toward modesty usually are instituted by children during this period and can be mildly encouraged by parents. Making haste slowly is a good axiom in the development of modesty during the latency period. Modesty should neither be ignored nor anxiously pressed. The behavior of healthily modest parents is usually the best help they can give in creating healthy modesty in the child.

In spite of satisfied curiosity during the pre-Oedipal period, a child may still wish to check secretively on any later changes in the body of his friends. Again, if other activities are fun, the average child will find—once his curiosity is satisfied—that the other activities are important. If he does not, there is some reason why not, and the cause needs to be found and corrective measures instituted.

All that is said above about the satisfaction of curiosity does not apply to the child's curiosity about the adult human figure. Ideas concerning this have gone through the cycles typical of so many theories of child care. At one time the modesty of parents was of such intensity it was considered a sin to let the child see and a sin for the child to look. This created anxiety, whetted curiosity, and made the adult human body a mystery enshrouded in wickedness. As the child grew into adulthood and discovered his own bodily changes

and those of the opposite sex, these implications often persisted and played a part in sexual maladjustment. To coun-
teract this the opposite parental behavior was recommended:
the child should become as familiar with the adult body
as with the child's body. But this too proved often unfortunate. More and more it seems that casual but effective modesty on the part of parents is the wisest pattern, and that
the child's verbalized curiosity is best gratified through
words even though the curiosity remains somewhat unsatisfied. If parental modesty is graciously handled, if the child's
curiosity is accepted, and the child is prepared as he approaches puberty for his own bodily changes and those of the
opposite sex, the limited early frustration of his curiosity
will not have significant repercussions.

The child's curiosity, as every parent knows, is not limited
to his body structure. He wants to know where he came
from, where other babies came from, and what role the
parents have in all this mystery. It is often glibly recommended that a child's curiosity about sexuality be respected
and gratified. This is much easier to say than to carry out.
In the past, when sexuality was a forbidden subject for a
child, the child was not as stupid or naïve as the parents
assumed. The child knew something happened; what it
might be was unknown except as his fantasy provided some
answer. Those fantasies were often, symbolically, surprisingly
close to the truth. Unfortunately, many of the fantasies the
child constructed were so isolated by the individual from the
conflicts with reality that necessitated this use of symbolism,
that a fissure occurred rather than a blending. The secrecy
implied in the parents' prohibition against learning reality
was undoubtedly in many instances responsible for this fissure; as a result the conflict was intensified.

Vicissitudes may influence the child's concept of procreation. A child at times will deny his intuitively known ideas
concerning sexuality because he wants to deny his origin.
He doesn't want to credit his parents with the gift of life. If

the child's curiosity and wish to clarify his fantasies by direct questioning is frowned upon, his fantasy will be isolated from reality because it meets some need that reality would seem to reveal as bad. This is particularly true in cases where parents refuse or are unable to answer the child's questions. The child who believes babies grow in the garden, to be plucked when ripe, may be only indicating and equating the growth of plants, which he enjoys observing, to the growth of a human being. If he is forbidden to clarify his concept further, he may suspect the growth of babies is not as delightful as the growth of flowers, and he will cling to his pleasant fantasy in order to avoid his uneasy feeling that reality is not pleasant.

Correcting a fantasy with the "facts of life" without helping the child to cross from fantasy to reality—and in so doing to maintain the emotional meaningfulness of his fantasy— may be equally disturbing. Barbara, at the age of 5, verbalized her need to deny the reality in order to preserve the emotional meaning of her fantasy. Her parents were "modern" people who believed truth lies only in facts; any questions that Barbara asked about the origin of life were answered in the framework of the parental concept of truth. Barbara returned from playing with Joan one day very puzzled. Joan, also 5 years old, had told her that God sent babies to parents. This puzzled Barbara because the sperm, ovum, the vagina and the penis were facts to her. Her mother answered her puzzled questioning by making it clear that Barbara knew the truth; the other child didn't. This was satisfactory until the next conversation between the children occurred. Then Barbara was again upset. Joan had claimed that Barbara's mother may have told the truth of Barbara's origin, but Joan's mother had explained Joan's. It was too bad, Joan pointed out, that Barbara didn't have a God to give a child and that the parents had to obtain a child in a much less wonderful way. Barbara was not easily consoled since she could grant her mother knew only how she had arrived but Joan's mother must have known how Joan arrived. Barbara finally resolved the conflict by fantasy. Joan's story avoided many difficulties, including the jealousy Barbara felt because of the mother's apparent position with the father. Over and above that it created an aura of warmth, something special about birth, something idealistic about the creation of life. Barbara decided her mother had not told the truth, Joan's mother had; Barbara was God's gift too. All of this turmoil and final retreat from facts to fantasy might have been avoided had Barbara's parents recognized that what Joan's parents referred to as God could have been translated into their own philosophy of life, which then would have enabled them to help Barbara fuse the emotional and the factual aspects of total living. She could have accepted the "facts of life" had the same aura of idealism and warmth enshrouded her concepts of the creation of life as Joan's, with the added advantage of knowing the reality. Too often facts are used to destroy feeling rather than to fuse facts and feelings.

A child may deny his knowledge of procreation because the knowledge itself creates conflicts. If the child senses parental conflict over sexuality, he may not be convinced by their verbal acceptance of it. By repressing the knowledge he can avoid the conflict, since a child does not like many unpleasant facts. He may also repress the knowledge because he cannot deal effectively with the urges in himself that the knowledge defines. This type of repression is often seen in early adolescence, when a boy or girl indicates that earlier given sexual information is "forgotten." It is forgotten because it relates too closely to the newly strengthened internal urges that he fears may not be controllable if their nature is identified. At times, the knowledge is repressed in order to deny the application to the parents as well as to himself. A child often denies the possibility of his parents being sexual. This may be not only because he, for a variety of reasons, considers sexuality improper and cannot accept an impropriety on the part of his parents, but also because he may reject it to deny the possibility of such intimacy between the parents, an intimacy from which he is excluded.

To the extent that parents are comfortable in answering questions their child raises about sexuality and reproduction, those questions should be answered. Parents usually are not wise to guess what additional questions the child may have that he doesn't ask. If the child finds his parents willing to answer questions, any question he can tolerate and really wishes answered he will usually ask. Parents who are casual and comfortable in discussing sexual questions with their child may go slightly beyond the child's direct verbalization without disturbing the child. Since most parents are not that relaxed in their discussion, however, it is wiser to limit any discussion to the specific question the child asks.

There are frequent discussions as to whether sex education should be given by parents, through books, or in the classroom. The first questions by a child occur typically before the child is in school or is able to read. The way those first questions are answered is particularly important in determining the child's attitude toward further questioning. The factual information in the reply is of secondary, even though major, significance compared to the ease and comfort with which the parent answers. Parents often find themselves better prepared if they do not trust solely to their own spontaneous response when the questions arise. Often reading a book meant for a child in which the reproductive functions are described in language the child can understand provides parents a language with which they can be comfortable in talking to their child. It is often difficult—especially on the spur of the moment—to translate an adult concept into child language.

If a child is able to read with facility, a book specifically written for a child may prove helpful. This is a pragmatic solution rather than an ideal one. Undoubtedly if the parents are skilled in handling a sexual discussion with their child and if the child has developed no uneasiness about asking his questions, it is better to rely on conversation than on books. Realistically, because of the parents' uncomfortableness or the child's reticence a book can serve as a substitute.

Sex education in the school is controversial. Ideally, if the school assumes this role, sex education should be incorporated into the regular curriculum as a logical part of a related course. Unfortunately, courses in physiology and psychology do not come early enough to gratify the child's curiosity so that many false ideas are accepted before the true ones are presented.

Any plan for the wise handling of sex education in the average school comes up against many snares. Educators may urge that sexual knowledge is a part of total knowledge and should be presented as such, yet many schools separate boys and girls when the information is given. They don't separate them when they discuss the digestive system. This differentiation suggests a recognition that the giving of facts is complicated by the feelings aroused by those facts. On the other hand, if this separation does not occur in the classroom, there may be discomfort on the part of the students which cannot always be successfully handled in a group. This would suggest that failure to separate the sexes also leads to difficulties.

Sexual knowledge is a part of total knowledge. It should not be given an exalted or mysterious position in the hierarchy of knowledge. Parents and teachers, in other words, should no more emphasize sex education than ignore it. Most children will handle sexual information with reasonable facility if it is given with reasonable skill. The child in whom the groundwork for sexual disturbances has already been laid may manifest dormant problems under the stimulus of sex education, no matter how it is given. It should also be borne in mind that a child talks not only to his parents and teachers. He also talks to his friends. In these conversations he may come upon some false information, but he will also find some truths. The child of today is often surprised that his parents feel sex education must be presented only under ideal conditions. He has already found many true answers under far from the best conditions.

Sex education, even ideally given, will not prevent sexual conflict nor assure good sexual adjustment. Long before physiologists solved some of the mysteries of digestion, food was digested by the human body. Long before primitive man knew how babies were started, babies were born. But good sex education can teach us how to recognize the danger signals and, more importantly, it can give us a more healthy view of sex within the total framework of our pursuit of lasting happiness.

28 : *School and the child*

THE FIRST DAY OF SCHOOL IS A DRAMATIC EVENT IN THE LIFE
of a child. So too in the life of his parents. A child, especially
if he has had contact with older children, looks forward to
it. Weekend and afternoon playmates have spent hours enjoying new experiences and play activities while he has remained at home bored with his own company. Starting
school means sharing these new experiences as well as uninterrupted companionship with those playmates. The child
may feel also that the first day of school is a step towards
being more grown up, a pleasant prideful sensation to the
emotionally healthy child. Now he will go to school too, just
like the admired, loved, or feared older sister, brother or
friend.

To the parents the step the child is about to take is
evidence that the child is growing up. The parents enjoy
their vision of the child's response to this new experience.
Furthermore, they have brought the child successfully
through infancy and with justified pride now present the
child to the broader world. The mother is especially de-
lighted, for, much as she may deny it, it will be a relief
to have someone else responsible for the child for a few
hours in the day.

Many children and many parents face disillusionment
when the day finally arrives. Parents may experience it first

because their anticipation of the day has been more ambivalent than perhaps the child's has been. The child's entering school represents the first good-sized crack in the closeness of the parent-child relationship. Many parents have mixed feelings about giving up their infant. In spite of the trials that infancy produced, it has also been the source of much parental gratification. The crack that now appears may seem to threaten the continuity of their gratification. Parents feel a little choked up as they introduce the child to new experiences which they will share only vicariously, if at all. To the extent that they really find pleasure in the maturing process of their child, to that extent will the pangs of separation be lessened though probably not always entirely erased.

Additional parental concern as the child is about to embark on a school career relates to the way the adults evaluate what they are doing to their child. They are committing him to supervision by another adult, and by an adult over whom, except in very broad ways, they have no control. They can pass laws that forbid corporal punishment in the school. They cannot pass laws that require a teacher to have a wise attitude towards their child. They, having tried to be especially wise parents, are fearful of the possibly disastrous effect that stupidity in regard to child development may have upon their child. They wonder if this precious psyche they have helped to develop will be shattered to bits by a teacher whose philosophy of child care must be wrong because it disagrees with their own theory or their favorite book on child psychology. It sometimes appears to the parents that, in sending their child to school, they are being as indiscreet as would be a housewife, who, having preserved her fine china by carefully washing it for many years, finally puts the dishes in the washing machine along with the dirty linen. At this point it is well for parents to remember that there is more than one method of effective child-rearing. Furthermore most children do quite well in many kinds of emotional environment. Lastly, most children show surprising toleration for the mistakes adults make. The psyche has a certain fragility but its fragility is not as great as parents may fear.

Furthermore, parents have heard that all children do not prove to be gratifying evidence of parental skills. The child may not accept school once he is exposed to it. He may show quiet resistance by not "socializing" well. He may deal with the displeasure by proving difficult for the teacher to handle. He may attempt to avoid the whole problem by refusing to go to school. He may evidence anxiety once he arrives. Parents are not as sure that school will be all joy to a child, in spite of their tongue-in-cheek enthusiasm in discussing school with him.

If the first school experience creates some conflict for the parents, they have at least some opportunity to prepare themselves for the difficulties that may arise. Most children are more confident of the positive aspects and less aware of the negative implications of the first days at school. Even though prepared for separation from the parents, the child may have little emotional awareness of what it will mean. He eagerly approaches his first day of school to find himself in a strange physical environment. He is often with a group of strange children who appear vaguely or obviously anxious. The anxiety is contagious. He is introduced to a strange adult who is occupied with the needs of many children, not just his. Into the chasm of the unknown his parent drops him and disappears.

There is another situation that at times causes the child to find school attendance difficult. Younger siblings in the home may be a source of a conflict. The child has been struggling to maintain his place in the family constellation in competition with younger brothers or sisters. To attend school means that the younger children have the mother all to themselves, a privilege he never enjoys because when he is at home the other children are always there. Some of the glamorous stories of school experiences with which he will entertain a younger brother or sister are not necessarily indicative of how well he likes school! They are rather an attempt to arouse the jealousy of the younger child so that the latter will also want to attend school, thus removing him from the privileged position of being home with mother.

The complication a younger child creates for the older child who has entered school suggests that a common practice among parents is of questionable merit. They introduce nursery school and a baby brother or sister to the child at the same time! The rationalization for this is that the older child will not be as jealous of the younger if he has other interests and is not exposed to the picture of the mother's care of the infant. Actually the nursery school experience may only confirm the child's fear of being displaced. He is sent away and the infant is kept at home. Circumstances may necessitate such unfortunate timing. When possible it is better that the child already be adjusted to nursery school before he is confronted with an infant rival or have found some answer to his conflict over a younger child before he meets the issue of school.

Some children accept this new experience with tolerance for the reality of school. They quietly experiment and find a satisfactory mode of adaptation. School becomes a challenge to them and they are gratified by their successful mastery of it. Secure in their belief of the parents' continued interest, confident of the benignity of the responsible adults and ready to find new pleasures in companionship with their own age group and in learning new tools for living, they slip into the classroom pattern happily.

A child may enjoy the experience with new toys, new surroundings, new faces, new noises. All of these things are exciting. The preoccupation of adults with other children may give a sense of freedom never experienced as long as adults could devote all their time to him. He has no em-

pathy with the anxiety of other children, so he is immune
to any effect from it. To such a child there is no immediate
disillusionment when he enters school. It may come later as
he recognizes that the freedom he thought he found is not
so complete. He may find the inevitable development of
classroom and group discipline difficult to integrate into his
own plan of life. He, the teacher and the parents will be
fortunate if the disillusionment comes so gradually that he
learns to adjust without being aware of how his dream has
been modified by reality.

Many children will have some difficulty in adapting to
the change that school attendance represents. The separation from home, from his own toys, from his own time
schedule, places new demands upon him. How children indicate the anxiety they are experiencing will differ. One will
make it quite apparent as he cries, clings to his parent and
resists all attempts on the part of others to interest him in
activities or equipment. Another will withdraw into a quiet
corner or a quiet activity, giving the impression of walling
himself off from any awareness of the disturbing environment.
Another will mask his anxiety by responding angrily and de-
structively; it is as if he hopes to destroy the equipment and
the other people so as to make it impossible for the school to
exist. A child may put his heart into any available activity, apparently enjoying himself, but probably defending himself
against discomfort by a whistling-in-the-dark technique. Sometimes a child who presents a picture of happy adjustment at
school returns home cross, fatigued or over-stimulated out of
all proportion to the day's events. In such instances his behavior at home may be the only sign of the struggle he is making to adjust at school.

The child who finds that entering school confronts him
with new problems too overwhelming to be handled quickly
is not necessarily manifesting alarming difficulty. He only
needs time to become acclimated. As he does become ac-

climated, he finds a source of security in the routine of the classroom, in the children and in the teacher. Until he can tap these new resources, he needs the security provided by the old. The mother's presence for a few days permits him gradually to become at home in the school.

Unfortunately, without being aware of it, parents may increase the difficulty the child has in accepting school and the separation from the familiar it entails. A child is extremely sensitive to the tension of his parents. If particularly his mother sees his entrance into school as a painful separation for her, the child will so interpret it also. In some cases in which a child shows stubbornly persistent anxiety about school, a careful evaluation of the mother's attitude discloses a parallel fear in her. She may fear the separation from the child, what the school will do to her child, or that the child will not be safe unless under her direct and constant surveillance. Under these circumstances the child's fear of school will not be handled successfully unless the mother accepts help for her own difficulty in meeting the problems her child's maturation is creating for her.

The younger the child is, the more the separation from parents and home will frighten him. Thus the child who is introduced to school by entering nursery school is usually not mature enough to adjust to a new environment without the support of a mother figure. The nursery school teacher functions in this role. The child cannot immediately shift from his real mother to a substitute mother. He has to *know* the teacher first. It may take quite a bit of time before he really does know her well enough to trust himself to her. Furthermore his classmates do not have the meaning to him that they will have in later years. Many children at the age of three are not ready psychologically to relate meaningfully to other children. Watching children of this age play together often reveals that the children are playing with the same toys, are physically in a group but in actuality are not sharing the play or the fantasy the play involves. The child would enjoy the play equally if he were alone.

In view of the fact that a child of nursery school age is not ready to socialize with his own age group and that he also still requires close proximity to parental figures, some question can be raised as to the worth of nursery-school experience. If a child lives in a neighborhood populated by several children his own age who do not attend nursery school either, there is in most instances no reason for a formal nursery school for one particular child. He is already living in a nursery school, with the parents of the other children serving as parent substitutes.

In the author's opinion the value of nursery-school experience is that it provides an opportunity for gradual development for the child rather than the abruptness of change that is demanded of the child who, to consider the opposite extreme, enters school at first grade. In the latter instance the child is ready to learn the fundamental academic tools, but if he has to utilize much of his psychic energy in adapting to the new environment, the separation from home, the presence of a group of children and the demands of schoolroom discipline, he will have less to devote to his first formal learning steps. Nursery school and kindergarten should provide surroundings that permit the child to prepare gradually for entrance into the formal school structure. The training of the nursery school teacher enables her to help the child attain that goal.

At what age a child should enter nursery school depends upon many factors. The type of nursery school available is one important consideration. A nursery school adequately equipped to handle the average four-year-old may be quite unable to give a three-year-old a constructive experience. Some children of three are ready to enter an adequate nursery school program; others are not. Some children of four are not. Even though those children who at four cannot accept nursery school may find it difficult to enter kinder-

garten the next year, they will have had a year of maturation which hopefully will enable them to accept the step
more easily.

Once a child has accepted school attendance, he will not
necessarily continue to enjoy it. There are realistic reasons
why children do not find school all pleasure. The discipline
in the schoolroom, while essential, is often difficult for an
active child to accept. A good part of the day he has to
occupy himself with what someone else says he should do.
The most skillful teacher cannot make every bit of learning
exciting. Much of school work is in the nature of a drill in
learning to use certain tools, tools that later will be a source
of pleasure. It may be exciting to learn to read "Dick sees
Mary" but after awhile the keen pleasure becomes dulled
unless the reader knows something about Dick and Mary
and whether Dick wants to see Mary or not! Parents and
the teacher know the joy to be found in reading. The child
may sometimes feel the ultimate pleasure is not worth the
struggle to achieve. While a skillful teacher will teach in a
way that minimizes the child's dissatisfaction, and a poor
teacher will make the potentially most exciting aspects of
learning dull, school is not an uninterrupted source of ecstasy
for the child! Parents too often deny the child the right to
be bored or disgruntled with school, or else they condemn
the school program because it does not provide a continually
exciting adventure to the child. One of the prices civilization
pays for the value received from education is the relinquishment of the fantasy of a totally joyful childhood.

If a child is chronically unhappy at school, if he refuses
to attend school, or if he is not learning at a rate compatible
with his known ability, the situation should be investigated.
The teacher may have a very clear concept of the difficulty.
If the teacher does not have a clue as to its nature, the
advice of others should be sought. Many schools have coun-
sellors on their faculty who have been trained to investigate
such problems. After the resources available in the school

have been utilized without results, professional help outside of the school is indicated. It is not safe to assume the child will "outgrow" his problem. It is wiser to know what if anything can be done to assure and to facilitate that process of "outgrowing."

29 : *The ill child*

REGRESSION IN ILLNESS

ILLNESS CREATES A PROBLEM IN ADJUSTMENT AND ADAPTATION
for anyone, be he child or adult. To understand the ill
person, to handle him constructively, and to avoid undesirable after-effects, it is important to understand how illness
affects the total person. The ill person is in many respects
different from the one he was before the onset of the illness
and from the one he will be after recovery. Physical well-
being is normally a part of the total personality. When physical illness replaces health the total personality may undergo
modification.

The nature of the individual's adjustment to his internal
needs and impulses and to his external environment changes
sharply in illness. Long-time goals, continued interests, and
the pressure of immediate demands must be abandoned,
modified or ignored. The energy previously available for
meeting daily pressures is now absorbed in the body's struggle to master the illness. The body, usually a more or less adequately functioning tool which the individual utilizes to a
large extent without awareness of its efficiency, in illness loses
much of its smooth functioning, and in many respects comes
to dominate rather than serve the person.

During illness, the individual withdraws his energy from
the task of actively adjusting to the external world. He also

becomes more dependent upon his interpersonal relationships. This is in part because the physician requires this change in adaptive patterns. The physician may insist upon inactivity, protection from external worries, and a period of physical rest.

On the other hand, acceptance of a more dependent pattern of adjustment is not only because it is advised. It is also a concomitant effect of illness. The ill person does not feel capable of dealing with the complexities of the world around him. His free energy is at low ebb and what remains often is engaged in his attempt to master his discomfort. Failing to handle the discomfort by his own effort, he reverts to that period of childhood in which the control of discomfort was delegated to the outside world, namely, the period of infancy when the essentials of survival were provided from the outside with minimum effort on his part.

This return to a more dependent relationship upon parents that occurs when a child is ill should be accepted by the meaningful adults in his environment. Because the child is supposed to be kept quiet and warm with the least possible expenditure of physical energy, gratification of some of his dependency needs is attained by wise nursing care. If the child reacts to illness by being a good patient, quietly obeying restrictions, and accepting the ministrations of the nursing person docilely, his return to infantile behavior is not recognized as such but is accepted as a part of the illness. In such instances the child has no conflict with his immediate role in life. His parents accept this response without concern as to its meaning.

The child who accepts his illness and his own desire to regress and withdraw is certainly easier to care for and will undoubtedly have more energy available for the curative process. The fact that he is a good patient does not justify failing to carry through those little aspects of care that make the episode more tolerable. The ill child needs the security that comes from being allowed some emotional gratification from his dependence on others. If he is the type of child who will lie for hours in bed with simple toys, making no demands for entertainment or service, his illness disrupts the family routine very little. Parents should not take undue advantage of this docility. They should be certain that adequate time is given to the child, particularly in those matters relating to aspects of his life other than his illness. Communication and interaction with people during an illness protects the child from insidious but progressive withdrawal during the period of confinement.

When the child is ill for only a few days, his withdrawal from the world is not long enough to crystallize into a permanent personality pattern. He may be very lonesome and consider that feeling simply a part of being sick. It is possible that a child, unhappy because he is lonesome, may not regain health as rapidly as will a happy child. Children who must endure a long illness and who are able to accept it without making overt demands on others, are the children in greatest danger of an ultimate and potentially permanent personality change. While it is excellent if any child can keep himself happy alone, it is important that this not be his only experience. The child with an extended illness who accepts a long period of bed regime, takes without protest what is given to him and makes no demands is the child who may eventually withdraw his interest from interpersonal relationships and create his own world from which others are totally excluded. Out of such withdrawal can develop many of the personality distortions that arise when, regardless of the cause, other people are unimportant to the maturing child.

A child who is not demanding certainly does not require constant attention to avoid the hazard of withdrawal. If it were provided he would probably become so restless under the constant demands to react that he would be converted into an irritable child simply because the over-stimulation would exhaust him. There is a middle-of-the-road way of handling this type of child. Parents can show their interest by periodically during the day making sure he is comfortable, bringing him some new toy with which to play, satisfying his particular appetite within the framework of his medical regime, and indicating by their behavior that they are well aware of his existence. Toys, books, radio and TV programs speed the passage of time. They are not adequate substitutes for interpersonal relationships!

Many children are not good patients. The ill child is frequently very demanding. Nothing seems to satisfy him. Because the pleasures that he seems to seek prove unsatisfactory in view of his general discomfort, he is cross, irritable, frustrating to himself and to his parents. He acts as if he doesn't know what he wants. Actually he does know what he wants, but can find nothing that meets those desires. What he wants most of all is to be comforted and to feel content in his environment. He cannot achieve this himself. Nothing that others offer to him really fulfills the role. When he makes demands, he believes that what he asks for will meet the difficulty. His judgment proves repeatedly wrong. The stupidity of his parents irritates him. According to his criteria of good parents they should be capable of providing what he seeks but cannot find. He wishes to be dependent upon his parents; they fail him.

A return to dependency during illness may result in irritability for another reason. This is seen more often in the older child and in certain adults. While the sick individual feels incapable of conducting his life on a mature level, reversion to a less mature pattern is shameful. He is angry, primarily at himself, secondarily at the regime imposed by others because of his illness. He resents the dependent implications in both his own needs and in the medical regime imposed. He may submit angrily to the nursing care, the forced rest, the required food and medication, unable to accept his status unless he can hide his basic longings behind a grumbling rejection.

The child may carry his wish to avoid this dependent relationship further and become the truly uncooperative patient who fights rest and tries at every opportunity to turn his regime from a wise to an unwise one. One of the most disturbing manifestations of this is in cases for which the doctor has recommended complete bed rest, a requirement that appears to serve only as a stimulation for increased activity. The child refuses to be quiet. How much a child's activity should be limited under such circumstances is a decision that the parents themselves cannot make. It should be discussed with the doctor since it is a medical decision. The doctor may feel that it is better for the child to be up and around with quiet activities rather than expending his energy in fighting the imposed bed rest. In other situations, bed rest may be an absolute necessity, but the child does not necessarily have to be put in a strait jacket! It is important that the parents use all of their knowledge of the child's interests and responses to make the bed rest period as pleasant as possible. It is more productive to help the child accept and even enjoy bed rest than to force it and thus strengthen the child's urge to rebel.

It is important that the parents struggling with a restless, fussy child not become discouraged. Even though their attention appears to be unsatisfactory it will in the long run have meaning. If the parental discouragement leads to impatience on their part, the resultant anger and irritation may serve only to exaggerate the child's unhappiness and irritability. Thus a vicious circle is established in which, as the parent becomes irritable the child becomes more disturbed, resulting in more irritability in the parent. In extreme instances both parent and child become preoccupied with their unsatisfactory interpersonal relationship and the reason for medically sound management is forgotten in the psychological battle between the two.

When a child is ill parents become concerned that if they allow the child to return to an infantile relationship he will become "spoiled" and continue to make the same demands when he is well. This concern may appear valid if the child is difficult to handle when ill. He already in illness is acting like a "spoiled" child. This apprehension does not take into account the healthy response on the part of most children to be more mature if they feel capable of being so. The child who is difficult to handle when ill in many instances does behave similarly to the child described in the chapter on the "spoilt" child, except that this behavior is evinced only during periods of illness. The salient difference is in the chronicity of the response. The ill child is unable to handle the discomforts of illness. This creates temporarily the same type of frustration the so-called "spoilt" child experiences. Once the illness is past, the severe frustration also passes. The typical "spoilt" child does not have this respite. If the parents can maintain some perspective, recognizing that the condition is temporary, they usually will find that they can endure it.

There is another type of response related to the dependent needs of children in prolonged illness that may not readily be recognized. A child when first ill may be quite demanding of attention. The adults, fearful of "spoiling" him, become overly eager not to spoil him or become irritated. They gratify only essential demands. The child becomes discouraged about the capacity of the outside world to give. He represses a normal desire for contact with others and creates a state within himself comparable to the yogi who fail to respond to either painful or pleasurable stimuli. He ceases to be a psychologically living person, although physiologically he survives. He asks for nothing because he has created a state in which he wants nothing. He complains about nothing, and accepts all discomfort without protest. In contrast to the child who is really a "good patient," this child does not respond to pleasurable stimuli any more than to unpleasant ones. This state of mind bodes poorly for his return to psychologically healthy living when his physical condition warrants it. If his difficulty is recognized and steps taken to draw him back to the world about him, often the first signs of psychological recovery are not responses indicating pleasure but rather of dissatisfaction over negative features of his situation, a disappointing response to the ministering adult but one to be understood and tolerated.

A return to a dependent relationship, so characteristic of the ill child, is a part of illness; it is not a permanent distortion of the basic personality. With the return to health, the infantile behavior will gradually disappear. It should be anticipated, however, particularly if the child has been ill for more than a few days, that a return to more mature behavior will not come at the same time that physical health returns. Often the child who has had several weeks of illness will only gradually retrace his steps towards more mature behavior. It is important that the parent recognize that in some instances the return cannot come immediately. The child must feel his way back to a more mature status. Parents who give their child real satisfaction during illness and then sharply shut it off the day the physician says the child is ready to return to physically normal living may press the child for more mature behavior too rapidly, inviting the child to define illness as the only time of real gratification.

The gradualness of the return to more mature behavior is not only because the child has found some satisfaction during the period of being cared for and requires time to accept the relinquishment of this pleasure; it is also related to the rate of his recovery. A return to physical well-being and adequate energy does not always occur simultaneously with the cure of the actual illness. Because children are apt to ignore signs of early fatigue, they may while recovering from the effects of an illness press themselves into activities that actually go beyond their returning strength. The fatigue is not recognized as such, but it is manifested in irritability or infantile behavior. If parents are graciously tolerant of the slow process of psychological recovery, the child will usually return to his old personality pattern unless that more mature behavior is less gratifying than the dependency of illness.

If a child does not return to his pre-illness patterns within a reasonable length of time, the question then arises as to whether the period of illness brought into sharper focus a significant sense of deprivation which was unknown to the child and which was relieved during the period of illness. Such a response would suggest that there is something perhaps of mild or possibly of great significance related to the child's overall interpersonal relationships, for which the illness has only been the clarifying experience.

What a reasonable length of time to allow for psychological recovery is, is not definable except through observation of the particular child. Evidence of steps toward psychological recovery indicate that the child is making progress and therefore, even though the progress is slow, the slowness should not be taken too seriously. If no steps are being taken within a time that the parents consider reasonable, it is important that the parents not trust their own judgment but seek the opinion of experts.

THE MEANING OF ILLNESS

Illness may arouse a great deal of fear and anxiety in either an adult or a child. The adult is better able to grasp the factual knowledge about his condition, a knowledge that may allay or intensify the anxiety he feels. To the child much more mystery shrouds his illness. One of the features of it, more easily evaluated by the adult than the child, is the unfamiliar sensations experienced. As has been discussed earlier, one of the first steps in psychological growth is the child's increasing awareness of his self as separated from his non-self, the differentiation of himself as a total being from that part of the external world of which he is aware. A great part of the early development of the self is based upon an awareness of bodily sensations. It is more or less assumed that if the external world undergoes a radical change, the child temporarily will respond with manifestations of insecurity and fear until he acclimates himself to the new world into which he has entered. Illness creates a different kind of unfamiliarity. During illness bodily sensations are different. The child himself, not the external world, is new. Not to be the familiar self is confusing and frightening.

That the sick child does not know who he is, is at times indicated in the night terrors that occur during illness. The night terrors may result when the child dreams he is lost. While such night terrors may have the same implication as those discussed in the material in regard to night terrors in general, they may have another significance. They may be indicative of the child's sense of lost identity. One child, subject to night terrors occurring characteristically during periods of illness, seemed to illustrate this rather clearly. Before he awoke, he would cry out that he didn't know where he was. When finally aroused he would always say, with a tone implying both self-reassurance and questioning, "I am John," as if he were responding to a dream, although he could never remember its details, in which he had lost himself. On waking he was reassuring himself, and asking for the assurance of those about him, that he really was the person he was when he was well.

This loss of identity during illness is a familiar experience to everyone. A person who is ill does not feel like himself. The adult is able to express the feeling not only to others but to himself, and in that expression implies that it is not a permanent loss but a transient one. In spite of this ability to recognize the temporary nature of the feeling of self-estrangement, adults often wonder when ill, if they will ever feel like their "old self" again. The small child may not be able to reassure himself as fully or grasp the significance of his feeling. It is frightening to seem like a different person, especially when that different person is defined by unpleasant body sensations. Under the circumstances it is not surprising that he shows evidence of anxiety or confusion.

Not only does the self become unfamiliar but in many illnesses the external world actually takes on distorted characteristics. This is particularly true when the illness, as it frequently is, is accompanied with toxicity. Toxicity affects the sensory responses and the interpretation given to sensory stimuli. Objects and ideas appear confusingly different to the patient. Their outlines may be vague, distorted, or no longer identifiable. This may result, particularly for the child, in anxious concern as to what these new shapes mean. Anyone who recalls a period of delirium can remember such distortions.

Instead of the child manifesting fears during his waking hours, nightmares of being attacked may occur during acute illness. In a way these nightmares have the same significance as nightmares of attack do at other times. The reason for their occurrence, however, may relate to the acute disturbance of conceptualization of reality during the illness. The child is failing to master the fear that the reality of his illness creates. Probably, too, many of these nightmares of being attacked indicate that the ego defenses against infantile fears are weakened. The nightmares, in such instances, represent the resurgence of old anxieties, a resurgence occurring because the child's adaptation is less effective during illness. A return to health will again lead to a more adequate adaptive pattern.

When a child manifests fears of this nature that are not part of his responsiveness during health, it does not necessarily indicate that the child has previously disguised a basic and serious anxiety, but rather that he is not able, with the handicap of his illness, to evaluate reality as well as previously. Undoubtedly the appearance of fears during illness that were not present previously is related to a low-grade anxiety that has always been present in the child but which he was able to master when well. His capacity to master those fears has been lessened as the result of the tax placed upon him by his illness. It is questionable whether these fears should be taken too seriously after the child recovers unless they persist or unless the child shows other evidence of a chronic emotional disturbance. The realization that fears occurring in illness, and not present otherwise, may indicate the child's ego is being overtaxed during health should cause the parents to evaluate carefully the child's picture after physical recovery. If, alerted by this manifestation during illness, the parents evaluate the picture during health as a satisfactory one, there is no reason for further exploration. If however a closer scrutiny suggests that previous symptoms have not been recognized, it is time again to seek the guidance of someone more objective than any parents can possibly be.

Anxiety may be aroused in the child by the actual illness, apart from the effect the illness has on his concept of himself and the external world. His body and the external world as symbolized by his parents and the doctor demand a different way of living from that to which he has become accustomed. The unfamiliarity means that possibly unknown dangers exist. This anxiety-arousing experience is another reason why the child returns to a more dependent relationship during his illness. He wants protection from this unknown danger that he cannot identify. There are ominous implications in the sensations he is experiencing. He does not know to what they will lead.

When the illness is of serious nature, the fear it engenders is augmented by the inevitable reaction of those dealing with him. If a child is seriously ill or if the early symptoms suggest the possibility of a serious illness, it is only natural for the parents to be alarmed. Parental anxiety, in spite of all attempts to disguise it, will be conveyed to a child. An adult patient recalled an episode in childhood which indicated how the unspoken concern of her parents during an illness she had as a child had been conveyed to her. A severe illness had resulted in her becoming apparently comatose. The onset had been so sudden the parents had not been prepared to handle this eventuality. It was necessary to take rapid steps towards hospitalization. Every attempt was made to maintain an air of calm casualness in the child's sick room, even though it was assumed that the child was unconscious. Since this was just before Christmas there was secreted in the house a rather special toy for the child. It was suggested that the toy be taken to the hospital so that when the child woke from the anticipated surgery, this toy, which she had eagerly looked forward to receiving, would be there for her. It was evident from their later comments that, in the minds of the adults, it was a way to deny to each other their fear that she would not awaken, a not unlikely outcome of the operation. Her parents were surprised when she awakened that her first gesture was to look around until she found the toy. As an adult she recalled that through the haze of her semi-comatose state had come a realization that they were taking this toy. Her only recall of the entire episode was her conviction at that moment that they must expect her to die or they would not take the toy to the hospital. Her parents may have deceived themselves. They had revealed something to her.

It is important that as little anxiety as possible be expressed in the presence of an ill child, regardless of the parents' or physician's awareness of the danger. An overt denial of the anxiety, however, rarely convinces a child. Over-protestations of assurance usually are seen through, so that the child recognizes that which consciously is being denied. The more completely the adult can master his own anxiety, the less frightened the child will become.

Adults who cannot achieve some mastery of their own concern should not have constant contact with an ill child. Complete absence of a parent simply because that parent cannot handle his own anxiety is not the answer either. Such a program only offers additional anxiety with which the child must deal. Because of intensified need for meaningful people, the absence of a parent can create additional fear. When parents are unable to deal with their fears, it is often the role of the physician to help them gain some perspective and some equilibrium. Many parents believe that they do not have a right to turn to the physician for assistance in dealing with their own fears; that he is primarily concerned with the child's condition; that it is an imposition to ask him to help with their problems. This is a false protection of the physician. His patient will do better if the parents are more adequate to the situation. A part of the effectiveness of the physician's treatment of the child rests in his success in treating parental anxiety.

An uncomfortable illness may have a further implication to the child concerning the role of his parents. Many childhood illnesses are accompanied by actual pain or other forms of discomfort. The child normally assumes that parents can relieve discomfort; this is inherent in his early confidence in them. Often parents, and the physician to whom the parents turn, are unable to provide the relief that the child seeks. To some children this has the implication that either the parents are inadequate or that they willfully fail to bring relief. To this failure of the adults to live up to the child's belief in them, the child may respond in various ways. The disillusionment may lead to real discouragement. What can one do if adults who are trusted fail? It may lead to fear beyond that created by the discomfort itself. It is frightening to have believed that one is safe because adults provide protections against danger and discomfort, only to find that one is at the mercy of bodily sensations that cannot be relieved. In addition, the adults' failure to give relief may arouse the child's anger because they do not carry out his wishes that they relieve his uncomfortable sensations.

This problem of the impotence of the parent to relieve

discomfort is unanswerable except indirectly. Certainly everything should be done to make the ill child as comfortable as possible. Those aspects of discomfort that cannot be relieved, the child must endure. He can endure it most adequately if he senses that the parents understand and provide support in meeting his total needs even though a specific one cannot be met. This support is not provided by anxious hovering, by much conversation and reassurance, by matching the child's moaning and groaning over the discomfort, or by purely verbal identification with the child's suffering. It is most effective when it can be conveyed to the child by the quiet presence of one or the other parent and by the parent's patient tolerance for the anxiety and irritability the child shows. Perhaps at no time are the verbal protestations and chatterbox dissertations of parents so hollow to the child as during the reality of physical discomfort. The sick child wishes to feel—not hear—the warmth of genuine empathy. Sick children, after all, are not so different from sick adults!

During illness itself, the part of the body that is involved often becomes the boundaries of the self and the rest of the total person is forgotten. Anyone with a severe headache may comment that his head aches so he cannot think. A severe pain in any part of the body brings about a complete absorption in the pain, effectively distracting the individual from any other conscious functioning. If a person does not feel well, even if not in pain, his interest in the outside world and the healthy parts of his body tends to become dormant. Most of his conscious response is to his feeling of malaise.

It is a familiar observation that, with children particularly, if they are uncomfortable in their illness it is often difficult to distract them from their symptoms. The child, if one attempts to distract him, may show considerable irritability, as if he were fighting the relinquishment of his absorption in this narrow aspect of himself. This by no means implies that he is enjoying his discomfort. His capacity to grasp the total situation is limited; his attention is directed chiefly toward his attempt to master that part of himself which is uncomfortable. It is not strange that a child reacts in this way. An adult who is ill will express the wish that everyone would just "leave him alone." A child may feel the same way. Sometimes he should just be left alone, as long as the periods of separation are not too long.

It is important, especially as the more severe discomfort subsides, to utilize every opportunity that spontaneously arises to foster the sick child's interest in something other than his symptoms. This of necessity should be geared to a level of stimulation compatible with the child's physical condition. When wisely done, it fosters the reawakening of the child's interest in his total world. In this regard it is probably unwise to verbalize to the child that since he is better he does not need as much attention as he did in the recent past. Such an attitude on the part of parents might perpetuate the child's absorption in his symptoms. It certainly suggests that health brings deprivations.

There is no "normal" response to illness for a child or an adult. During acute illness, most of the child's energy should ideally be directed towards the natural bodily effort to get well. An unhappy child, an anxious child, or an angry child will probably recover with less facility from any illness than will the happy child who is not too worried, too frustrated, or too deprived. It is impossible for parents of most children to create a situation in illness that will provide this optimum state for recovery. A failure to do so does not mean that the child is doomed to an unnecessarily prolonged illness. Parents can only strive to reach a reasonable goal in achieving this state of mind in the child.

CHRONIC ILLNESS AND PHYSICAL DISABILITIES

Chronic illness or an illness that extends over several weeks has the same meaning to a child as an acute illness, but the effect of that meaning is more readily discernible because of its chronicity. It also has the potentiality of being more permanently damaging in its effect upon the developing personality. The implications to the child of an acute illness readily pass with the illness. A long illness may result in a solidifying of certain responses and therefore less readiness for them to evaporate with returning health. This is particularly true if the illness results in a permanent handicap, such as the paralysis following poliomyelitis or in damage to some organ with danger of a recurrence with further damage as in rheumatic fever.

For the child with a long continued or chronic illness or with a residual handicap following the illness the dependent relationship upon adults continues for a long period of time. The child may react to this with real enjoyment. He may become bored with it and fight it. He may see it as a threat to his own respect for himself, and therefore do everything to deny it. As his condition improves he may mobilize all his strength to rebel against the continued requirements that he remain relatively helpless. He may, on the other hand, resist any pressure to become more self-reliant, having come to accept the pleasures of dependency and having lost the sense of pleasure that greater freedom provides.

The child with a chronic illness is often very frightened by his condition. He does not understand it. He has lost his awareness of what it meant to be well. He may experience vague fears which he cannot clearly define but which are related to his apprehension about the outcome of his illness. An older child actually may recognize the possibility of a fatal end to his illness. Even though his awareness of the danger may be ill-defined, it is rooted in the same factors that may cause the acutely ill child to be anxious. As time passes and health does not return, the anxiety is increased.

The anxiety of the chronically ill child is often intensified by the anxiety of those around him. Part of this is unavoidable. If the child has a chronic illness that may have a serious outcome, the type of care that is needed and the insistence that it be carried out, the solemnity with which the doctor deals with the symptoms and the normal anxiety of the parent, all convey a feeling of uneasiness to the child. The child soon recognizes that the thermometer when studied by the doctor, nurse or parent brings different responses at different times. He soon learns that an elevation of temperature brings anxiety into the sickroom atmosphere, a drop in temperature brings relaxation and cheerfulness. The concern with which physical examinations are repeatedly given is not ignored by the child. The eagerness with which parents or nurse follow the doctor out of the room for a whispered conference is not interpreted as originating in the pleasure adults get from a tête-a-tête conversation.

In an attempt to avoid the transmission of their anxiety some doctors and parents make a great gesture of hiding it in the presence of the child. This can have some undesirable side-effects. Firstly, if the doctor and parents do not seem to be taking the illness seriously, the imposed rest may seem ridiculously excessive to the child. Then he may have contempt for the doctor's orders, and see the imposition of them as an attack by the doctor or the parents rather than a logical, medically sound program. No adult would accept docilely a doctor's recommendation that he stay at complete bed rest for six weeks if the doctor insisted that there was nothing wrong with the patient. The adult would probably defy his doctor's orders, change doctors, or begin to struggle with fantasies as to what the doctor really thought.

Likewise the child might want to change doctors. The child knows he is uncomfortable; he knows there is something really wrong. If the doctor is so casual about it, will he really recognize the discomfort involved and do something to relieve it? Undoubtedly some children (and some adults) exaggerate their discomfort because the bedside manner of those caring for them suggests a casualness that implies the degree of discomfort is not recognized. A squeaky wheel has to squeak loudly to be heard by a deaf mechanic!

On the other hand, just as the adult patient fantasies about the doctor's ideas, the child may also. He may recognize that the adults over-protest their lack of anxiety; he may sense in their eagerness not to be anxious how deep their anxiety really is. In the author's experience, the sounder approach to the child, particularly in those cases involving a chronic illness requiring long convalescence, is frankness within the bounds of the child's capacity to comprehend. This frankness is best vested in the doctor since he is more familiar with the actual nature of the illness. It appears wise in most instances for the doctor to have a discussion with any child facing a chronic illness. In this discussion the doctor can explain to him in simple terms the nature of the illness and the reason for a period of slow recovery. This obviously should not be couched in terms that will alarm the child. It should be presented truthfully, but positively in terms of the ultimate outcome, an outcome that will be facilitated if the child is cooperative in carrying out the medical regime. There is no reason to keep the child in the dark in regard to the truth of his physical condition as long as the way in which he is told is not motivated by the wish to terrify the child, to punish him for his lack of cooperation, or to overwhelm him with terminology he cannot possibly comprehend.

Most importantly, in cases of chronic illness or in those cases that may leave a permanent handicap, the anxiety of parents cannot be ignored or denied. The parents should turn to the physician for an understanding of the child's illness. They must believe in the doctor and he must give them reason to trust his frankness. The emphasis by the doctor and by the parents should be in terms of what can be done rather than the possible disastrous eventualities. Again it should be pointed out that parents who feel embarrassed at their ignorance and hesitate to question the doctor, who believe that the doctor is so busy that he doesn't have time to explain, or who think they should bear their anxieties alone in order not to bother the physician, complicate the work of the doctor. He may not know of the parents' embarrassment over their ignorance, and he may not, in the rush of his work, be alert to the underlying anxiety in the parents. The parents are not wasting the doctor's time when they ask him to discuss the disease from which the child suffers, its requirements for optimum recovery, and the complications that may occur during the process of the illness. They are actually saving his time because, with this knowledge, parental anxiety will tend to be less overwhelming, parents will be wiser nurses for the child, and the child's recovery will be expedited.

One of the psychological hazards of a chronic illness relates to the tendency of the child to lose the conception of his total self and to become focused on the diseased part of his body. This tendency may in a chronic illness play a considerable part in the ultimate psychological development of the individual. The individual comes to see himself as a diseased organ rather than as a total person. This is reflected in the verbalization of some chronically ill adults. They will refer to themselves as a cardiac, as a polio case, or as an ulcer patient. While any patient with a chronic illness may sometimes use such expressions, there is a certain implication to the wording. It implies that the person's identity is created by the diseased organ rather than by his total personality. Such remarks are in contrast to the person who says, "I have a bad heart," "I have an ulcer," or "I have a weak arm, because as a child I had infantile paralysis." This wording implies that the total individual has an illness or a handicap rather than that the illness or handicap is the total individual.

Some tendency to focus upon a diseased organ is almost inevitable during a critical period of any illness. The doctor particularly is preoccupied with the need of the diseased organ. His concern about the rest of the body is primarily in the framework of its effect upon the recovery of the diseased organ. Increasingly doctors are becoming aware of the necessity of always considering the total person, the total person having a part that is functioning poorly. It is not wise, however, to depend solely upon the doctor for this awareness of the total individual. It is much more the responsibility of those who care for the child, particularly the parents. They themselves, unless they check the tendency, are apt to lose sight of their total child and see him only as the diseased organ. This certainly increases the child's tendency to do likewise.

Once the acute discomfort of a chronic illness is passed, the child, even though he cannot return to normal activity, does have the same needs as any child has. Those needs have to be gratified in different ways. It is important, during the convalescent period, that the child be helped to see his illness as a part of himself rather than his total self. This often can be done by stimulating interests that are compatible with his age and his general developmental level but which do not place additional strain in the area of the illness. Perhaps one of the best examples to illustrate this is that of a child recovering from rheumatic fever with a residual damaged heart that will have some effect on his future plans. Consider, as a case in point, a boy who had been interested in sports, had always played active, masculine games and had made a social adjustment on an athletic level. At the age of nine, he contracted rheumatic fever which left him with damage to the heart requiring a year of considerable restriction upon activity and which indicated that he would have some restrictions through the rest of his life. In other words he could not anticipate being captain of the college football team. This was a severe blow to the boy's concept of himself as an adequately masculine in-dividual. He saw himself as defeated in any attempt to become a total man, visualizing himself as an ambulatory damaged heart. This child needed help to re-orient himself gradually to his own concept of himself as a man. If the primary attempt to give him this orientation were by a definition of his limitations, his focus upon his heart could become even greater. There are two general ways to define this type of problem. It can be said to such a boy "You can never play football because of your heart"—a statement that would leave him, as far as he could see, in a vacuum for the future. On the other hand, his interest could be stimu-lated in listening to football games, studying football tech-niques, and possibly, as an oversimplified example, directing him towards the goal of managing a football team. It is not a question of imposing foreign interests upon the child, but rather of stimulating his interest in new activities or, more importantly, of directing interests he already has into chan-nels compatible with his physical handicap. This goal does not have to be achieved over night. It probably cannot be. It involves long planning.

Sympathy for a chronically ill or physically handicapped child is certainly a valid response. It is important, however, that this sympathy be in the framework of the total life situation of the child rather than in regard solely to his illness. The mother who says to the diabetic child or to others in the child's presence, "Isn't it a shame! Children love candy so; it is so good and Johnny can't have it because he has diabetes," may be expressing sympathy but in doing so is creating a greater problem of frustration for the child. In such an instance wise sympathy is that which offers to the child other pleasures in eating that are compatible with his diabetic condition, accepting the restriction on sweets as a part of the child's life which is neither ignored nor focused upon. To say a child cannot do a certain thing creates in the child a sense of frustration; to define what he can do stimulates anticipation. By either method the same restrictions are imposed, but the attitude towards that imposition is different.

In cases of chronic illness or permanent disability knowledge on the part of the child as to the rationale for any restrictions placed upon him or any form of treatment given is extremely important. If a diet, restriction of activity or any other form of medical surveillance is indicated, the child should know why. Some parents hesitate to do this for fear it will make the child "hypochondriacal." There is nothing hypochondriacal about following a wise regime that takes into consideration the particular nature of the individual's bodily functioning. A child may become very anxious or very angry at medical requirements that do not make sense to him. A diabetic child will handle dietary restrictions much better if he knows the reason for them than if he sees the restrictions only as a depriving attitude on the part of the parents. The child with a poorly functioning heart will accept physical restrictions better if he knows there is a rationale for the restriction than if he sees it only as an attempt to make a sissy of him.

There is an additional value to the child being aware of the reason for continued caution or restriction in certain respects. He will much more reliably and wisely control his behavior away from the family monitoring if he knows the reasons for precautions rather than if he believes they are imposed because of parental idiosyncrasies.

The child with a chronic illness will become hypochondriacal if his parents are over-zealous in their care and place unwarranted emphasis on any symptom. When a doctor recommends medication, the wise parent does not double the medication on the theory that if one dose is good two will be better. Overdosing of care is as dangerous as under-dosing.

It is typically human to be rather optimistic about one's own future irrespective of some of the alarming aspects. It is also part of the psychology of most people to strive towards health and maturity. In some instances this drive loses its force during a prolonged illness. This may reflect a previously unsatisfactory life, in which the individual's gratifications in health and maturity were limited.

There are children (and adults) who enjoy being ill. It is during this time that they find they enjoy the most attention and have the least demands made upon them. It is a relief to escape from unsatisfactory relationships in the reality world of health and indulge in the less demanding, more attentive life created by illness. When this is observed, even though the observation leads to the valid conclusion that the individual prefers illness to health, it does not mean that the child or adult should not receive attention. It is simply an indication that there is something wrong with the experiences of health in a reality world which only illness corrects.

HOME CARE AND HOSPITALIZATION

The ill child is not the only member of a family. There is always the danger that parental anxiety, the demands of the child, and the demands of the illness will make the ill child the hub of all family activity. Other members of the family can usually adjust to the disruption of the family routine resulting from an acute illness. To make this adjustment to a chronic illness is a very different matter.

Husbands need dinner when they return home. Other children in the family need time for activities with their parents. The dishes have to be washed, the clothes ironed, the house cleaned. The requirement that the mother be at home to care for the ill child often deprives her of an essential aspect of living, her social contact with people outside the home.

In the event of the prolonged illness, a mother will be a better nurse if she has some time away from the ill child. The other children will adjust better to the illness of one of their siblings if they find that they too continue to be important to their parents. The husband will be more helpful if he is not deprived of all the satisfactions of returning home. Certain things have to be left undone when there is illness in the home. Each member may have to make some shift in their adaptation and in their demands. Careful thinking through of the problem will usually result in fewer demands for adjustment upon other members of the family than seem indicated in the first days of the illness.

It often seems that the demands of the sick child are of such nature that no one else's demands can be met. If it is really so, the possibility should be considered that the child will have more adequate care and the total family will not be so disrupted if the child is hospitalized. Hospitalization for a sick child is an answer that should come only after thoughtful consideration by both the physician and the family. Obviously in certain illnesses only the hospital can provide the necessary conditions for recovery. In those cases the decision is made more easily. The more difficult evaluation is under those circumstances where hospitalization is optional, with the necessity of deciding whether the child can be properly cared for at home, whether the other essential demands of the family can still be met, and whether both can be accomplished without overly straining the parents. Fathers cannot work all day after sitting up all night with a sick child. Mothers cannot do twenty-four-hour nursing. An infant cannot be put on a closet shelf to lie dormant until an older child requiring continuous nursing is well again.

Hospitalization can offer more effective care for a child under certain circumstances than the home possibly can. While there are disadvantages to hospitalization for the child, there are also advantages, and the two should be carefully balanced before one or the other is arbitrarily chosen. The way hospitalization is managed may have a great deal of bearing upon its efficacy. Going to the hospital often is a frightening experience to a child. Whenever a child is to be hospitalized, if sufficient time is available to prepare him, he should be told what the hospital routine will be. He should know of the type of care he'll get, what will be expected of him at the hospital, and the visiting program that is allowed.

As in all areas of child care there is always the swing from one extreme to the other. There was a time when if a child was to be hospitalized he was kept completely in the dark as to what was going to happen to him. He was required to make an adjustment to an unfamiliar and unpredictable world with no preparation. The anxiety that resulted from this type of handling resulted in recommendations of the very opposite approach. Children were overprepared for hospitalization. They were given a dissertation on the details of hospital living, of surgery and the like that resulted in excessive anxiety because the whole picture was unrealistically built up and made to appear much more at variance with ordinary living than it is. After all, there are not many details to be described, and they can be described briefly and correctly. Preparation for hospitalization should not be long drawn out and melodramatically offered. It should be done factually, though not coldly. The questions that the child asks should be answered but the immediate pre-hospitalization period should not become focused solely on the impending hospitalization. This is not easy for parents to do because, again, of their own underlying concern. A doctor who is empathetic with children can often achieve this preparation more wisely, with the parents simply alert to answering any further questions the child may raise.

A child is often quite lonesome in the hospital. It is certainly important that the family keep in as close touch with him as is permitted by the routine of the hospital. It is meaningful to him if he recognizes by the parents' action when they visit him that they thought about him when they were away. The bringing of a small toy may be extremely gratifying to the child. Aside from the pleasure he derives from the toy itself, it often indicates to him the continued interest of his parents. It is not at all unusual for a child to value a toy brought by the parent in spite of the fact that the hospital provides very adequate play material for the youngster. A present from the parent has a very specific meaning.

In recent years there has been a gradual modification in the attitude of hospital managements towards the parents of the sick child. It has been recognized that the child has a greater need for the parent during illness than he has in health. The hospitals therefore have liberalized their visiting hours. Many hospitals not only permit but urge that one parent, usually the mother, spend most of her time with the child during the hospitalization period.

Other considerations being equal it is wise for one parent, particularly when the child is acutely ill or has had surgery, to remain with the child. This gives the child a sense of security that no amount of efficient nursing can provide. This generalization has certain risks inherent in it. If a hospital is not set up to allow the parent to live there, the parent who insists upon staying may actually disrupt the effective routine of the hospital. The tension that may result between the nursing staff and the parent may actually increase the child's feeling of uneasiness.

When the hospital encourages the parent to remain with the child, this encouragement should be accepted only if the parent feels comfortable in dealing with the situations that may arise with the child. A mother who faints at the sight of blood should certainly not be at the child's bedside when he awakens from a tonsillectomy. Parents who are extremely upset by the child's physical condition or paralyzed with anxiety about the outcome of an illness will not serve the function that they should by being present in the sick room. They can only increase the child's anxiety.

Parents should not be self-conscious about their ineffectiveness in the sick room. When parents are ill-suited to the sick room, the answer, if it is financially possible, is to provide special nursing care for the child. If that is not practical or necessary, the hospital nurses in their sympathy for the child will give more because of the absence of the child's own parents. If the hospitalization is to be long, the total family situation must also be taken into consideration. Often, in those cases, as the child becomes acquainted with the nurses and the other patients, he becomes more at ease in the hospital and can tolerate a gradual decrease in parental attention.

It is impossible to spell out in any detail how the chronically or acutely ill child should be handled. It will depend a great deal upon the individual child. One will accept home care with minimal difficulty; another will be difficult at home but, if hospitalization is indicated, will make a surprisingly good adjustment to that regime. One child will require a great deal of entertaining if he is to tolerate the confinement his illness imposes; another will prefer solitude and quiet play.

If parents trust their own intuitive understanding of the child's needs and their own responsiveness to it, they will often come to the wisest way of handling the child in view of the type of child he is and the type of parents they are. To behave artificially contrary to an intuitive response will rarely convince the child or even more rarely correct the difficulties.

30 : *When and where to seek help*

PARENTS CANNOT EXPECT THAT THEIR INTUITIVE EVALUATION of any situation will always be a correct one. They are bound to make many mistakes, though with the best intentions in the world. They will also make mistakes at times because their own ego is as exhausted as the child's. Under such circumstances they will deal with a particular problem with irritation rather than insight and wisdom. Parents make many mistakes and children survive them. If parents make too many mistakes the child points it out through his behavior. When parents feel unable to grasp the significance of their mistakes or the child's behavior, they should seek the objective evaluation that a professional person can give. Once the situation is understood there are ways to repair the damage that seems to have been done. Nothing inhibits sound and intuitive reactions so much as a fear that one will do the wrong thing. Parents need to believe in themselves as parents but they need also to realize that as parents they may be too close to a situation, too emotionally involved in it to be able to evaluate it.

Often a child's behavior which baffles his parents is not alarming in significance. It may be only a manifestation of a normal step in development. If parents are anxious and confused, their response may not only cause the particular behavior to appear more alarming; it may create tension, anxiety and provocativeness in the child that will result in that which was actually of no significance becoming a serious disturbance. A simple example of this may indicate the possibilities. Harry at the age of six was not learning to read as rapidly as his sister had. Parental concern was expressed by urging him to work harder at his reading. Try as he would he met defeat. He became anxious about his achievement and the anxiety resulted in greater difficulty in reading. As a consequence the parents became more concerned and, in their concern, became more impatient with him. Previously a relatively secure child, he lost confidence in himself and in the stability of his parents' affection for him. He interpreted their behavior as indicative that they would not love him as dearly if he could not read. He was aware that part of their irritation stemmed from his inability to live up to the standards his sister had met so easily at the same age. Girls, it appeared to him, were more adequate and as a consequence more gratifying to parents. Even if he couldn't succeed as she did in reading, perhaps by pretending to be a girl he could win their love. His interest and behavior changed from those of budding masculinity to femininity. He still could not read as well as his parents wished, but he could at least try to woo them with his femininity. He was also convinced that if he could become a girl he would read better! A superstructure of character distortion had been built upon a simple difficulty. Had his parents sought advice when first they became concerned about his reading, they would have learned that Harry was learning to read as well as any child whose mental ability is somewhat above average. His sister's rate of learning had been a direct indication that she had superior mental ability. But there was nothing alarming about Harry's reading picture; he would learn quite adequately if given time.

If a child appears fearful to leave a level of development there is some reason for this fear. If, for example, he clings to an infantile adjustment to reality when according to his chronological age he should feel gratified at a more mature level, there is a legitimate question as to whether he is a child whose maturation is slower than the typical, whether he has had adequate gratification at the more immature level or whether he sees dangers in going beyond that stage. Sometimes parents have certain ideas as to why this condition exists. They should try to correct those obvious aspects of which they are aware. If the correction proves ineffective, it is time to obtain the opinion of someone who can be more objective.

A child who is chronically hostile, who is overly submissive, overly fearful, overly preoccupied with sexuality or sexual play, may find a modified environment of help in clarifying his own confusion. A child who is not learning at a rate commensurate with his ability should be evaluated. A child at an age when he could be expected to deal with certain frustrations but is unable to do so except by a temper outbreak may be indicating that something in him or around him should be changed. Bedwetting beyond the age of four is frequently an indication for seeking advice. A child who chronically lies, steals, truants from school or runs away from home should be studied. If every additional integrative task that confronts the child's ego results in a sign of ego inadequacy, the parents should consult a trained person.

When parents recognize the necessity of outside help, it does not mean that the only person to consult is a psychiatrist with the prospect of becoming involved in a long program of psychoanalysis of the child, mother, father and perhaps siblings. There are many other people skilled in evaluating certain problems. With the acceptance of modern psychology as an essential part of medical training, the family physician and the pediatrician are frequently qualified to assist parents with many of the common problems of childhood. They are also in a position to measure more objectively the significance of the particular problem the child presents in relationship to the child's overall behavior and adjustment. They have a perspective because they are less emotionally involved than the parents and still have a background of knowledge of the child based upon their long contact with the child and the family. Although the family physician or pediatrician is not equipped by training to do intensive treatment directed towards the resolution of emotional problems they frequently are able to suggest simple procedures to try and, in other cases, are able to determine whether a specialist should be consulted.

When the child has reached school age, teachers who are sympathetic to the needs of the total child rather than interested only in his academic achievement, are, like the family physician or pediatrician, frequently able to evaluate the picture the child presents. Teachers see the child against the backdrop of children his own age in the actualities of living. They also often have an opportunity to gain clues concerning the child's inner living through spontaneous remarks, writings and drawings. One little girl in her art class characteristically drew a bird cage with a bird pecking at the bars. Asked casually one day by the teacher whether the bird was unhappy in the cage, the little girl answered that it was. The bird would be afraid to fly away even if she could, but, if the people who owned her would let her be free in the house, she wouldn't want to fly away. A little questioning of the parents brought out that this child who was quiet and withdrawn in the classroom was being over-controlled by well meaning but anxious parents.

Parent study groups, if competently conducted, can often clarify the confusion that parents experience. It is also validly reassuring to find that other parents have similar experiences. It is for the leader, however, to decide whether the similarity of problems revealed in a group is indicative of psychological health!

Neighbors and close friends are the poorest source of help when the parents have a question about their child. Neighbors and friends are rarely objective. Furthermore the child should not be held up to friends and neighbors for dissection. His immediate environment should accept him as a total living person, not as an object of scientific study. Parents should not be so objective that they can discuss freely with everyone the undesirable traits of their child or indicate how impossible he is to live with.

Family physicians, pediatricians, school teachers and leaders of parent groups can evaluate the external picture of the child in his environment. The internal conflicts and the subtlety of the external environment usually are not within their function to evaluate. When more intensive study is indicated, other professional people—specially trained—are available. Many communities have community-supported agencies, staffed by trained workers who can offer counseling service to parents about child problems. Some of them have people on their staff who are equipped to work directly with children. Also, more and more schools are employing psychologists or social workers who not only study the child in the school but aid parents in the home problems.

Parents often feel humiliated when they become aware of the need to seek help about their child's emotional development or health. They believe they should be able to find the answers within themselves. In the past a similar pride often prevented some people from consulting physicians about physical health: it was assumed that the individual had home remedies, was able to read a book on herbs, and could be his own physician. Now if a person has a headache he tries aspirin. If the headache persists, he knows he should consult a physician who will determine its cause and suggest a way to relieve the pain. No one considers it a sign of weakness and inadequacy to have the physician investigate the headache, even if the physician ends by indicating the headache is not serious; the patient just needs a vacation.

People still have difficulty in translating this attitude into the psychological area and accepting the idea of consulting a trained person about persistent psychological headaches. It is particularly true if they decide, or are advised, to consult a psychiatrist! The idea that a person is human psychologically and thus subject to psychological ills is less tenable than the idea that a person is human physically and thus subject to human physical ills. Parents cannot expect to know all about psychological health and illness. It is no more or no less a reflection of parental inadequacy to consult a psychiatrist than it is to consult a pediatrician or the family physician.

If parents consult a psychiatrist there are certain things they should be prepared for. The psychiatrist will usually want to spend some time with both parents, together or separately. During these interviews he will ask detailed questions not only about the problems at present but the history of the child from birth. He does not expect the parents to recall all the details of the past but he does want to know all that the parents can recall. Since he cannot ask all the pertinent questions that will bring out significant information, he hopes the parents will tell of episodes of the child's past life or reactions of the child when younger that might have some significance. This part of the interview parents can usually understand and accept. Often however he seeks information that may at first seem more like gossipy prying since it appears unrelated to the child's problem. The psychiatrist often wishes to know in some detail the background of the parents, the problems they struggled with as children, their picture of their relationship with their own parents, brothers, sisters and friends. He is interested in this in order to learn what forces shape the personality of the adults who are living with the child he wishes to help. He is not seeking this in order to find a reason to blame the parents. He is seeking it so as to understand them. Only by understanding them as individuals can he hope to know how to help them with their child.

He will also ask questions about the relationship that exists between the parents. That relationship is meaningful because of the effect the relationship has on the child's environment and the role the child is playing for each parent. Parents who attempt to hide their own difficulties from the psychiatrist they are consulting about their child, are unintentionally but seriously handicapping the psychiatrist. They are like the patient who describes an abdominal pain, but refuses to let the physician examine him because the patient feels that this would violate his modesty. A psychiatrist does not pass judgment upon the parents' morals or ethics; he is only interested in helping.

Many times parents are asked to tell facts they would not want known. The confidential nature of interviews is a basic law for psychiatrists. To tell those previously hidden facts is a basic law for a patient or the parents of a patient.

Psychiatric advice may take one of several forms. The problem that has developed may appear rather typical for a child of the particular age. Often then suggestions are made as to how to handle it with the accompanying recommendation that the child be seen again in three months or so in order to evaluate any change in the picture. At times, even though the problem is not typical for the age but seems to be directly related to and proportionate to some ill-advised handling on the part of the parents, the psychiatrist makes specific recommendations for a change in the child's environment. Again he may suggest a later follow-up contact in order to determine the efficacy of the changes. In some instances the psychiatrist may suggest seeing the child once a week over a period of time. Through this form of treatment he may help to give the child some understanding of his behavior and help him see other possible ways in which to handle his life situation.

The form of treatment that involves the longest period of time, often an increase in manifestations of the underlying disturbance before improvement sets in, and the most taxing kind of parental cooperation, is child psychoanalysis. When a psychiatrist recommends an analysis for a child he does not imply the child is more disturbed than those children for whom other approaches are recommended. He recommends it rather because whatever may have been the original reason for the difficulty the problem has now become incorporated into the child's adjustment patterns and he will be more likely to resolve the current difficulty and any future ones adequately if he has insight into the meaning his experiences have had to him. It is not unusual during analytical therapy for a child to act out, in a primitive form, impulses which previous to his treatment were under control. At that point parents often feel discouraged. They need close contact with the therapist not only to understand what is happening and have support from the therapist but also to have some guidance as to how to deal with the behavior. From successful psychoanalytic therapy with a child comes improved integrative patterns.

Parents often resent the therapist's secretiveness about the material the child gives to him. This secretiveness is an essential part of therapy. The average child will not expose his inner feelings and thoughts to a therapist unless he is certain they will be handled confidentially. Furthermore, a therapist will at times make suggestions to the parents based upon his knowledge of the child for which he cannot give an explanation because he cannot reveal the child's secrets. The parents feel excluded. This feeling of exclusion must be tolerated because of the ultimate gains that will result.

Parents at times fear the child will transfer his love for them to the therapist. In successfully progressing treatment the therapist often becomes a very important person to the child. If the problem with which the child is dealing is a painful one and if the child feels only the therapist knows, understands and can help, he may temporarily be more closely tied to his therapist than to anyone else. In the end however, no one replaces parents permanently except in those rare cases in which the parents have nothing to give. Usually those parents don't mind being displaced!

One other form of recommended treatment that may prove disconcerting to parents is the advice that they, not the child, need help. This again seems to imply that the parents are to blame. In one sense this is true because problems of their own that they are unable to recognize may make it impossible for them to give that which the child requires. Often these parents are eager to do the most constructive thing, will seem to understand advice that is given but will be unable to carry out their intentions. Their difficulties may be quite unrevealed in their superficial behavior so that their first impression tends to justify a conclusion that their child is deeply disturbed, whereas in reality the child is reacting normally to the difficulties the parents present to him. The nature of the parental conflicts are as multiple as are the number of parents who need help. In a large percentage of these cases the parents are unaware of the nature of their difficulties. They are only aware that their child's behavior is atypical. The most effective help for a child under such circumstances is the help given to the parents.

Psychiatrists cannot perform miracles. Furthermore, even though great progress has been made in the last century towards more complete understanding of human personality and although constructive ways have been found to prevent the development of undesirable personality traits or correct those when they do occur, the knowledge is still far from complete. Psychiatry is not the only branch of medicine in which large unknown islands still exist. Physicians do not as yet know the cause of the common cold, nor do they know an effective way to prevent or cure a cold. They do know something about prevention, something about relieving the symptoms and something about preventing complications. The family physician is not rejected because of this inadequacy but is valued for what he can give. Psychiatrists as well as those people in the allied fields of education, psychology and social work should be utilized with the same tolerance for the shortcomings in their specialty.

Index